CIVIL WAR BATTLE FLAGS

of the Union Army and Order of Battle

KNICKERBOCKER
PRESS

CIVIL WAR BATTLE FLAGS

of the Union Army and Order of Battle

Foreword by Steven J. Wright

Introduction by Robert Younger

Order of Battle Compiled by General C. McKeever,
Quartermaster General of the U.S. Army

KNICKERBOCKER
PRESS

CIVIL WAR BATTLE FLAGS
OF THE UNION ARMY AND ORDER OF BATTLE

Foreword by Steven J. Wright
Introduction by Robert Younger

Published by
KNICKERBOCKER PRESS
276 Fifth Avenue
New York, NY 10001

Copyright © 1997 by Knickerbocker Press

Published by arrangement with Morningside House, Dayton, Ohio.

Originally published as
FLAGS OF THE UNITED STATES ARMY CARRIED DURING THE WAR
OF THE REBELLION, 1861 & 1863
and
TABULAR STATEMENTS SHOWING NAMES OF COMMANDERS OF ARMY CORPS,
DIVISIONS AND BRIGADES OF THE UNITED STATES ARMY, 1861-1865
Both by General C. McKeever, quartermaster general

ISBN 1-57715-007-4

MANUFACTURED IN CHINA

FOREWORD

The thirty-five years between the end of the Civil War and the turn of the century saw perhaps the greatest effort to record and preserve the history of "the recent unpleasantness." It was during this period that we see the creation of such associations as The Southern Historical Society and the publishing of its papers, and the establishment of numerous veterans' organizations and their efforts to tell the story from their perspective. Almost every researcher is familiar with the endeavors of the Grand Army of the Republic, the United Confederate Veterans and the Military Order of the Loyal Legion of the United States.

It was also during this period that the War Department began the monumental task of collecting, and eventually publishing, *The War of the Rebellion: A Compilation of the Official Records of the Union and Confederate Armies* and its accompanying atlas. Not to be outdone, the Quartermaster General of the United States Army prepared *Flags of the Army of the United States* and *Commanders of Army Corps, Divisions and Brigades,* originally published in 1887. While printed in very limited quantity, these volumes, from the beginning, served as valuable companions to the plethora of material being published about the war, particularly the *Official Records.* Over the years the *Official Records* and other nineteenth century works about the war have been reprinted many times and are readily available to scholars, but *Commanders of Army Corps, Divisions and Brigades* became so rare that it was known to only the most dedicated Civil War bibliophile.

The obscurity of this volume does not diminish its significance to scholars and researchers. With attrition, casualties, and necessary constant reorganization, it is impossible for even the most organized student of the Civil War to maintain order of any army organization that was continually changing. While volumes such as the *Official Records* preserve the reports and correspondence of the Army, one can easily be confused by a particular unit's place in that organization. Other classic works, such as Frederick Dyer's *A Compendium of the War of the Rebellion,* present Army organization, but, again, in a most confusing way. It took the methodical coordination of the Quartermaster General's office to present this information in a concise, accurate format. The significance of this work cannot be overstated and time has not diminished its contribution to Civil War scholarship.

STEVEN J. WRIGHT, Curator
The Civil War Library and Museum
Philadelphia, PA
May 1996

INTRODUCTION

Flags of the Army of the United States Carried During the War of the Rebellion 1861-1865 and *Tabular Statements Showing the Names of Commanders of Army Corps, Divisions and Brigades, United States Army, During the War of 1861 to 1865,* both compiled by the Quartermaster General of the U.S. Army, were originally published in 1887. The two volumes appeared in a limited edition published by Burk & McFetridge of Philadelphia, and were available bound separately or together in atlas-size editions. They are herein reprinted in one valuable volume.

Flags of the Army of the United States contains beautifully reproduced color plates of many of the flags used to designate headquarters, corps, brigades, divisions, and armies. Included here are reproductions of the individual flags that flew over the headquarters of such generals as Burnside, Grant, Reynolds, Custer and Sykes. In addition, individual pages are devoted to each army corps on which every brigade flag as well as the flag displayed at each corps headquarters are reproduced together. In *A Practical Guide to American Nineteenth Century Color Plate Books*, an annotated bibliography compiled by Whitman Bennett, *Flags of the Army of the United States* is said to contain "87 full pages of the most beautiful lithographs possible, so fine that not only the colors but the textures and fabrics are clearly distinguishable. Many have just one figure to a page but numerous others display groups of small flags." It is indeed an interesting and valuable book.

The second companion volume, *Commanders of Army Corps, Divisions and Brigades*, contains clear, easy-to-read charts of command for every army corps that fought for the United States during the Civil War. The information was compiled and published soon after the war's end; the accuracy of the volume is therefore very reliable. Each of the "Tabular Statements" show the names of all corps, division and brigade commanders along with their dates of service. The command structure of each army corps is conveniently displayed across two facing pages. An index of names is also included.

Command information and flag designation can be easily researched in the one-volume *Flags of the Army of the United States* and *Commanders of Army, Corps, Divisions and Brigades*. It is indeed a valuable addition to the modern Civil War research library.

—ROBERT YOUNGER

ARTILLERY.   NATIONAL.   INFANTRY.

REGIMENTAL COLORS.

FLAGS

OF THE

ARMY OF THE UNITED STATES

CARRIED DURING

The War OF THE Rebellion

1861-1865,

to designate the Headquarters
of the different
Armies, Army Corps, Divisions and Brigades.

---·❊·---

Compiled under direction of the
Quartermaster General U.S. Army.

1887

BURK & M^cFETRIDGE LITH. PHILA.

❧ NOTE ☙

The illustrations contained in this volume are based upon official orders, and such other data as the Quartermaster's Department has been able to gather through private correspondence. It has not been practicable to obtain definite information in all cases, and the Quartermaster-General will be thankful for any authentic correction of errors.

TABULAR

——SHOWING

COMMANDERS OF ARMY CO

UNITED ST

——DUR

WAR OF 186

——COMPILED FROM DATA ON

QUARTERMASTER G

1

ATEMENTS

AMES OF ——

S, DIVISIONS AND BRIGADES,

S ARMY,

HE ——

TO **1865.**

IN THE OFFICE OF THE ——

ERAL OF THE ARMY.

7.

Gen. C. McKeever.

INDEX.

NAME.	BRIGADE.	DIVISION, DISTRICT, &c.	CORPS.
A			
Abbott, H. L.,	3	Defenses of Washington.	22
do	4	Defenses south of the Potomac.	22
do	3	Defenses south of the Potomac.	22
do	2	Defenses south of the Potomac.	22
Abbott, J. C.,	2	1st Division.	24
do	2	1st Division.	10
Abercrombie, J. C.,	3	4th Division.	17
Abercrombie, J. J.,	——	Abercrombie's Division.	22
do	2	1st Division.	5
do		1st Division.	4
do	2	1st Division.	4
Abert, W. S.,	5	Defenses of Washington.	22
do	2	Defenses north of the Potomac.	22
Adams, C. W.,	1	District of the Frontier.	7
do	2	District of the Frontier.	7
Adams, R. N.,	2	4th Division.	15
do	2	2d Division.	16
Albright, Chas.,	3	3d Division.	2
Alcott, J. H.,	2	3d Division.	19
Alden, A.,	3	2d Division.	10
Alexander, C. M.,	——	King's Division.	22
do	1	"Irish Legion," King's Division.	22
Alexander, F. N.,	2	1st Division, District of Kentucky.	23
Alexander, J. I.,	1	2d Division.	17
do	1	7th Division.	17
do	1	3d Division.	15
Alexander, J. M.,	1st Colored.	District of Memphis.	16
Alford, S.. M,	1	2d Division.	7
do	2	U. S. Forces, north end of Folly Island, S. C.	10
do	2	U. S. Forces, Folly Island, S. C.	10
do	2	Vogdes's Division.	10
do	1	2d Division.	10
do	1	2d Division.	10
do	1	Getty's Division.	18
Allabach, P. H.,	2	3d Division.	5
Allard, T. B.,	1	2d Division.	9
Allcock, T.,	4	Defenses south of the Potomac.	22
do		Defenses north of the Potomac.	22
Allen, D. B.,	1	2d Division.	11
Allen, J. A. P.,	2	Defenses north of the Potomac.	22
Allen, Thos. S.,	3	1st Division.	6
Ames, A.,	——		10
do	2	U. S. Forces, south end of Folly Island, S. C.	10
do	——	U. S. Forces, Folly Island, S. C., North. Dist.	10
do	2	U. S. Forces, Folly Island, S. C.	10
do	——	District of Florida.	10
do	——	1st Division.	10
do	——	3d Division.	10
do	——	2d Division.	10
do	——	1st Division.	11
do	2	1st Division.	11
do	——	2d Division.	18
do	3	2d Division.	18
do	——	2d Division.	24
Ames, J. W.,	2	3d Division.	18
do	3	3d Division.	18
do	2	1st Division.	25
do	2	3d Division.	25
Ammen, Jacob,	——	4th Division.	23
Amory, J. J. C.,	——	1st Division.	18
do	1	District of Beaufort, S. C.	18
do	——	Defenses of New Berne, District of N. C.	18
Anderson, Dan'l,	3	Cavalry Division.	7
Anderson, N. L.,	2	3d Division.	4
Anderson, Robert,	3	3d Division.	1
Andrews, C. C.,	——	2d Division.	7
do	2	2d Division.	7
do	——	2d Division.	13
Andrews, Geo. L.	2	2d Division.	5
do	1	3d Division.	19
Andrews, J. W.,	3	3d Division.	2
Anthony, D. C.,	1	2d Division.	16
Armstrong, J. B.,	2	3d Division.	10
Armstrong, S. C.,	2	2d Division.	25
Asboth, A.,	——	6th Division.	16
do	——	District of Columbus.	16
do	2	3d Division.	19
Augur, C. C.,	1	3d Division.	1
do	——	U. S. Forces, Baton Rouge, La.	19
do	——	1st Division.	19
do	——		22
do	——	2d Division.	2d of Va.
Averill, W. W.,	4th Separate.		8
Ayres, R. B.,	1	1st Division.	5
do	4	1st Division.	5
do	——	2d Division.	5
do	1	2d Division.	5
B			
Bacon, Geo. A.,	Cavalry.	Left Wing.	16
Bailey, B. P.,	1	3d Division.	3
Bailey, G. W. K.,	1	1st Division.	13
Bailey, W. P.,	4	1st Division.	2
Baird, A.,	——	1st Division.	14
do	——	3d Division.	14
Baird, J P.,	2	1st Division.	11
Baker, J. B.,	Burns'.	Sedgwick's Division	2
Baldwin, P. P.,	2	2d Division, Right Wing.	14
do	3	2d Division.	20
Banbury, J.,	3	3d Division.	15
do	3	2d Division.	17
Bane, M. M.,	3	District of Corinth.	13
do	3	District of Corinth, Left Wing.	16
do	3	2d Division.	16
Banks, N. P.,	——	——	5
do	——	——	19
do	——	——	2d of Va.
Barlow, F. C.,	——	——	2
do	——	1st Division.	2
do	——	Sedgwick's Division.	2
do	2	2d Division.	11
do	——	1st Division.	11

NAME.	BRIGADE.	DIVISION, DISTRICT, &c.
Barnes, Chas.,	2	Defenses south of the Potomac.
Barnes, Jas.,	——	1st Division.
do	1	1st Division.
do	——	U. S. Forces, Norfolk and Portsmouth.
do	——	St. Mary's District.
Barnes, Jos. H.,	1	1st Division.
do	2	1st Division.
do	3	1st Division.
Barnes, M.,	2	1st Division.
Barnes, S. M.,	2	1st Division.
do	3	3d Division.
Barney, A. M.,	1	2d Division.
Barney, V. G.,	2	3d Division.
Barnum, H. A.,	3	2d Division.
Barrett, T. H.,	3	1st Division.
do	——	2d Division.
do	2	2d Division.
Barrett, W. W.,	2	3d Division.
Barry, H. W.,	1	2d Division.
Barry, Wm. F.,	——	Light Artillery Depot and Camps of Instr'n.
Barten, Rich. F.,	1	1st Division.
Bartholomew, O. A.,	1	2d Division.
Bartleson, F. A.,	1	1st Division.
Bartlett, J. J.,	——	1st Division.
do	3	1st Division.
do	2	1st Division.
do	——	3d Division.
do	——	2d Division.
Bartlett, W. C.,	1	4th Division.
Bartlett, W. F.,	——	1st Division.
do	1	1st Division.
Barton, T. M. L.,	3	Defenses south of the Potomac.
Barton, W. B.,	——	U. S. Forces, Hilton Head, S. C.
do	Barton's.	U. S. Forces, Hilton Head, S. C.
do	Barton's.	Hilton Head District.
do	Barton's.	District of Florida.
Bassett, Isaac C.,	3	1st Division.
Bates, D.,	1	3d Division.
do	——	3d Division.
do	1	3d Division.
do	1	1st Division.
do	1	3d Division.
Bates, T. I.,	2	2d Division.
Baxter, D. W. C.,	——	Sedgwick's Division.
do	Gorman's.	Sedgwick's Division.
do	Burns'.	Sedgwick's Division.
do	Dana's.	Sedgwick's Division.
Baxter, H.,	——	2d Division.
do	2	2d Division.
do	——	2d Division.
do	2	2d Division.
do	2	3d Division.
Bayley, T.,	1	1st Division.
do	2	1st Division.
Beach, B.,	3	4th Division.
Beach, Frank,	2	Getty's Division.
do	1	Sub-District of Albemarle.
Beadle, W. H. H.,	3	Defenses south of the Potomac.
Beal, L. W.,	2	2d Division.
Beale, Geo. L.,	1	1st Division.
do	2	1st Division.
Beatty, J.,	2	1st Division.
do	1	2d Division.
do	2	2d Division.
Beatty, S.,	——	3d Division.
do	2•	3d Division.
do	3	3d Division.
do	1	3d Division, Left Wing.
do	——	3d Division.
do	1	3d Division.
Beaver, Jas. A.,	1	1st Division.
do	3	1st Division.
do	4	1st Division.
Beckwith, E. G.,	——	4th Division.
Beecher, Jas. C.,	3d or African.	U. S. Forces, north end of Folly Island, S. C.
do	3	Vogdes' Division.
Belknap, J. S.,	1	4th Division.
Belknap, W. W.,	——	4th Division.
do	3	2d Division.
Bell, Louis,	3	2d Division.
do	3	3d Division.
Bendix, Jno. E.,	1	3d Division.
Benedict, Lewis,	3	1st Division.
do	3	1st Division.
Bennett, J. E.,	3	1st Division.
Bennett, T. W.,	2	3d Division.
do	——	——
Benton, W. P.,	——	1st Division.
do	1	1st Division.
do	2	2d Division.
do	——	3d Division.
do	1	14th Division.
Benton, T. H.,	2	3d Division, Arkansas Expedition.
Bentzoni, C.,	——	District of Eastern Arkansas.
Berdan, H ,	2	3d Division.
do	3	3d Division.
Berry, H. G.,	3	1st Division.
do	——	2d Division.
do	3	3d Division.
Berry, W. W.,	3	2d Division.
Berthoud, Alex F.,	3	1st Division.
Bertram, H.,	1	2d Division.
do	2	2d Division.
Biddle, Chapman,	1	3d Division.
Biddle, Geo. H.,	2	1st Division.
Bidwell, D. D.,	3	2d Division.
Bintliff, Jas.,	1	1st Division
do	3	1st Division.
Birge, H. W.,	——	1st Division.
do	——	2d Division.
do	1	2d Division.
do	2	2d Division.
do	1	4th Division.
do	3	4th Division.

INDEX.

INDEX--Continued.

INDEX--Continued.

INDEX--Continued.

NAME.	BRIGADE.	DIVISION, DISTRICT, &c.	CORPS.
Jones, W. S.,	2	2d Division.	15
do	3	4th Division.	15
Jourdan, J.,	1	2d Division.	18
do	2	5th Division.	18
do	Jourdan's.		18
do	2	Defenses of New Berne, N. C.	18
do	—	Sub-District of Beaufort, District of N. C.	18
do	4	1st Division.	24
Judah, H. M.,	—	2d Division.	23
do	—	3d Division.	23
Judd, H. B.,	—	District of Delaware.	8
Judson, Wm. R.,	—	District of the Frontier.	7
do	2	District of the Frontier.	7
do	3	District of the Frontier.	7
Judy, J. W.,	3	8th Division.	16
K			
Kammerling, G.,	2	3d Division.	14
Kane, Thos. L.,	2	1st Division.	12
do	2	2d Division.	12
Karge, Joseph,	1	Cavalry Division.	16
Kautz, A. V.,	3	1st Division.	23
do	—	1st Division.	25
Kearney, Ph.,	1	1st Division.	1
do	—	1st Division.	3
do	—	3d Division.	3
Keifer, J. W.,	2	3d Division.	3
do	2	3d Division.	6
Keigwin, J.,	2	1st Division.	13
do	3	1st Division.	13
do	1	9th Division.	13
Keim, W. H.,	2	3d Division.	4
Kellogg, Jno. A.,	1	3d Division.	5
Kelly, B. F.,	—	Railroad District.	8
do	—	Defenses of the Upper Potomac.	8
do	—	1st Division.	8
Kelly, P.,	2	1st Division.	2
Kenly, J. R.,	—	3d Division.	1
do	—	District of Eastern Shore of Maryland.	8
do	—	District of Delaware.	8
do	Maryland.	Defenses of the Upper Potomac.	8
do	—	District of Delaware and the Eastern Shore.	8
do	1st Separate.	—	8
do	3d Separate.	—	8
do	1	1st Division.	8
Kent, L.,	3	1st Division.	13
Keys, E. D.,	—		4
Kimball, N.,	1	3d Division.	2
do	Kimball's Independ't.		2
do	—	1st Division.	4
do	1	2d Division.	4
do	—	2d Division.	7
do	—	3d Division.	16
do	—	Arkansas Expedition, 2d Division.	16
do	—	Arkansas Expedition, 3d Division.	16
Kimball, Wm. K.,	2	4th Division.	19
King, E. A.,	2	4th Division.	14
King, J. H.,	—	1st Division.	14
do	2	1st Division.	14
do	3	1st Division.	14
King, Rufus,	—	3d Division.	1
do	—	1st Division.	4
do	Independent.	—	4
do	—	King's Division.	22
King, W. S.,	3	Defenses south of the Potomac.	22
Kinney, P.,	2	12th Division.	13
Kinney, T. J.,	1	3d Division.	16
do	4th Cavalry.	5th Division.	16
Kinsey, W. B.,	3	1st Division.	13
Kirby, J. M.,	1	1st Division.	4
Kirk, E. N.,	2	Right Wing, 2d Division.	14
Kitching, J. H.,	3	2d Division.	5
do	1	Defenses north of the Potomac.	22
Kittridge, C. W.,	1	13th Division.	16
do	1	Arkansas Expedition, 3d Division.	16
Kleckner, Chas.,	3	1st Division.	4
Knefler, F.,	1	3d Division.	21
do	3	3d Division.	4
Knipe, J. F.,	—	1st Division.	12
do	1	1st Division.	12
do	—	1st Division.	20
do	1	1st Division.	20
Kockersperger, C.,	Burns'.	Sedgwick's Division.	2
Krebs, J. M.,	Cavalry.		19
Krez, C.,	3	3d Division.	13
Kryzanowski, W.,	2	3d Division.	11
L			
Laibold, B.,	2	Right Wing, 3d Division.	14
do	2	3d Division.	20
Landrum, W. J.,	—	4th Division.	13
do	1	4th Division.	13
do	2	4th Division.	13
do	2	10th Division.	13
Lane, J. C.,	2	2d Division.	12
Lane, J. Q.,	2	2d Division.	4
Langley, J. W.,	3	2d Division.	14
Lanman, J. G.,	—	Right Wing, 4th Division.	13
do	—	4th Division.	16
Lawler, A. J.,	2	1st Division.	2
Lawler, M. K.,	2	1st Division.	13
do	2	1st Division.	13
do	3	1st Division.	13
do	—	4th Division.	13
do	2	14th Division.	13
do	—	District of Jackson, Left Wing.	16
do	2	3d Division.	16
do	—	3d Division.	19
Lazelle, H. M.,	Independent Cavalry.	—	22
Leasure, Daniel,	—	1st Division.	9
do	2	1st Division.	9
do	3	1st Division.	9
Ledlie, J. H.,	—	1st Division.	9

NAME.	BRIGADE.	DIVISION, DISTRICT, &c.
Ledlie, J. H.,	1	1st Division.
do	—	District of the Currituck.
Lee, A. C.,	Lee's Cavalry.	
Lee, A. L.,	—	12th Division.
do	—	3d Division.
do	1	3d Division.
Lee, F. L.,	Lee's.	
Lee, H. C.,	2	1st Division.
do	2	Getty's Division.
Lee, H. T.,	3	Defenses south of the Potomac.
Lee, J. C.,	2	1st Division.
do	1	Defenses south of the Potomac.
Leggett, M. D.,	2	Right Wing, 3d Division.
do	—	3d Division.
do	1	3d Division.
do	2	3d Division.
Lehman, T. F.,	—	4th Division.
do	1	District of the Albemarle.
do	—	Sub-District of the Albemarle.
Leman, J. A.,	3	1st Division.
Lemert, Wilson C.,	3	2d Division.
Leonard, John,	2	2d Division.
Leonard, S. H.,	—	2d Division.
do	1	2d Division.
do	3	2d Division.
do	1	2d Division.
Lewis, G. W.,	Cavalry.	
Lewis, Jas. M.,	2	3d Division.
do	2	Arkansas Expedition, 3d Division.
Lightburn, J. A. J.,	2	2d Division.
do	—	2d Division.
Lincoln, W. S.,	1	Independent Division.
Lindsey, D. W.,	4	1st Division.
do	2	9th Division.
Little, Jno. S.,	—	2d Division.
do	2	2d Division.
Littlefield, M. S.,	3d or African.	U. S. Forces, north end of Folly Island, S. C.
do	3	District of Florida, 1st Division.
Livingston, R. R.,	—	District of Northeastern Arkansas.
Lockman, J. I.,	2	3d Division.
Lockman, J. S.,	2	2d Division.
Lockwood, H. H.,	—	2d Division.
do	—	
do	—	District of Eastern Shore of Maryland.
do	1st Separate.	—
do	3d Separate.	—
Logan, J.,	2	4th Division.
Logan, John A.,	—	Right Wing, 3d Division.
do	—	
do	—	3d Division.
Long, C. H.,	1	Defenses north of the Potomac.
Loomis, J. M.,	2	Stanley's Division, Left Wing.
do	1	4th Division.
do	1	1st Division.
Lord, N. B.,	Cavalry.	Getty's Division.
Love, Geo. M.,	1	1st Division.
do	3	1st Division.
Love, S. P.,	1	3d Division.
do	2	District of Kentucky, 2d Division.
Lovell, Chas. S.,	2	2d Division.
Lowell, jr., C. R.,	Independent Cavalry.	
Lum, C. M.,	1	2d Division.
do	1	4th Division.
Lyle, P.,	1	2d Division.
do	2	2d Division.
do	2	2d Division.
do	1	2d Division.
do	1	3d Division.
Lynch, J. C.,	1	1st Division.
Lynch, W. F.,	1	3d Division.
Lynde, E.,	3	District of the Frontier.
Lytle, W. H.,	1	3d Division.
M		
Macauley, D.,	2d Separate.	—
do	1	3d Division.
do	3	2d Division.
MacDonald, C. R.,	2	2d Division.
MacDougall, C. D.,	3	1st Division.
do	Consolidated.	1st Division.
do	3	3d Division.
MacGregor, J. D.,	3	3d Division.
MacKenzie, R. S.,	2	1st Division.
Mackey, C. H.,	1	1st Division.
Macy, G. N.,	1	1st Division.
Madill, H. J.,	3	1st Division.
do	1	3d Division.
do	2	3d Division.
do	1	1st Division.
Magilton, A. L.,	2	3d Division.
do	3	3d Division.
Mallon, J. E.,	Dana's.	Sedgwick's Division.
Malloy, A. G.,	2	1st Division.
do	3	3d Division.
Malmborg, A.,	2	2d Division.
Maltby, Jasper A.,	—	3d Division.
do	3	3d Division.
Mann, A.,	1	3d Division.
Mansfield, J. K. F.,	—	Division at Suffolk, Va.
Manson, M. D.,	—	
do	—	2d Division.
do	1	3d Division.
do	2	3d Division.
Manter, F. H.,	1	1st Division.
Marble, J. M. C.,	1	Defenses north of the Potomac.
do	2	Defenses north of the Potomac.
Marsh, C. C,	1	3d Division, Right Wing.
do	1	3d Division.
Marshall, E. G.,	3	1st Division.
do	Provisional.	1st Division.
do	1	Defenses north of the Potomac.
Marshall, J. W.,	3	3d Division.
Marshall, W. A.,	3	1st Division.
Marston, G.,	1	3d Division.
do		1st Division.

INDEX--Continued.

NAME.	COMMAND.			NAME.	COMMAND.	
	BRIGADE.	DIVISION, DISTRICT, &c.	CORPS.		BRIGADE.	DIVISION, DISTRICT, &c.,
Wilder, J. T.,	1	4th Division.	14	Winslow, E. F.,	2	Cavalry Division.
do	1	5th Division.	14	Winthrop, F.,	1	2d Division.
Wilder, T. F.,	1	Independent Division.	24	do	——	3d Division.
Wiles, G. F..	2	3d Division.	17	Wisewell, M. N.,	——	Military District of Washington.
Wilhelm, T.,	2	Defenses south of the Potomac.	22	do	1	Veteran Reserve Corps Division.
Wilkin, Alex.,	2	1st Division.	16	Wistar, I. J.,	Reserve.	Division at Suffolk, Va.
Wilkinson, N.,	6	1st Division.	8	do	——	2d Division.
Willard, G. L.,	3	3d Division.	2	do	2	2d Division.
do	3	Abercrombie's Division.	22	do	——	U. S. Forces, Yorktown and vicinity.
Willett, J. M.,	Gorman's.	Sedgwick's Division.	2	Wistar, Langhorne,	1	3d Division.
do	Burns'.	Sedgwick's Division.	2	do	2	3d Division.
Williams, A. S.,	——	1st Division.	5	Withington, W. H.,	1	1st Division.
do	——	——	12	do	2	1st Division.
do	——	1st Division.	12	Wolfe, E. H.,	3	3d Division.
do	——	Temporary Division.	14	Wood, G. A.,	2	1st Division.
do	——	——	20	Wood, J.,	1	2d Division.
do	——	1st Division.	20	Wood, jr., J.,	3	3d Division.
do	——	1st Division.	2d of Va.	Wood, Oliver,	1	1st Division.
Williams, J. M.,	2	District of the Frontier.	7	do	2	2d Division.
do	2	1st Division.	7	do	4	District of Jackson, Left Wing.
do	Colored.	——	7	do	2	2d Division Arkansas Expedition.
Williams, R.,	1	4th Division.	15	Wood, T. J.,	——	——
Williamson, J. A.,	2	1st Division.	15	do	——	3d Division.
do	3	1st Division.	15	do	——	Left Wing, 1st Division.
Willich, August,	——	3d Division.	4	do	——	——
do	1	3d Division.	4	do	——	1st Division.
do	1	Right Wing, 2d Division.	14	do	Dana's.	Sedgwick's Division.
do	——	2d Division.	20	Woodall, Dan'l,	1	3d Division.
do	1	2d Division.	20	Woodbury, D. P.,	——	District of Key West and Tortugas.
Wilson, J. M.,	——	District of Delaware and Eastern Shore.	8	Woodruff, W. E.,	3	1st Division, Right Wing.
Wilson, Wm ,	1	1st Division.	2	Woods, C. R.,	——	1st Division.
do	Consolidated.	1st Division.	2	do	1	1st Division.
do	1	4th Division.	19	do	2	1st Division.

INDEX--Continued.

ERRATA.

1st Army Corps, J. W. Hofman should be J. W. Hoffman.
4th Army Corps, T. E. Champin should be T. E. Champion.
4th Army Corps, F. D. Sedgwick should be T. D. Sedgewick.
4th Army Corps, J. Conrad should be Col. 15th Mo. Vols.
5th Army Corps, W. W. Robison should be W. W. Robinson.
7th Army Corps, S. M. Alvord should be S. M. Alford.
11th Army Corps, W. Kryzonowski should be W. Kryzanowski.
13th Army Corps, J. C. Pugh should be I. C. Pugh.
13th Army Corps, C. C. Washburn should be C. C. Washburne.
16th Army Corps, W. W. Sandford should be W. W. Sanford.
16th Army Corps, B. Domblaser should be B. Dornblaser.
16th Army Corps, Geo. W. Waring, jr., should be Geo. E. Waring, jr.
16th Army Corps, Henry E. Burgh should be Henry B. Burgh.
16th Army Corps, E. D. Murray should be C. D. Murray.
16th Army Corps, F. Steel should be F. Steele.
17th Army Corps, I. C. Pugh should be Col. 41 Ill. Vols.
18th Army Corps, A. Zabriski should be A. Zabriskie.
19th Army Corps, J. I. Alexander should be Col. 59th Ind. Vols.
20th Army Corps, J. F. Knife should be J. F. Knipe.
20th Army Corps, G. W. Mindil should be G. W. Mindel.
20th Army Corps, C. Canby should be C. Candy.
21st Army Corps, T. D. Sedgwick should be T. D. Sedgewick.
22d Army Corps, C. C. Merservey should be C. C. Messervey.
22d Army Corps, J. Stahel should be J. H. Stahel.
23d Army Corps, Rich. F. Barter should be Rich. F. Barten.
23d Army Corps, John O. Dowd should be John O'Dowd.

GEN. GRANT'S HEADQUARTERS

SCALE

GEN. SHERMAN'S HEAD QUARTERS.

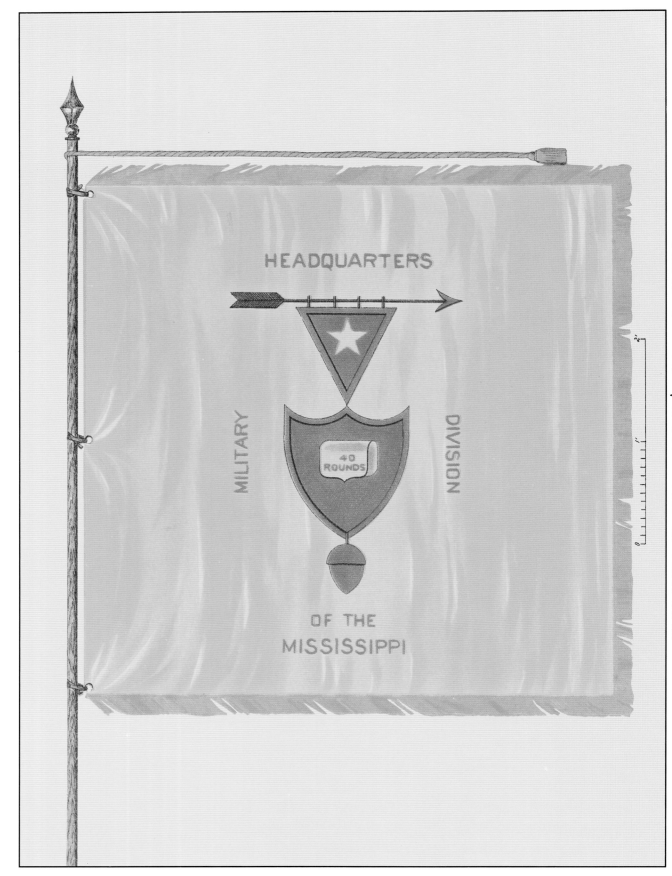

FLAG USED AT GEN. SHERMAN'S HEADQUARTERS.

FROM CHATTANOOGA TO THE END OF THE WAR.

SCALE

GEN. SHERIDAN'S BATTLE FLAG.

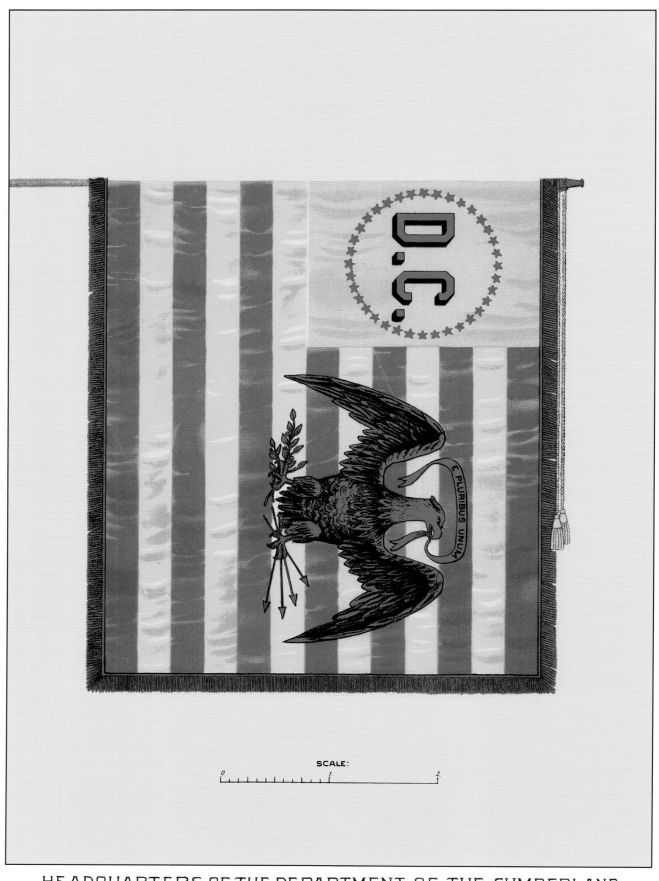

SCALE:

HEADQUARTERS OF THE DEPARTMENT OF THE CUMBERLAND.

USED BY GEN. GEORGE H. THOMAS.

HEADQUARTERS OF THE ARMY OF THE POTOMAC

USED FROM MAY 1864 PRIOR TO WHICH TIME THE NATIONAL FLAG WAS USED

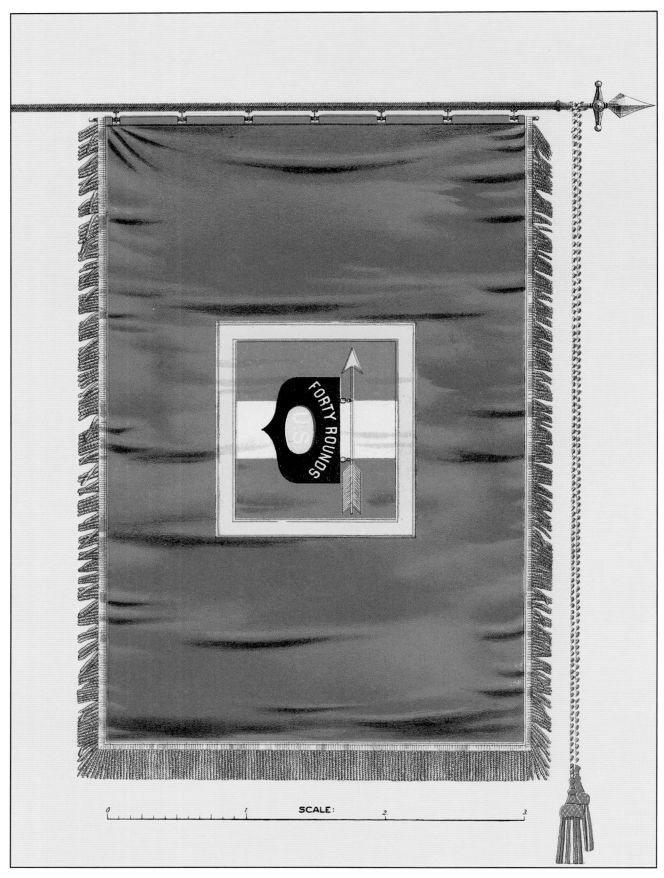

SCALE:

ARMY OF THE TENNESSEE.

HEADQUARTERS OF THE ARMY OF THE OHIO.

HEADQUARTERS OF GEN. BURNSIDE'S COMMAND.

PREVIOUS TO CONSOLIDATION WITH THE ARMY OF THE POTOMAC.

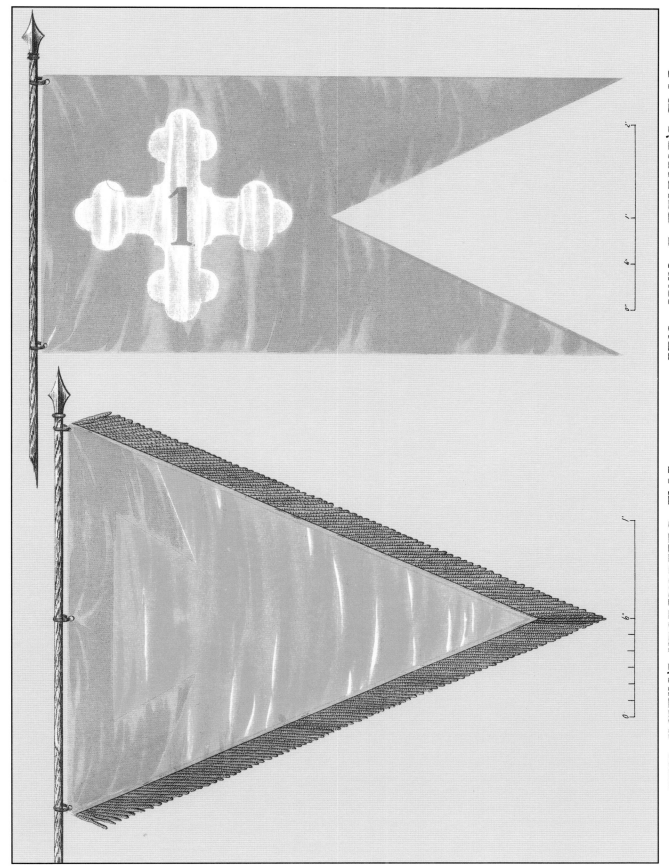

GEN. AVERILL'S HEADQUARTERS FLAG
WEST VIRGINIA.

GEN. JOHN F. REYNOLD'S FLAG
FIRST CORPS AT GETTYSBURG

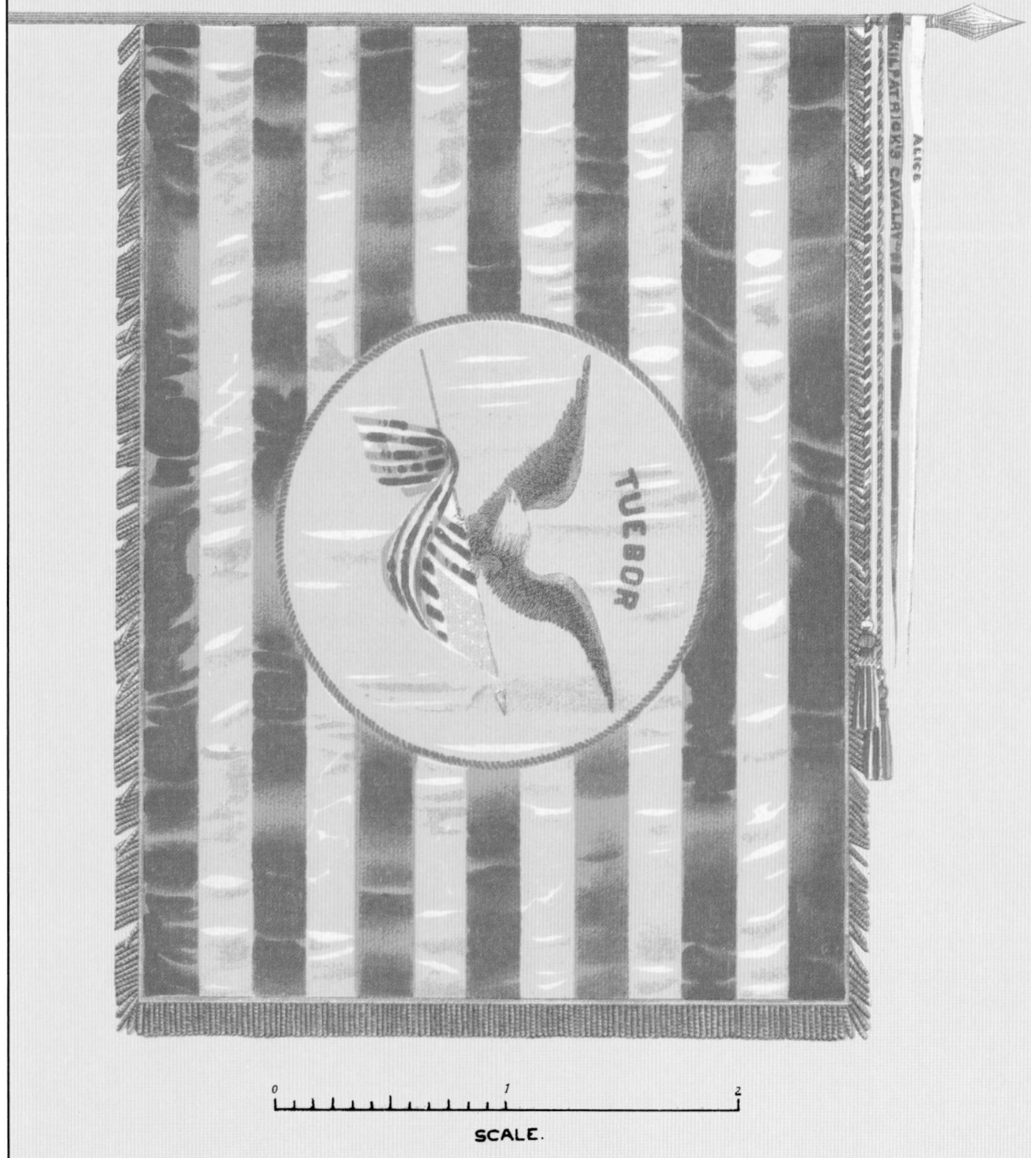

9TH ARMY CORPS.

THIS FLAG WAS PRESENTED TO THE 9TH CORPS HDQRS. BY LADIES OF LEXINGTON KY. PRIOR TO THE MOVEMENT TO VICKSBURG AND CARRIED UNTIL THE CORPS WAS TRANSFERRED TO THE EAST. A 9 IN THE LOOP OF THE 9 ON REVERSE SIDE.

SCALE.

GEN. KILPATRICK'S FLAG.

SCALE.

TUEBOR

KILPATRICK'S CAVALRY

Alice

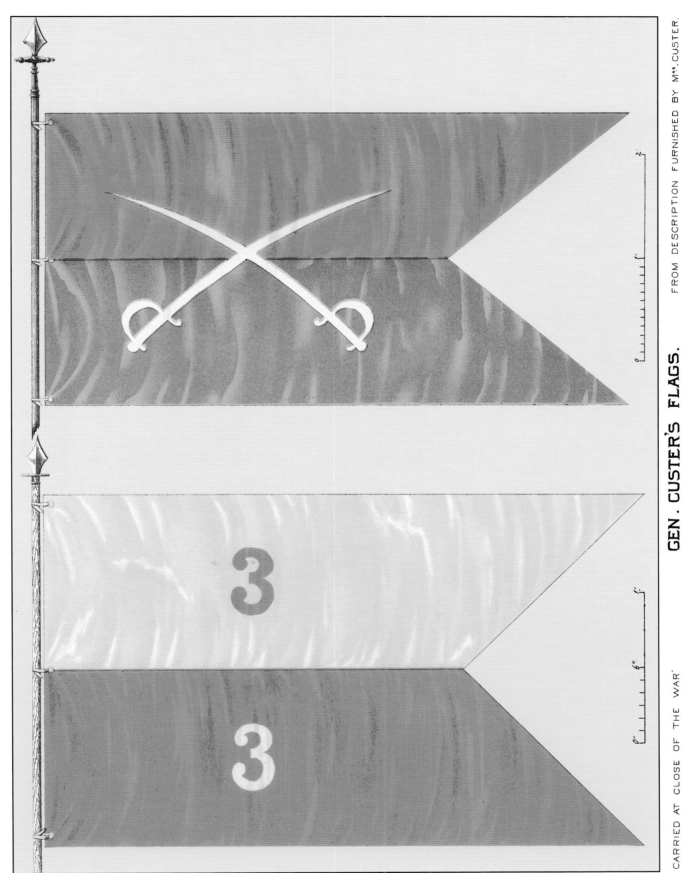

GEN. CUSTER'S FLAGS.

CARRIED AT CLOSE OF THE WAR. FROM DESCRIPTION FURNISHED BY M^{RS.} CUSTER.

RED STAR BRIGADE.

ADOPTED IN NOV. 1862 BY GEN'L C.A.HICKMAN'S BRIGADE AND USED
THEREAFTER WHEN ORIGINAL REGIMENTS SERVED TOGETHER.

THE REGULAR BRIGADE FLAG.

CARRIED BY BRIGADE OF REGULAR INFANTRY (GEN'L GEO. S.KYES COMDG)
ARMY OF POTOMAC THROUGHOUT CAMPAIGN OF 1862.

1ST CAVALRY DIVISION
MILITARY DIVISION OF WEST MISSISSIPPI

1ST CAVALRY DIVISION
ARMY OF THE POTOMAC & ARMY OF THE SHENANDOAH

34

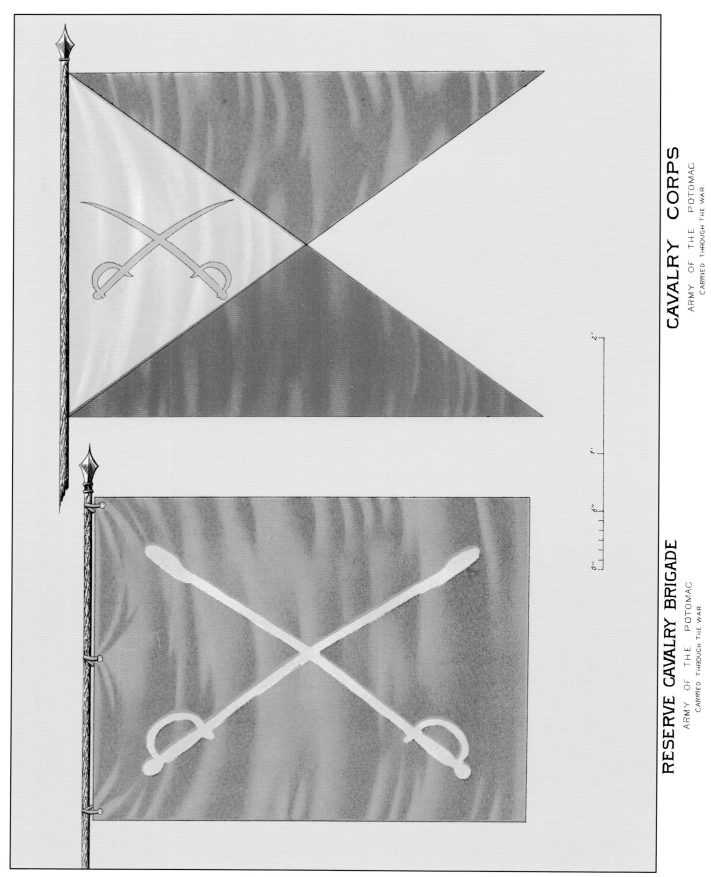

RESERVE CAVALRY BRIGADE

ARMY OF THE POTOMAC

CARRIED THROUGH THE WAR.

CAVALRY CORPS

ARMY OF THE POTOMAC

CARRIED THROUGH THE WAR.

REGIMENT

ARTILLERY.

U.S.

ARTILLERY REGIMENTAL.

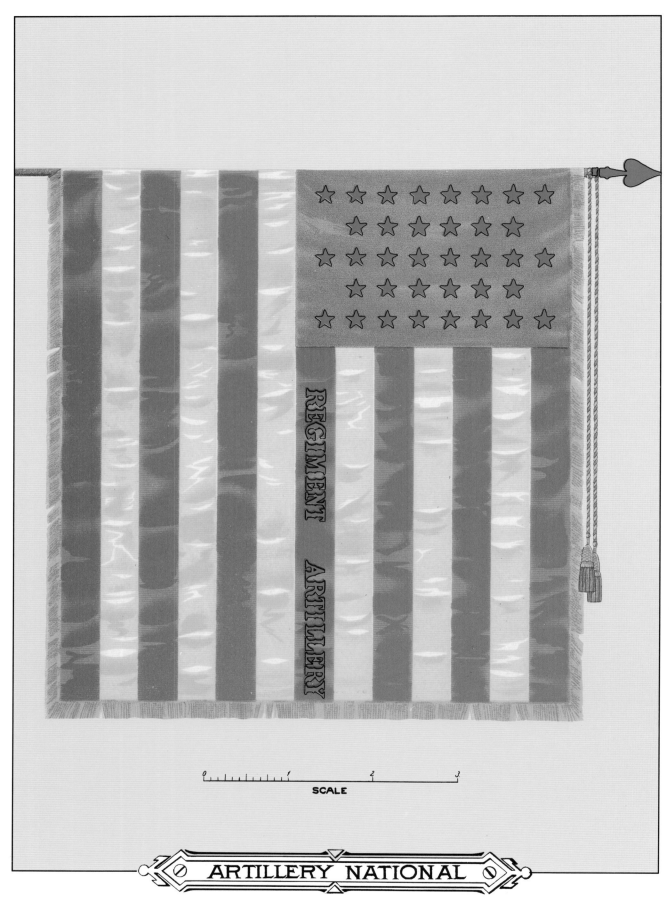

REGIMENT ARTILLERY

ARTILLERY NATIONAL

ALTHOUGH THE REGULATIONS OF 1863 PRESCRIBED WHITE STARS THE COLORS ACTUALLY CARRIED HAD GOLD STARS

SCALE

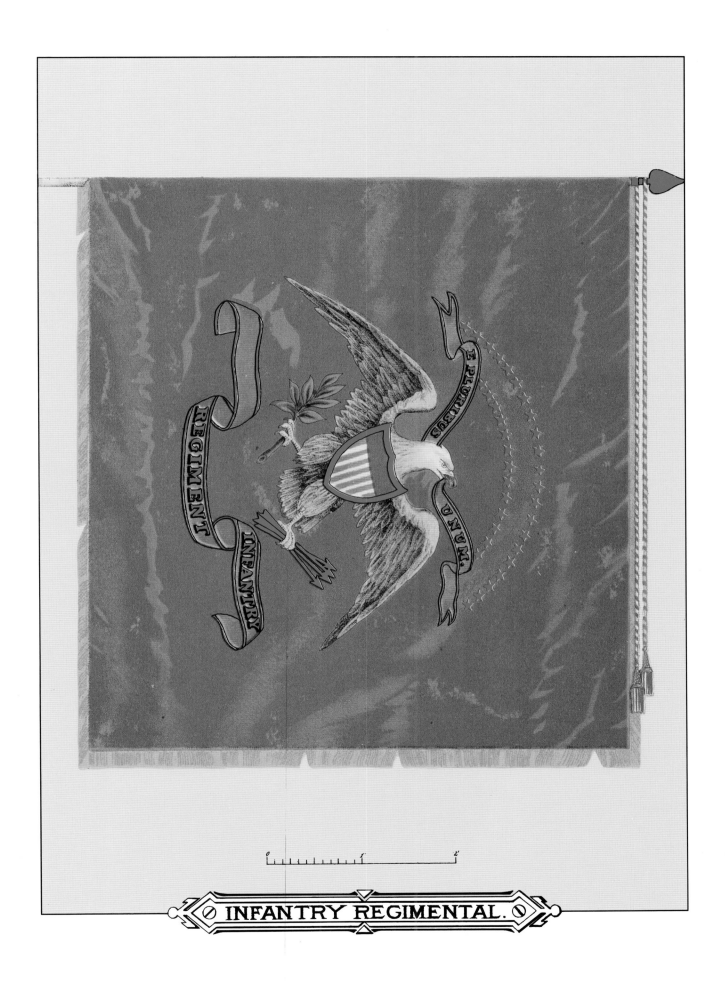

INFANTRY REGIMENTAL.

GUIDON.
CAVALRY AND LIGHT ARTILLERY.

STANDARD.
CAVALRY.

CAVALRY AND LIGHT ARTILLERY.

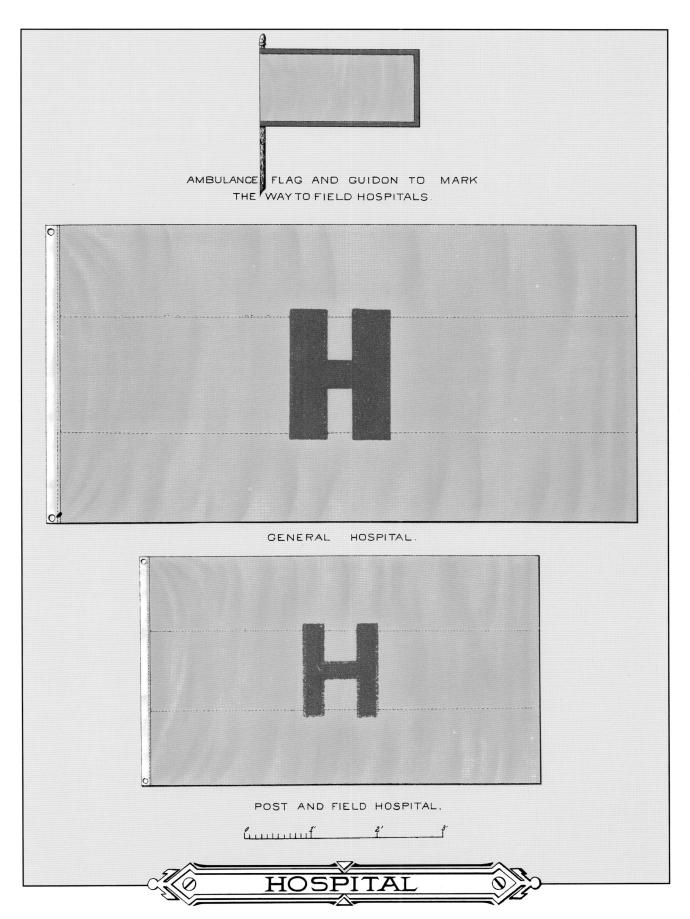

AMBULANCE FLAG AND GUIDON TO MARK
THE WAY TO FIELD HOSPITALS.

GENERAL HOSPITAL.

POST AND FIELD HOSPITAL.

HOSPITAL

FROM JANUARY 1864

FIRST A

Ordered March 3, 1862. Order of the President of the U. S.   Announced March 13, 1862, G. O. No. 101, Army of the Potomac.   Merged into the Depar

Transferred to 5th Army Corps, G. O. Army of the Potomac, March 24, 1864.   Recreated G. O. No. 287

COMMANDERS.

IRVIN McDOWELL,	Major-Gen
JOHN F. REYNOLDS,	Brigadier-
"	Major-Gen
"	"
J. S. WADSWORTH,	Brigadier-
"	"
JOHN NEWTON,	Major-Gen
WINFIELD S. HANCOCK,	"

1st Division—1st Army Corps.

Merged into Department of the Rappahannock, April 4, 1862.   Transferred to 5th Army Corps, March 23, 1864.
Organized and known as 1st Division, 1st Army Corps, or U. S. Vet. Vols., May, 1865.   Discontinued July, 1865.

COMMANDERS.		DATE.	
Wm. B. Franklin,	Brigadier-General.	March,	1862
Abner Doubleday,	"	September 14,	"
James S. Wadsworth,	"	January 4,	1863
"	"	March,	"
Solomon Meredith,	"	February 27,	"
"	"	November 13,	"
L. Cutler,	"	July 15,	"
"	"	September 23,	"
"	"	November 13,	" Temporary.
"	"	February 10,	1864
H. S. Briggs,	"	August 13,	1863 Temporary.
J. C. Rice,	"	August 23,	"
"	"	January 14,	1864 Temporary.
"	"	March,	" "
S. S. Carroll,	Bvt. Major-General.	May 8,	1865

Geo. A
J. B. R
Nelson
John G
J. C. R
S. H.
Henry

1st Brigade—1st Division.

Merged into Department of the Rappahannock, April 4, 1862.
Transferred to 2d Brigade, 1st Division, June, 1863.
Reorganized June, 1863.   Formerly 4th Brigade, 1st Division.
Transferred to 5th Army Corps, March 23, 1864.
Reorganized May, 1865, and known as 1st Brigade, 1st Division,
1st A. C. or U. S. Vet. Vols.
Discontinued July, 1865.

COMMANDERS.		DATE.	
Philip Kearney,	Brigadier-General.	March,	1862
Walter Phelps, Jr.,	Col. 22d N. Y. Vols.	Sept.,	"
"	" 22d " "	April,	1863
Wm. M. Searing,	" 30th " " Temp.,	March,	"
E. B. Fowler,	" 14th " S. M.	May 30,	"
Solomon Meredith,	Brigadier-General.	June,	"
W. W. Robinson,	Col. 7th Wis. Vols.	July 2,	"
"	" 7th " "	Feb. 28,	1864
Henry A. Morrow,	" 24th Mich. "	Jan. 3,	"
Oliver Wood,	" 4th U. S. Vet. Vols.	May,	1865
Francis Fessenden,	Brigadier-General.	June,	"

2d Brigade—1st Division.

Merged into Department of the Rappahannock, April 4, 1862.
Transferred to 5th Army Corps, March 23, 1864.
Reorganized May, 1865, and known as 2d Brigade, 1st Division,
1st A. C. or U. S. Vet. Vols.
Discontinued July, 1865.

COMMANDERS.		DATE.	
Henry W. Slocum,	Brigadier-General.	March,	1862
J. W. Hofman,	Lt.-Col. 56th Pa. Vols.	Sept.,	"
"	" 56th " "	Jan. 14,	1864
James Gavin,	" 7th Ind. "	Nov. 10 to 20, 1862
"	" 7th " "	Jan. 18,	1863
Abner Doubleday,	Brigadier-General.	Dec. 24,	1862
"	"	Jan. 4,	1863
Geo. H. Biddle,	Col. 95th N. Y. Vols.	Dec. 28,	1862
"	" 95th " "	Aug. 16,	1863
L. Cutler,	Brigadier-General.	July 15,	"
E. B. Fowler,	Col. 14th N. Y. S. M.	Sept. 24,	"
"	" 14th " "	Oct.,	"
J. C. Rice,	Brigadier-General.	Feb. 21,	"
"	"	Feb. 10,	1864
W. H. Morgan,	Col. 3d U. S. Vet. Vols.	May,	1865

3d Brigade—1st Division.

Merged into Department of the Rappahannock, April 4, 1862.
Discontinued June 16, 1863.
Reorganized May, 1865, and known as 3d Brigade, 1st Division,
1st A. C. or U. S. Vet. Vols.
Discontinued July, 1865.

COMMANDERS.		DATE.	
John Newton,	Brigadier-General.	March,	1862
M. R. Patrick,	"	Sept.,	"
W. F. Rodgers,	Col. 21st N. Y. Vols.	Oct. 6,	"
G. R. Paul,	Brigadier-General.	" 14,	"
"	"	March 1,	1863
"	"	April 20,	"
H. M. Bossert,	Col. 137th Pa. Vols.	Feb. 17,	"
Alex. T. Berthoud,	" 31st N. Y. "	March 29,	"
M. F. Gallagher,	Lt.- " 7th U. S. Vet. Vols.	May,	1865
T. H. Neill,	Brigadier-General.	June 11,	"

1st B

Merged into Depart
Transferred t

COMM	
John F. Reynolds,
A. Duryea,
T. F. McCoy,
"
A. R. Root,
S. H. Leonard,
"
G. R. Paul,
Peter Lyle,

4th Brigade—1st Division.

Organized September, 1862.   Designated 1st Brigade, 1st Division, June, 1863.

COMMANDERS.		DATE.	
John Gibbon,	Brigadier-General.	September,	1862
L. Cutler,	Col. 6th Wis. Vols.	November 5,	"
Solomon Meredith,	Brigadier-General.	" 26,	"
"		March,	1863
W. W. Robinson,	Col. 7th Wis. Vols.	February 27,	"

Edw.
Rich.
N. Ta
S. H.
Chas.

appahannock, April 4, 1862.   Recreated September 12, 1862, G. O. No. 129, War Department.   Announced G. O. Army of the Potomac, September 28, 1862.

ent, November 28, 1864.   Corps discontinued and troops ordered to be mustered out of service, July 11, 1866.

	DATE.
	March 14, 1862.
	September 29, "
	January 4, 1863.
	Early in March, 1863.
	A few days in January, 1863.
	February 27, 1863.
	July 2, "
	November 28, 1864.

2d Division—1st Army Corps.

d into Department of the Rappahannock, April 4, 1862.

ANDERS.		DATE.
	Brigadier-General.	March, 1862
	"	September, "
	"	November 4, "
	"	From Dec., 1862, to Dec. 30, 1862
	"	November 5, 1862
	"	December 30, "
	"	April, 1863
	Col. 13th Mass. Vols.	February, " Temporary.
	Brigadier-General.	A few days in December, 1863

3d Division—1st Army Corps.

Merged into Department of the Rappahannock, April 4, 1862.   Transferred to 5th Army Corps, March 23, 1864.

COMMANDERS.		DATE.
Rufus King,	Brigadier-General.	March, 1862
Geo. G. Meade,	"	September 12, "
H. G. Sickel,	Col. 3d Pa. V. R. C.	December 25, "
Abner Doubleday,	Brigadier General.	January 18, 1863
R. P. Cummins,	Col. 142d Pa. Vols.	Short time in February, 1863
John R. Kenly,	Brigadier-General.	January 11, 1863
"	"	" 1864
N. T. Dushane,	Col. 1st Md. Vols.	December 29, 1863 .

ivision.

hannock, April 4, 1862.
March 23, 1864.

	DATE.
al.	March, 1862
	Sept., "
ols.	Oct., "
"	Dec. 11, 1863
"	Nov. 15, 1862
"	May 21, 1863
al.	Jan. 31, 1864
	June 17, 1863
ols.	July 5, "

2d Brigade—2d Division.

Merged into Department of the Rappahannock, April 4, 1862.
Transferred to 5th Army Corps, March 23, 1864.

COMMANDERS.		DATE.
Geo. G. Meade,	Brigadier-General.	March, 1862
Peter Lyle,	Col. 90th Pa. Vols.	Sept., "
Henry Baxter,	Brigadier-General.	April 21, 1863
"	"	Feb., "
Richard Coulter,	Col. 11th Pa. Vols.	Dec., 1863
Chas. Wheelock,	" 97th N. Y. Vols.	Jan , 1864

1st Brigade—3d Division.

Merged into Department of the Rappahannock, April 4, 1862.
Reformed by consolidation of 2d Brigade, 3d Division,
December 28, 1863.
Transferred to 5th Army Corps, March, 23, 1864.

COMMANDERS.		DATE.
Ch. C. Augur,	Brigadier-General.	March, 1862
Truman Seymour,	"	Sept., "
W. Sinclair,	Col. 6th Pa. V. R. C.	Nov. 14, "
W. McCandless,	" 2d " "	Dec. 13, "
Jas. R. Porter,	" 135th Pa. Vols.	Feb. 17, 1863
Thos. A. Rowley,	Brigadier-General.	March 28, "
Chapman Biddle,	Col. 121st Pa. Vols.	July, "
"	" 121st " "	Oct., "
A. B. McCalmont, Lt.-	" 142d " "	Sept., "
Langhorne Wister,	" 150th " "	Dec. 28, "
E. L. Dana,	" 143d " "	Feb., 1864

2d Brigade—3d Division.

Merged into Department of the Rappahannock, April 4, 1862.
Consolidated with 1st Brigade, 3d Division,
December 28, 1863.
Reorganized December 28, 1863.   Formerly 3d Brig., 3d Div.
Transferred to 5th Army Corps, March 23, 1864.

COMMANDERS.		DATE.
Jas. S. Wadsworth,	Brigadier-General.	March 13 to 17, 1862
M. R. Patrick,	"	" " "
A. L. Magilton,	Col. 4th Pa. Res. Corps.	Sept., "
R. P. Cummins,	" 142d " Vols.	Dec. 27, "
Roy Stone,	" 149th " "	Feb., 1863
E. L. Dana,	" 143d " "	July 1, "
Langhorne Wister,	" 150th " "	Aug. 22, "
Chas. E. Phelps,	" 7th Md. "	Dec. 28, "
N. T. Dushane,	" 1st " "	Jan., 1864

3d Brigade—2d Division.

ment of the Rappahannock, April, 1862.   Discontinued May 20, 1863.

ANDERS.		DATE.
	Brigadier-General.	March, 1862
	Col. 11th Pa. Vols.	September, "
	" 11th " "	March, 1863
	Brigadier-General.	October 4, 1862
	"	December 30, 1862
	Col. 13th Mass. Vols.	From Dec. to Dec. 30, 1862
	" 13th " "	January 23, 1863
	" 13th " "	April, "
	" 97th N. Y. "	February, "

3d Brigade—3d Division.

Merged into Department of the Rappahannock, April 4, 1862.   Discontinued February, 1863.
Reorganized by assignment of Regiments, July 11, 1863.   Termed 2d Brigade, 3d Division, December 28, 1863.

COMMANDERS.		DATE.
L. Cutler,	Col. 6th Wis. Vols.	March, 1862
C. F. Jackson,	Brigadier-General.	September, "
Robt. Anderson,	Lt.-Col. 9th Pa. Res. Corps.	December 13, "
M. D. Hardin,	" 12th " "	" 30, "
J. W. Fisher,	" 5th " "	January, 1863
N. T. Dushane,	" 1st Md. Vols.	July, "

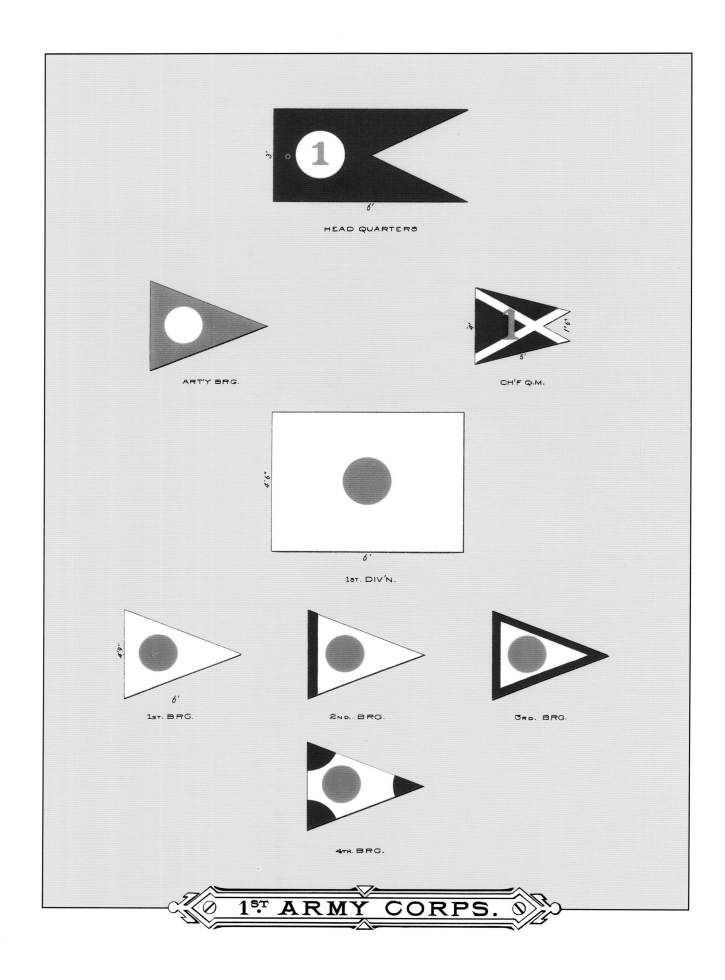

HEAD QUARTERS

ART'Y BRG.

CH'F Q.M.

1ST. DIV'N.

1ST. BRG.

2ND. BRG.

3RD. BRG.

4TH. BRG.

1ST ARMY CORPS.

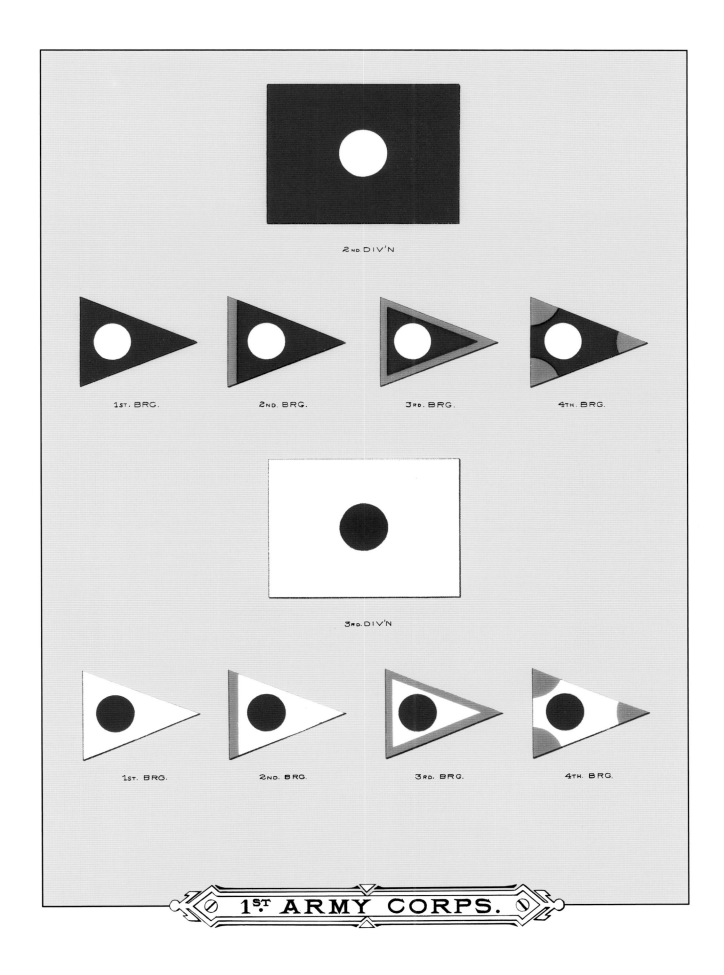

2ND DIV'N

1ST. BRG.   2ND. BRG.   3RD. BRG.   4TH. BRG.

3RD. DIV'N

1ST. BRG.   2ND. BRG.   3RD. BRG.   4TH. BRG.

1ST ARMY CORPS.

SECOND AR

Created March 3, 1862, by Order of the President of the U. S.   Announced March 13, 1862.

COMMANDERS.

E. V. SUMNER,	Brigadier-Gene
D. N. COUCH,	Major-General.
JOHN SEDGWICK,	"
O. O. HOWARD,	"
W. S. HANCOCK,	"
WM. HAYS,	Brigadier-Gene
G. K. WARREN,	Major-General.
J. C. CALDWELL,	Brigadier-Gene
A. A. HUMPHREYS,	Major-General.
F. C. BARLOW,	Bvt. Major-Ge
G. MOTT,	" "

First Division—Formerly Richardson's Division—2d Army Corps.

Discontinued G. O. No. 35, Army of the Potomac, June 28, 1865.

COMMANDERS.		DATE.
I. B. Richardson,	Brigadier-General.	March 13, 1862, and August, 1862
W. H. French,	"	July, 1862, Temporary
W. S. Hancock,	"	September 17, 1862
"	Major-General.	February 20, 1863
S. K. Zook,	Brigadier-General.	January 24, 1863, Temporary
J. C. Caldwell,	"	May, 1863, and February, 1864
Paul Frank,	Col. 52d N. Y. Vols.	15 days in December, 1863, and temporary in March, 1864
H. L. Brown,	" 145th Pa. "	January, 1864
F. C. Barlow,	Brigadier-General.	April, "
N. A. Miles,	"	July, "
John Ramsey,	Bvt. Brigadier-General—Col. 8th N. J. Vols.	May 20, 1865

Meagher's Brigade— Richardson's Division.

Changed to 1st Brigade, 1st Division, September, 1862.
Designation exchanged with 2d Brigade, 1st Division, November, 1862.

COMMANDERS.		DATE.
T. F. Meagher,	Brigadier-General.	March, 1862
"	"	Sept., "
Robt. Nugent,	Col. 69th N.Y.Vols.	July, "
John C. Caldwell,	Brigadier-General.	Nov., "
G. Von Schack,	Col. 7th N.Y. Vols.	Dec., "

1st Brigade— 1st Division.

Discontinued G. O. No. 35, Army of the Potomac, June 28, 1865.

COMMANDERS.		DATE.
J. C. Caldwell,	Brigadier-General.	Feb., 1863
E. C. Cross,	Col. 5th N.H.Vols.	May, "
Jas. A. Beaver,	" 148th Pa. "	June, "
N. A. Miles,	" 61st N.Y. "	July, "
"	" 61st " "	April, 1864
H. B. McKeen,	" 81st Pa. "	Dec , 1863
K. O. Broady,	Lt.- " 61st N. Y. "	March, 1864
J. C. Lynch,	" 183d Pa. "	July, 1864
Wm. Wilson,	Lt.- " 81st " "	Oct., "
"	" 81st " "	June, 1865
G. N. Macy,	" 20th Mass. "	Nov. 1, 1864
"	" 20th " "	March, 1865
G. W. Scott,	Col. 61st N.Y.Vols.	Feb. 22, "
"	" 61st " "	March 15, "
"	" 61st " "	May 31, "
John Fraser,	" 140th Pa. "	April 17, "

Howard's Brigade— Richardson's Division.

Name changed to 2d Brigade, 1st Division, September, 1862.

COMMANDERS.		DATE.
O. O. Howard,	Brigadier-General.	March, 1862
J. C. Caldwell,	"	June, "

2d Brigade— 1st Division.

Designation exchanged with 1st Brigade, 1st Di November, 1862.
Consolidated with 3d Brig., 1st Div., June 27, and termed Consolidated Brigade, 1st Divisi Reorganized November, 1864.
Discontinued G. O. No. 35, A. of P., June 28,

COMMANDERS.		DA
J. C. Caldwell,	Brigadier-General.	Sept.
T. F. Meagher,	"	Nov.,
"	"	Feb.
P. Kelly,	Col. 88th N. Y. Vols.	Dec.,
"	" 88th " "	May,
R. Byrnes,	" 28th Mass. "	Jan.,
"	" 28th " "	May,
A. J. Lawler,	Maj. 28th " "	Feb.,
T. A. Smyth,	Col. 1st Del. "	March
Robert Nugent,	" 69th N.Y. "	Nov.
"	" 69th " "	Feb.,
R. C. Duryea,	" 7th " Hy.Art.	Jan.,

French's Brigade— Richardson's Division.

Designation changed to 3d Brigade, 1st Division, September, 1862.

COMMANDERS.		DATE.
Wm. H. French,	Brigadier-General.	March, 1862
"	"	Aug., "
Jno. R. Brooke,	Col. 53d Pa. Vols.	July, "

3d Brigade— 1st Division.

Consolidated with 2d Brigade, 1st Division, and termed 1st Brigade, 1st Division, June 27, 1864.
Reorganized November, 1864.

COMMANDERS.		DATE.
Jno. R. Brooke,	Col. 53d Pa. Vols.	Sept., 1862
S. K. Zook,	" 57th N.Y. "	Oct., "
"	" 57th " "	March, 1863
R. P. Roberts,	" 140th Pa. "	Jan., "
Paul Frank,	" 52d N.Y. "	Feb., "
"	" 52d " "	July 28, "
"	" 52d " "	Dec., 1863
"	" 52d " "	Feb., 1864
"	" 52d " "	April, "
J. A. Beaver,	" 148th Pa. "	Oct., 1863
"	" 148th " "	Jan., 1864
A. Funk,	" 39th N.Y. "	March, "
"	" 39th " "	May 28, 1865
C. D. MacDougall,	" 111th " "	1864
"	" 111th " "	Nov., "
"	" 111th " "	April 2, 1865
G. Von Schack,	" 7th " "	Jan., 28, "
H. J. Madill,	" 141st Pa. "	Feb. 25, "

4th Brigade— 1st Division.

Organized April 13, 1863, S. O. No. 87, 2d Army Corps.

COMMANDERS.		DATE.
J. R. Brooke,	Col. 53d Pa. Vols.	April 13, 1863
"	" 53d " "	June, "
"	" 53d " "	Sept "
"	" 53d " "	March 25, 1864
W. F. Bailey,	" 2d Del. "	May, 1863
"	" 2d " "	Dec. 29, "
J. A. Beaver,	" 148th Pa. "	Aug. 29, "
L. W. Bradley,	Maj. 64th N.Y. "	Jan., 1864
H. L. Brown,	Col. 145th Pa. "	Feb., "
John Hastings,	Lt.- " 7th N.Y.Hy.Art.	June, "
K. O. Broady,	" " 61st " Vols.	July 25, "
Wm. Glenny,	" " 64th " "	Aug. 25, "
"	" " 64th " "	Dec. 30, "
St. C. A. Mulholland,	Lt.-Col.116th Pa.Vols	Oct. 15, "
"	" 116th " "	May 20, 1865
J. Ramsey,	Col. 8th N. J. Vols.	Jan. 13, "
W. M. Mintzer,	" 53d Pa. "	April 20, "
G. T. Egbert,	" 183d " "	June, "

Consolidated Brigade— 1st Divisio

Organized June 27, 1864.
Discontinued S. O. 276, 2d A. C., November 2

COMMANDERS.		DA
C. D. MacDougall,	Col. 111th N.Y.Vols.	June
"	" 111th " "	Oct.
L. Crandall,	" 125th " "	July
Wm. Wilson,	Lt.- " 81st Pa. "	Aug.,
J. E. McGee,	" " 69th N.Y. "	Sept.

..I, Army of the Potomac. Discontinued G. O. No. 35, Army of the Potomac, June 28, 1865.

DATE.

March 13, 1862.
October 7, 1862, and February 7, 1863.
December 26, 1862.
January 26, 1863.
{ Temporary May 22, 1863, and Permanent }
{ June 24 and Dec. 29, 1863, and March 24, 1864. }
Temporary July 3, 1863.
Temporary Aug. 16, 1863, Jan. and Feb., 1864.
15 days, Dec., 1863, and Jan. 27, 1864.
Nov. 25, 1864, and May 5, 1865.
Temporary, April 22, 1865.
From June 9 to 19, 1865.

Sedgwick's Division—2d Army Corps.

Designation changed to 2d Division, September, 1862. Discontinued G. O. No. 35, Army of the Potomac, June 28, 1865.

COMMANDERS.		DATE.
John Sedgwick,	Brigadier-General.	March 13, 1862
O. O. Howard,	"	September, 1862
"	Major-General.	February 7, 1863
J. T. Owen,	Brigadier-General.	Temporary, January 26, 1863, and 10 days in February, 1863
John Gibbon,	"	April 1, 1863, and April 4, 1864
"	Major-General.	August 20, 1864
Wm. Harrow,	Brigadier-General.	Temporary, July 4, 1863, and September, 1863
A. S. Webb,	"	Temporary, August 15 and October 7, 1863, and December, 1863
D. W. C. Baxter,	Col. 72d Pa. Vols.	From December 10 to 21, 1863
T. A. Smyth,	" 1st Del. "	Temporary, July 31, 1864, and December, 1864
Wm. Hays,	Brigadier-General.	February 25, 1865
F. C. Barlow,	Bvt. Major-General.	April 6, 1865
J. P. McIvor,	Col. 170th N. Y. Vols.	May 28, 1865

..rman's Brigade— Sedgwick's Division.

..gnation changed to 1st Brigade, 2d Division, September, 1862.
..ntinued G. O. No. 35, A. of P., June 28, 1865.

COMMANDERS.		DATE.
..orman,	Brigadier-General.	March, 1862
"	"	Sept., "
"	"	Oct., "
"	"	March 10, 1863
..orehead,	Col. 106th Pa. Vols.	Dec. 19, 1862
"	" 106th " "	May 13, 1863
..well,	" 19th Me. "	Jan. 25, "
..ard,	" 15th Mass. "	Feb. 7, "
..rrow,	Brigadier-General.	June, "
..ath,	Col. 19th Me. Vols.	July, "
"	" 19th " "	Oct. 6, "
..Baxter,	" 72d Pa. "	Aug. 28, "
"	" 72d " "	Oct. 22, "
"	" 72d " "	Jan. 2, 1864
..aith,	" 71st " "	Sept. 28, 1863
..udson,	" 82d N.Y. "	Dec. 10, "
..en,	Maj. 152d " "	Feb. 10, 1864
..onnor,	Col. 19th Me. "	Feb. 27, "
..ebb,	Brigadier-General.	April, "
..cKeen,	Col. 81st Pa. Vols.	May, "
..erce,	Brigadier-General.	June 4, "
..erce,	Lt.-Col. 108th Pa. Vols.	" 27, "
..igg,	" " 59th N. Y. "	Aug. 13, "
..gan,	Brigadier-General.	Sept., "
..illett,	Col. 8th N.Y.Hy.Art.	Nov. 15, "
..lmstead,	" 59th N. Y. Vols.	Jan. 19, 1865
"	" 59th " "	March 14, "
..est,	" 17th Me. "	March 1, "

Burns' Brigade— Sedgwick's Division.

Designation changed to 2d Brigade, 2d Division, September, 1862.
Discontinued G. O. No. 35, A. of P., June 28, 1865.

COMMANDERS.		DATE.
W. W. Burns,	Brigadier-General.	March, 1862
D. W. C. Baxter,	Col. 72d Pa. Vols.	July, "
"	" 72d " "	Aug., "
"	" 72d " "	Sept., "
"	" 72d " "	Jan., 1863
"	" 72d " "	Oct., "
O. O. Howard,	Brigadier-General.	Sept., 1862
J. T. Owen,	Col. 69th Pa. Vols.	Oct., "
"	" 69th " "	March, 1863
"	" 69th " "	April, 1864
A. S. Webb,	Brigadier-General.	June 28, 1863
"	"	Sept., "
W. L. Curry,	Lt.-Col. 106th Pa. Vols.	Aug., "
F. E. Heath,	" 19th Me. "	Oct. 21, "
A. F. Devereux,	" 19th Mass. "	Nov. 17, "
R. P. Smith,	" 71st Pa. "	Jan. 9, 1864
C. Kockersperger,	Lt.- " 71st " "	March 18, "
T. G. Morehead,	" 106th " "	" 26, "
J. P. McIvor,	" 170th N.Y. "	June 3, "
"	" 170th " "	June 23, "
"	" 170th " "	Nov. 3, "
"	" 170th " "	Feb. 5, 1865
J. Ramsey,	Col. 8th N. J. Vols.	June 7, 1864
W. Blaisdell,	" 11th Mass. "	" 20, "
M. Murphy,	" 69th N.Y. "	July, "
"	" 69th " "	Nov., "
J. M. Willett,	" 8th "Hy.Art.	Oct., "
J. B. Baker,	" 8th "	May 28, 1865
Wm. DeLacy,	Lt.- " 164th " Vols.	June 29, "

Dana's Brigade— Sedgwick's Division.

Designation changed to 3d Brigade, 2d Division, September, 1862.
Discontinued G. O. No. 35, A. of P., June 28, 1865.

COMMANDERS.		DATE.
N. J. T. Dana,	Brigadier-General.	March, 1862
Wm. L. Tidball,	Col. 59th N.Y.Vols.	Aug., "
N. J. Hall,	" 7th Mich. "	Sept., "
"	" 7th " "	March, 1863
J. R. Brooke,	" 53d Pa. "	Dec. 27, 1862
J. E. Mallon,	" 42d N.Y. "	July 18–27, 1863
"	" 42d " "	Oct. 1–14, "
R. P. Smith,	" 71st Pa. "	July 27, "
D. W. C. Baxter,	" 72d " "	Aug. 11, "
A. D. Wass,	Lt.- " 19th Mass. "	" 28, "
T. G. Morehead,	" 106th Pa. "	Oct. 15, "
S. S. Carroll,	" 8th Ohio "	March, 1864
T. A. Smyth,	" 1st Del. "	May 17, "
"	" 1st " "	Aug., "
"	Brigadier-General.	Feb. 28, 1865
S. A. Moore,	Lt.-Col. 14th Conn.Vols.	July 31, 1864
F. E. Pierce,	" " 108th N.Y. "	Dec. 23, "
Dan'l Woodall,	" 1st Del. "	Feb., 1865
"	" 1st " "	April 7, "

4th Brigade— 2d Division.

Organized May, 1864.
Designation changed to 2d Brigade, 2d Division, June, 1864.

COMMANDER.		DATE.
R. O. Tyler,	Brigadier-General.	May 9, 1864

Blenker's Division—2d Army Corps.

Transferred to the Department of the Rappahannock, April 4, 1862.

COMMANDER.		DATE.
L. Blenker,	Brigadier-General.	March 13, 1862

Third D

Organized Septem

The 1st Division, 3d Corps, joined 2d Corps March, 1864, and w

COMMANDERS.

Wm. H. French,	Brigadier-Gene
A. Sully,	"
Alex. Hays,	"
J. T. Owen,	"
D. B. Birney,	Major-General.
G. Mott,	Brigadier-Gene
"	Bvt. Major-Ger
R. DeTrobriand,	Brigadier-Gene

Stahel's Brigade—Blenker's Division.

Transferred to Department of Rappahannock, April 4, 1862.

COMMANDER.		DATE.
J. H. Stahel,	Brigadier-General.	March, 1862

Von Steinwehr's Brigade—Blenker's Division.

Transferred to Department of Rappahannock, April 4, 1862.

COMMANDER.		DATE.
A Von Steinwehr,	Brigadier-General.	March, 1862

1st Brigade—3d Division.

Organized September, 1862.
Known as Kimball's Independent Brigade prior to September, 1862.
Discontinued G. O. No. 35, A. of P., June 28, 1865.

COMMANDER.			DATE.	
N. Kimball,	Brigadier-General.		Sept.,	1862
J. S. Mason,		"	Dec.,	"
John Coons,	Col.	14th Ind. Vols.	Feb.,	1863
Jos. Snyder,	"	7th Va. "	March,	"
"	"	7th " "	July,	"
S. S. Carroll,	"	8th Ohio "	April,	"
"	"	8th " "	Sept.,	"
T. W. Egan,	"	40th N.Y. "	March,	1864
"	"	40th " "	May 12,	"
H. J. Madill,	"	141st Pa. "	June 16,	"
R. DeTrobriand,	Brigadier-General.		July 12,	"
"		"	March 2, 1865	
"		"	May 19,	"
J. H. H. Ward,		"	April,	1864
G. W. West,.	Bvt. Brigadier-Genl.		Feb. 17, 1865	
R. B. Shepherd,	Col. 1st Me. Hy. Art.		April 6,	"

2d Brigade—3d Division.

Organized September, 1862.
Discontinued G. O. No. 35, A. of P., June 28

COMMANDER.			L
D. Morris,	Col.	14th Conn. Vols.	Sept
"	"	14th " "	Jan.
			Fe
O. H. Palmer,	"	108th N.Y. "	Dec.
R. C. Johnson,	"	12th N. J. "	"
Wm. Hays,	Brigadier-General.		Feb.
T. A. Smyth,	Col.	1st Del. Vols.	May
"	"	1st " "	Sept
"	"	1st " "	Feb.
T. H. Davis,	Lt.- "	12th N. J. "	Aug
C. J. Powers,	"	108th N. Y. "	Dec.
Alex. Hays,	Brigadier-General.		Marc
T. R. Tannatt,	Col. 1st Mass.Hy.Art.		May
B. R. Pierce,	Brigadier-General.		June
"		"	Aug
"		"	Feb.
H. J. Madill,	Col.	141st Pa. Vols.	July
C. A. Craig,	"	105th " "	Aug
Jno. Pulford,	"	5th Mich. "	"
G. W. West,	"	17th Me. "	Jan.

Bohlen's Brigade—Blenker's Division.

Transferred to Department of the Rappahannock, April 4, 1862.

COMMANDER.		DATE.
H. Bohlen,	Brigadier-General.	March, 1862

Kimball's Independent Brigade.

Designation changed to 1st Brigade, 3d Division, September, 1862.

COMMANDER.		DATE.
N. Kimball,	Brigadier-General.	July, 1862

…my Corps.

…inued March 26, 1864.
…on. Discontinued G. O. No. 35, Army of Potomac, June 28, 1865.

DATE.
September 12, 1862, and January, 1863
Temporary, December 20, 1862
June 28, 1863; September 6, 1863, and January 4, 1864
August, 1863; December, 1863, and February, 1864
March, 1864
July 23, 1864, and March 2, 1865
May 19, 1865
Temporary, Feb. 15, 1865, and April 6, 1865, and from June 9 to 19, 1865

4th Division—2d Army Corps.

Late 2d Division, 3d Army Corps. Consolidated with 3d Division, 2d Army Corps, May 13, 1864.

COMMANDER.		DATE.
J. B. Carr,	Brigadier-General.	March 24, 1864

3d Brigade— 3d Division.

…d September, 1862. Discontinued May, 1863.
…organized June, 1863, formerly 3d Brigade,
Department of Washington.
Discontinued March, 1864.
…d May, 1864, formerly 1st Brigade, 4th Division.

COMMANDERS.		DATE.
…er,	Brigadier-General.	Sept., 1862
…rews,	Col. 1st Del. Vols.	" "
…shall, Lt.-	" 10th N.Y. "	Nov., "
…Gregor,	" 4th " "	Jan., 1863
	" 4th " "	April 27, "
…right,	" 132d Pa. "	Feb. 24, "
…ndix,	" 10th N.Y. "	March 16, "
…s,	Brigadier-General.	June, "
…ard,	Col. 125th N.Y. Vols.	June 28, "
	" 14th Ind. "	July 17, "
…n,	Brigadier-General.	Aug., "
	"	Sept., "
	"	Jan., 1864
…ll,	Col. 125th N.Y. Vols.	Dec., 1863
	" 39th " "	Feb., 1864
	Brigadier-General.	May, "
…ster,	Col. 11th N. J. Vols.	July, "
	" 11th " "	Jan., 1865
…sey,	Bvt. Brigadier-General.	Dec., 1864
…ice,	Col. 7th N. J. Vols.	June 7, 1865

4th Brigade— 3d Division.

Organized May, 1864, formerly 2d Brigade, 4th Division.
Discontinued July 3, 1864.

COMMANDER.		DATE.
Wm. R. Brewster,	Col. 73d N. Y. Vols.	May, 1864

1st Brigade— 4th Division.

Consolidated with 3d Division, 2d Corps, May 13, 1864.

COMMANDERS.		DATE.
G. Mott,	Brigadier-General.	March, 1864
"	"	April, "

2d Brigade— 4th Division.

Consolidated with 3d Division, 2d Corps, May 13, 1864.

COMMANDER.		DATE.
W. R. Brewster,	Col. 73d N. Y. Vols.	March 25, 1864

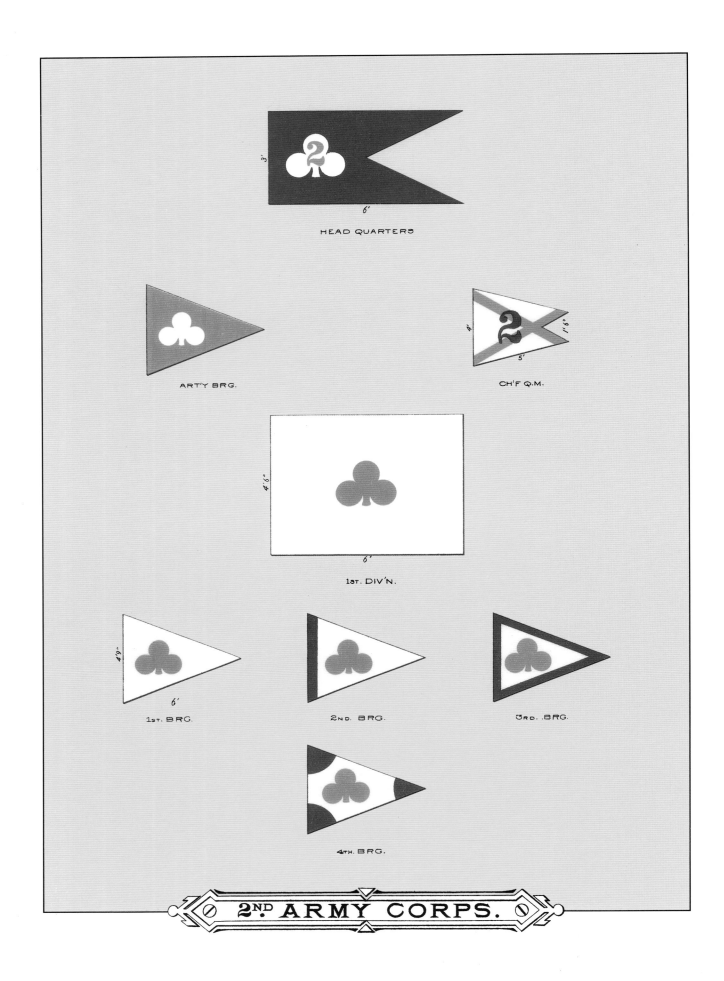

HEAD QUARTERS

ART'Y BRG.

CH'F Q.M.

1st. DIV'N.

1st. BRG.

2nd. BRG.

3rd. BRG.

4th. BRG.

2ND ARMY CORPS.

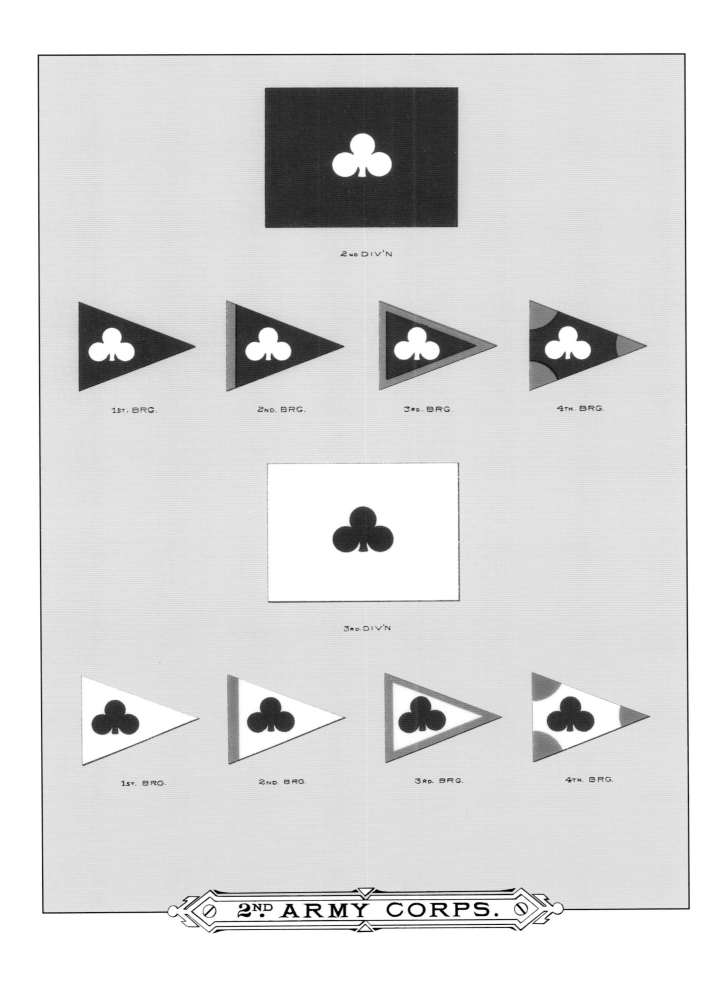

2ND DIV'N

1ST. BRG.   2ND. BRG.   3RD. BRG.   4TH. BRG.

3RD. DIV'N

1ST. BRG.   2ND. BRG.   3RD. BRG.   4TH. BRG.

2ND. ARMY CORPS.

THIRD A[RMY CORPS]

Created March 3, 1862.　By Order of the President of the U. S.　Announced March 13, 1862.

COMMANDERS.

S. P. HEINTZELMAN,	Brigadier-G[eneral]
GEO. STONEMAN,	"
D. E. SICKLES,	Major-Gene[ral]
D. B. BIRNEY,	"
WM. H. FRENCH,	"

Porter's Division—3d Army Corps.

Transferred to 5th Corps, May 18, 1862.

COMMANDER.		DATE.
F. J. Porter,	Brigadier-General.	March 13, 1862

1st Division—3d Army Corps.

Known as 3d Division, 3d Corps, from organization of Corps until August, 1862.
Transferred to 2d Army Corps, March 24, 1864.

COMMANDERS.		DATE.
P. Kearney,	Brigadier-General.	August, 1862
Geo. Stoneman,	"	September, 1862
D. B. Birney,	"	November, 16, 1862
"	Major-General.	June, 1863, and February 17, 18[
J. H. H. Ward,	Brigadier-General.	Temporary June, 1863, and Jan.

1st Brigade—Porter's Division.

COMMANDER.		DATE.
J. H. Martindale,	Brigadier-General.	March, 1862

2d Brigade—Porter's Division.

COMMANDER.		DATE.
Geo. W. Morell,	Brigadier-General.	March, 1862

1st Brigade—1st Division.

Known as 1st Brigade, 3d Division, until August, 1862.

COMMANDERS.		DATE.
J. C. Robinson,	Brigadier-General.	Aug., 1862
S. B. Hayman,	Col. 37th N.Y.Vols.	Dec., 30, "
J. Van Volkenburg,	" 20th Ind.	" Jan., 1863
C. H. T. Collis,	" 114th Pa.	" Feb., "
"	" 114th "	" Aug., "
C. K. Graham,	Brigadier-General.	March, "
"	"	June, "
A. H. Tippin,	Col. 68th Pa. Vols.	May 14, "
H. J. Madill,	" 141st "	" July 2, "

2d Brigade—1st Division.

Known as 2d Brigade, 3d Division, until Aug[

COMMANDERS.		
D. B. Birney,	Brigadier-General.	Aug
"	"	Oct
J. H. H. Ward,	Col. 38th N.Y.Vols.	Sept
"	Brigadier-General.	Nov
"	"	Feb.
"	"	Apri
"	"	Jan.
"	"	Feb.
R. DeTrobriand,	Col. 38th N.Y.Vols.	Jan.
"	" 38th " "	Mar
E. Walker,	" 4th Me. "	Dec
"	" 4th " "	Jan.

3d Brigade—Porter's Division.

COMMANDER.		DATE.
D. Butterfield,	Brigadier-General.	March, 1862

3d Brigade—1st Division.

Known as 3d Brigade, 3d Division, until August, 1862.

COMMANDERS.		DATE.
O. M. Poe,	Col. 2d Mich. Vols.	Aug., 1862
H. G. Berry,	Brigadier-General.	Sept., "
"	"	Nov., "
R. DeTrobriand,	Col. 55th N. Y. Vols.	Oct., "
"	" 38th " "	June 3, 1863
T. A. Roberts,	" 17th Me. "	Jan., "
S. B. Hayman,	" 37th N. Y. "	Feb., "
T. W. Egan,	" 40th " "	Nov. 22, "
"	" 40th " "	Feb., 1864
B. R. Pierce,	" 3d Mich. "	Dec. 30, 1863
G. W. West,	" 17th Me. "	Jan., 1864

MY CORPS.

, Army of the Potomac.   Discontinued March 24, 1864.   Troops transferred to 2d and 6th Corps.

DATE.
March 16, 1862.
October 30, 1862.
February 8, and June, 1863.
June, 1863, and January 28, 1864.
July 7, 1863, and February 17, 1864.

2d Division—3d Army Corps.

Transferred to 2d Army Corps, March 24, 1864.

COMMANDERS.		DATE.
Jos. Hooker,	Brigadier-General.	March 13, 1862
D. E. Sickles,	"	September, 1862
J. B. Carr,	"	Jan., 1863, and Temporary May, 1863
H. G. Berry,	Major-General.	February 8, 1863
A. A. Humphreys,	Brigadier-General.	May 23, 1863
H. Prince,	"	July 10, 1863

3d Division—3d Army Corps.

Designated 1st Division, 3d Corps, August, 1862.   Reorganized November, 1862.
Transferred to 1st and 2d Divisions, 3d Corps, June, 1863.   Reorganized July, 1863.
Transferred to 6th Army Corps, March 24, 1864.

COMMANDERS.		DATE.
C. S. Hamilton,	Brigadier-General.	March 13, 1862
Philip Kearney,	"	May 2, "
A. W. Whipple,	"	November, "
C. K. Graham,	"	May 14, 1863
W. L. Elliott,	"	July 13, "
J. B. Carr,	"	October 3, "

1st Brigade—2d Division.

COMMANDERS.		DATE.
,	Brigadier-General.	Dec. 31, 1862
	"	Feb., 1863
dell,	Col. 11th Mass.Vols.	Jan., "
	" 11th " "	Nov. 15, "
ster,	" 11th N.Y.	Oct. 5, 1863

2d Brigade—2d Division.

COMMANDERS.		DATE.
Z. B. Tower,	Brigadier-General.	July 31, 1862
P. Lyle,	Col. 90th Pa. Vols.	Aug., "
J. W. Revere,	Brigadier-General.	Dec. 24, "
	"	March, 1863
C. K. Graham,	"	Feb., "
J. E. Farnum,	Col. 70th N.Y.Vols.	April, "
W. R. Brewster,	" 73d " "	May, "
	" 73d " "	Aug., "
	" 73d " "	Feb., 1864
F. B. Spinola,	Brigadier-General.	July, 1863
Thos. Rafferty,	Maj. 71st N.Y.Vols.	July 23, "
John Leonard,	Lt.-Col. 72d " "	Jan., 1864

1st Brigade—3d Division.

Changed to 1st Brigade, 1st Division, August, 1862.
Reorganized November, 1862.   Reorganized July, 1863.

COMMANDERS.		DATE.
C. D. Jameson,	Brigadier-General.	March, 1862
J. C. Robinson,	"	June 12, "
A. S. Piatt,	"	Nov., "
	"	Jan., 1863
B. P. Bailey,	Col. 86th N.Y.Vols.	Dec. 17, 1862
	" 86th " "	Feb., 1863
E. Franklin,	" 122d Pa.	April, "
A. Van H. Ellis,	" 124th N.Y.	May, "
W. H. Morris,	Brigadier-General.	July, "

2d Brigade—3d Division.

Changed to 2d Brigade, 1st Division, August, 1862.
Reorganized November, 1862.

COMMANDERS.		DATE.
D. B. Birney,	Brigadier-General.	March, 1862
S. S. Carro l,	Col. 8th Ohio Vols.	Nov., "
J. H. Potter,	" 12th N. H. "	Jan., 1863
H. Berdan,	" 1st U. S. S. S.	Feb. 19, "
S. M. Bowman,	" 84th Pa. Vols.	March, "
J. W. Keifer,	" 110th Ohio "	July 12, "
	" 110th " "	Sept., "
J. W. Horn,	" 6th Md. "	Aug. 14, "

3d Brigade—2d Division.

COMMANDERS.		DATE.
F. E. Patterson,	Brigadier-General.	May 3, 1862
J. W. Revere,	"	Nov., "
G. Mott,	"	Dec. 24, "
	"	Aug. 31, 1863
W. J. Sewell,	Col. 5th N. J. Vols.	May, "
	" 5th " "	Feb. 16, 1864
G. C. Burling,	" 6th " "	June, 1863

3d Brigade—3d Division.

Changed to 3d Brigade, 1st Division, August, 1862.   Reorganized March 13, 1863.

COMMANDERS.		DATE.
H. G. Berry,	Brigadier-General.	April 2, 1862
H. Berdan,	Col. 1st U. S. S. S.	March 13, 1863
B. F. Smith,	" 126th Ohio Vols.	July 10, "
	" 126th " "	Sept. 17, "
J. W. Schall,	" 87th Pa. "	Aug. 28, "

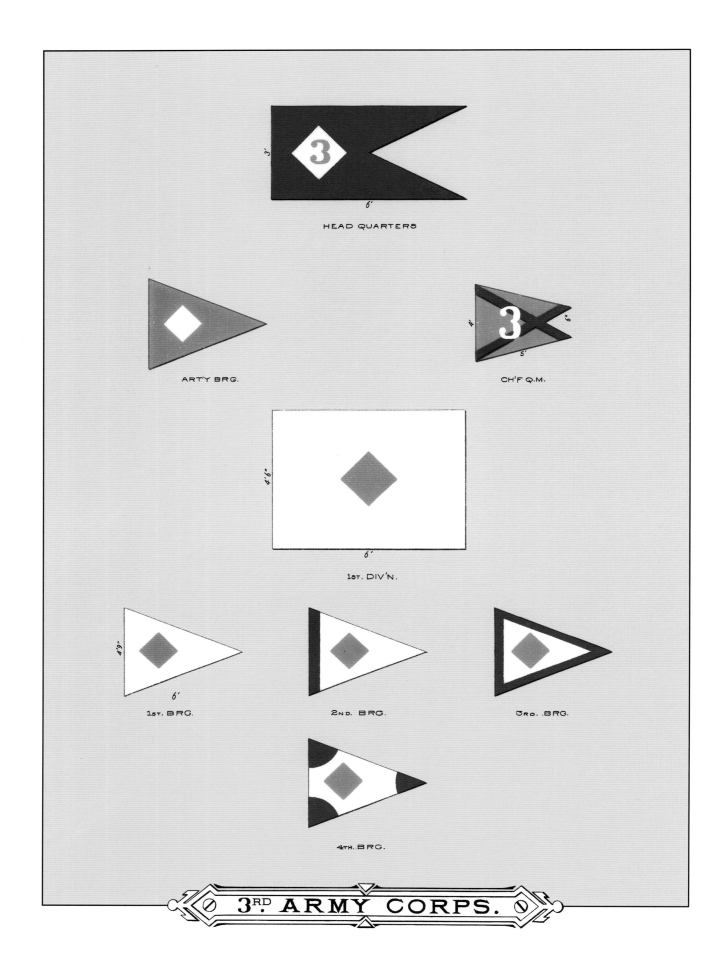

HEAD QUARTERS

ART'Y BRG.

CH'F Q.M.

1ST. DIV'N.

1ST. BRG.

2ND. BRG.

3RD. BRG.

4TH. BRG.

3RD. ARMY CORPS.

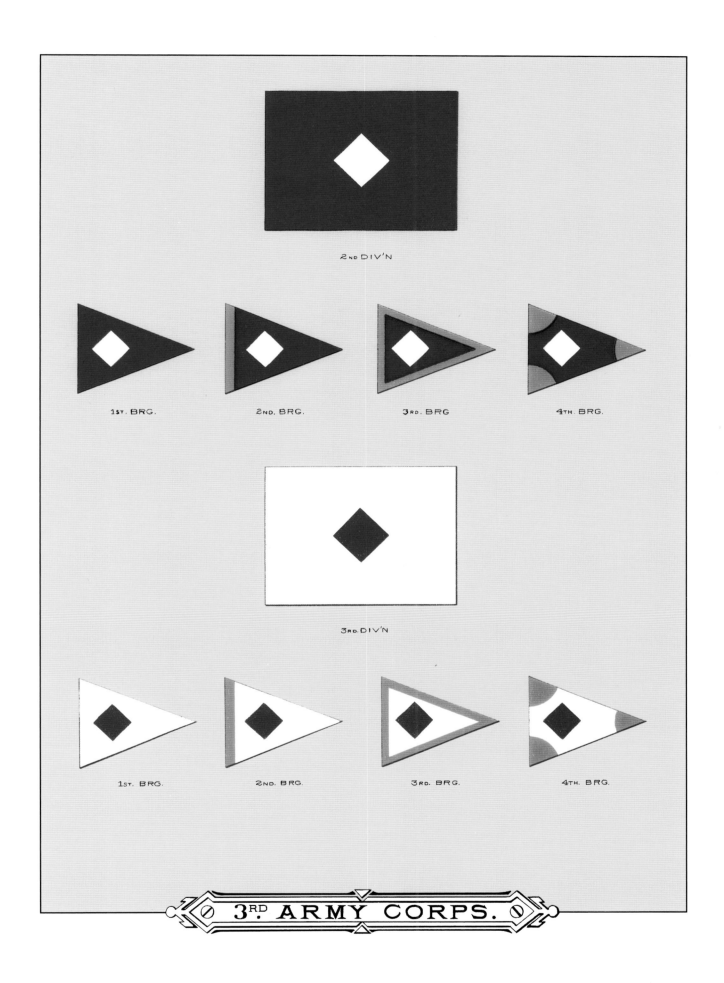

2ND DIV'N

1ST. BRG. 2ND. BRG. 3RD. BRG 4TH. BRG.

3RD. DIV'N

1ST. BRG. 2ND. BRG. 3RD. BRG. 4TH. BRG.

Created March 3, 1862, by order of the President of the United States.   Announced March 13, 1862, G. O. No. 101, A

Order carried into effect October 9, 1863.   Formed by consolidation

COMMANDERS.

E. D. KEYS,	Brigadier-G
GORDON GRANGER,	Major-Gene
O. O. HOWARD,	"
D. S. STANLEY.	"
"	"
T. J. WOOD,	Brigadier-G

1st Division—4th Army Corps.

Transferred to 6th Army Corps, September, 1862.   Reorganized June, 1863.   Reorganized June 7, 1865.

COMMANDERS.		DATE.
D. N. Couch,	Brigadier-General.	March 13, 1862
"	Major-General.	August, "
J. J. Abercrombie,	Brigadier-General.	July, "
Rufus King,	"	June, 1863
John M. Palmer,	Major-General.	October, "
C. Cruft,	Brigadier-General.	October 27, 1863
"	"	February 13, 1864
D. S. Stanley,	Major-General.	November 21, 1863
"	"	March, 1864
Wm. Grose,	Col. 36th Ind. Vols.	July, "
"	Brigadier-General.	Temporary, February 16, 1865
N. Kimball,	"	August, 1864
"	"	November 28, "
"	"	March, 1865
"	Bvt. Major-General.	June, 1865
W. C. Whitaker,	Brigadier-General.	September 19, 1864

2d Di

2d and 3d Brigades transferred to C
1st Brigade transferred to Gen. Foster's comm

COMMANDERS.

W. F. Smith,	Brigadier-
J. J. Peck,	"
Geo. H. Gordon,	"
P. H. Sheridan,	Major-Gen
G. D. Wagner,	Brigadier-
"	"
John Newton,	"
W. L. Elliott,	"
E. Opdyke,	Col. 125th
J. Conrad,	" 15th

1st Brigade—1st Division.

Reorganized June 7, 1865.

COMMANDERS.		DATE.
H. S. Briggs,	Col. 10th Mass. Vols.	March, 1862
C. Devens, Jr.,	Brigadier-General.	May 1, "
"	"	July 26, "
C. H. Innes,	Col. 36th N. Y. Vols.	May 31, "
I. N. Palmer,	Brigadier-General.	June 7, "
H. Tyndale,	"	June 17, 1863
F. D. Sedgwick,	Col. 2d Ky. Vols.	Oct. 26, "
D. A. Enyart,	" 1st " "	Nov., "
"	" 1st " "	Feb. 13, 1864
C. Cruft,	Brigadier-General.	Jan., "
"	"	March, "
J. M. Kirby,	Col. 101st Ohio Vols.	June 10, "
"	" 101st " "	Oct , "
W. E. McMackin,	Lt.- " 21st Ky. "	Sept., "
T. E. Rose,	" 77th Pa. "	June 7, 1865

2d Brigade—1st Division.

Reorganized June 7, 1865.

COMMANDERS.		DATE.
L. P. Graham,	Brigadier-General.	March, 1862
H. W. Wessells,	"	May 19, "
J. J. Abercrombie,	"	" 24, "
John Cochran,	Col. 65th N. Y. Vols.	July, "
Geo. E. Church,	" 11th R. I. "	June, 1863
W. C. Whitaker,	Brigadier-General.	Oct., "
"	"	March 15, 1864
"	"	Nov. 27, "
S. M. Barnes,	Col. 8th Ky. Vols.	Dec. 8, 1863
J. H. Moore,	" 115th Ills. "	Jan., 1864
"	" 115th " "	Dec. 23, "
J. E. Taylor,	" 40th Ohio "	June, 1864
T. E. Champin,	" 96th Ills. "	Sept. 21, "
Jas. C. Evans,	Lt.- " 21st Ky. "	Oct., "
I. C. B. Suman,	" 9th Ind. "	June 7, 1865

1st Brigade—2d Division.

No returns on file for May, June and July, 1862.
Transferred to Gen. Foster's command December, 1862
Reorganized May, 1863.

COMMANDERS.		D
W. S. Hancock,	Brigadier-General.	Marc
W. H. Emory,	"	July
H. M. Naglee,	"	Sept
Wm. Gurney,	Col. 127th N. Y. Vols.	May
Jas. B. Steedman,	Brigadier-General.	Oct.
F. T. Sherman,	Col. 88th Ills. Vols.	"
"	" 88th " "	Apr
J. F. Jacques,	" 73d " "	Mar
N. Kimball,	Brigadier-General.	May
E. Opdyke,	Col. 125th Ohio Vols.	Aug.
"	" 125th " "	Marc
John Russell,	Lt.- " 44th Ills. "	Feb.
"	" " 44th " "	June

3d Brigade—1st Division.

Discontinued June 7, 1865.

COMMANDERS.		DATE.
J. J. Peck,	Brigadier-General.	March, 1862
A. P. Howe,	"	June, "
Chas. Kleckner,	Col. 172d Pa. Vols.	" 1863
Wm. Grose,	" 36th Ind. "	October, "
"	" 36th " "	January, 1864
"	Brigadier-General.	August 5, "
"	"	November 29, "
"	"	March, 1865
"	"	May, "
J. E. Bennett,	Col. 75th Ills. Vols.	December, 1863
"	" 75th " "	September 5, 1864
"	" 75th " "	February 16, 1865
"	" 75th " "	March 31, "
P. S. Post,	" 59th " "	July, 1864
L. H. Waters,	" 84th " "	October 21, "
"	" 84th " "	April 9, 1865

3d B

No returns on file for May, June and J
D

COMMANDERS

J. W. Davidson,	Brigadie
H. W. Wessells,	
C. G. Harker,	Col. 65th
L. P. Bradley,	" 51st
"	Brigadie
J. Conrad,	Col. 15th

Independent Brigade—4th Army Corps.

Organized December, 1862.   Discontinued June, 1863.

COMMANDERS.		DATE.
R. Busteed,	Brigadier-General.	December, 1862
Rufus King,	"	April 1, 1863

West's B

COMMANDER.

R. M. West,	Col. 1st Pa. Lt

MY CORPS.

...omac.   Discontinued August 1, 1863, G. O. No. 262, A. G. O.   Recreated September 28, 1863, G. O. 322, A. G. O.

...t Corps.   Discontinued G. O. No. 131.   A. G. O. August 1, 1865.

DATE.
March   13, 1862.
October   10, 1863.
April,   1864.
July   27, 1864.
January   30, 1865.
Temporary, December   1864.

...ny Corps.

Dept. of Va., September, 1862.
...December, 1862. Reorganized May, 1863.

DATE.
March   13, 1862
June,   "
May   4, 1863
October,   "
Temporary, February,   1864
September 30, "
April,   "
December 2, 1864
Temporary, June   24, 1865
July   11,   "

3d Division—4th Army Corps.

Dropped from 4th Corps, June, 1862.

COMMANDERS.		DATE.
Silas Casey,	Brigadier-General.	March 13, 1862
T. J. Wood,	"	October, 1863
"	"	February 12, 1864
"	Major-General.	January, 1865
"	"	March 20, "
August Willich,	Brigadier-General.	Temporary, January 8, 1864
Samuel Beatty,	"	" December 2, "
"	"	February 7, 1865

2d Brigade—2d Division.

No returns on file for May, June and July, 1862.
Transferred to Gen. Dix's command, September, 1862.
Reorganized May, 1863.

COMMANDERS.		DATE.
...Brooks,	Brigadier-General.	March, 1862
...ry,	"	Aug. 31, "
...gner,	Col. 40th Mass. Vols.	May, 1863
...	Brigadier-General.	Oct., "
...	"	April 21, 1864
...e,	Col. 97th Ohio Vols.	Jan., "
...	" 97th " "	Nov. 29, "
...ke,	" 40th Ind. "	Sept. 30, "
...se,	Brigadier-General.	Oct., "
...ervecr,	"	Feb. 8, 1865
...	Col. 15th Mo. Vols.	June 16, "
...ain,	Lt.- " 42d Ills. "	July 12, "

1st Brigade—3d Division.

No Returns on File.

COMMANDERS.		DATE.
August Willich,	Brigadier-General.	Oct., 1863
"	"	May, 1864
"	"	June 2, 1865
R. H. Nodine,	Col. 25th Ills. Vols.	Jan. 8, 1864
C. T. Hotchkiss,	" 89th " "	March 11, "
"	" 89th " "	Aug. 25, "
"	" 89th " "	March, 1865
W. H. Gibson,	" 49th Ohio "	April 20, 1864
"	" 49th " "	May 15, "
J. A. Martin,	" 8th Kans. "	Sept. 15, "
A. D. Streight,	" 51st Ind. "	Nov. 17, "
C. R. Doolittle,	Brigadier-General.	May 17, 1865

2d Brigade—3d Division.

No Returns on File.

COMMANDERS.		DATE.
W. H. Keim,	Brigadier General.	March, 1862
W. B. Hazen,	"	Oct., 1863
"	"	April 17, 1864
N. L. Anderson,	Col. 6th Ohio Vols.	March, "
P. S. Post,	" 59th Ills. "	August, "
H. K. McConnell,	" 71st Ohio "	Dec., "
S. Beatty,	Brigadier-General.	June 7, 1865

...ision.

...ed to Gen. Dix's command, September, 1862.
...865.

DATE.
March,   1862
August   31, "
October   1863
June,   1864
May   1865
December,   1864

3d Brigade—3d Division.

No Returns on File.

COMMANDERS.		DATE.
I. N. Palmer,	Brigadier-General.	March, 1862
S. Beatty,	"	October, 1863
"	"	April 16, 1864
"	"	November 6, "
"	"	March 20, 1865
Alex. M. Stout,	Col. 7th Ky. Vols.	February, 1864
F. Knefler,	" 79th Ind. "	March, "
"	" 79th " "	May, "
"	" 79th " "	December 2, "
G. F. Dick,	" 86th " "	February 21, 1865

...my Corps.

...63.

DATE.
April,   1863

Terry's Brigade—4th Army Corps.

Organized June, 1863.

COMMANDER.		DATE.
H. D. Terry,	Brigadier-General.	June, 1863

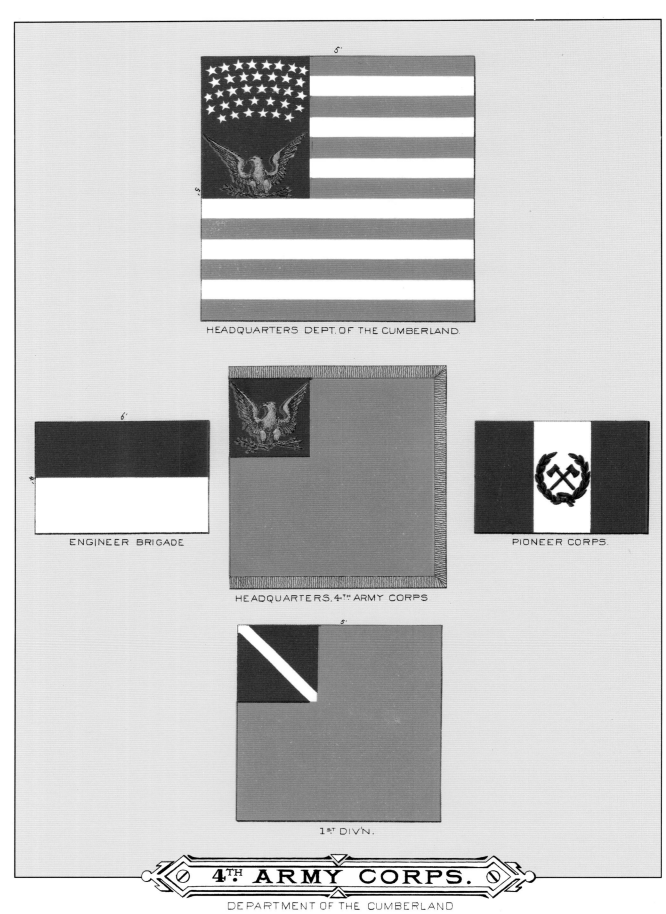

HEADQUARTERS DEPT. OF THE CUMBERLAND.

ENGINEER BRIGADE

HEADQUARTERS, 4TH ARMY CORPS

PIONEER CORPS.

1ST DIV'N.

4TH ARMY CORPS.

DEPARTMENT OF THE CUMBERLAND

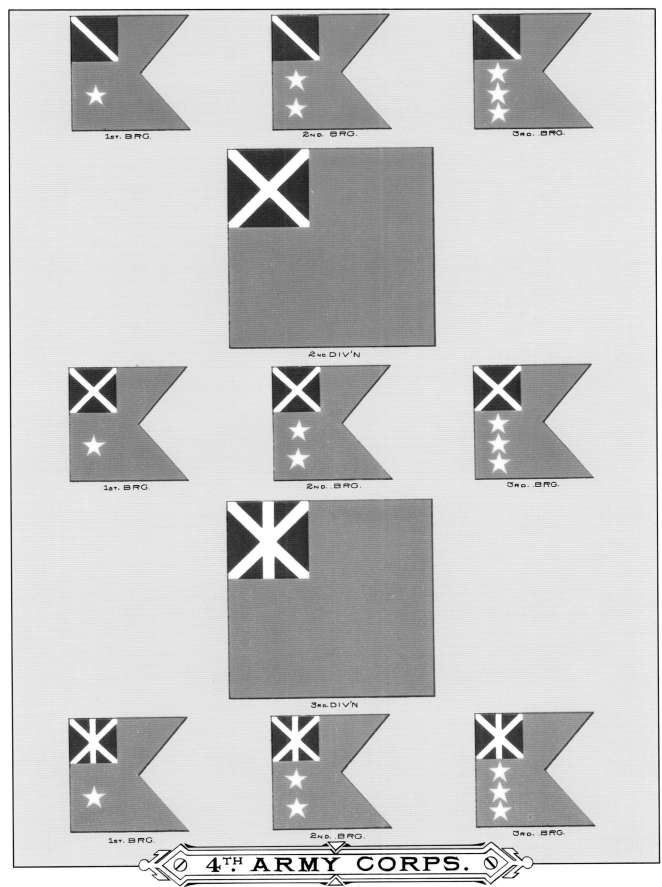

1st. BRG.

2nd. BRG.

3rd. BRG.

2nd. DIV'N

1st. BRG.

2nd. BRG.

3rd. BRG.

3rd. DIV'N

1st. BRG.

2nd. BRG.

3rd. BRG.

4TH ARMY CORPS.

DEPARTMENT OF THE CUMBERLAND

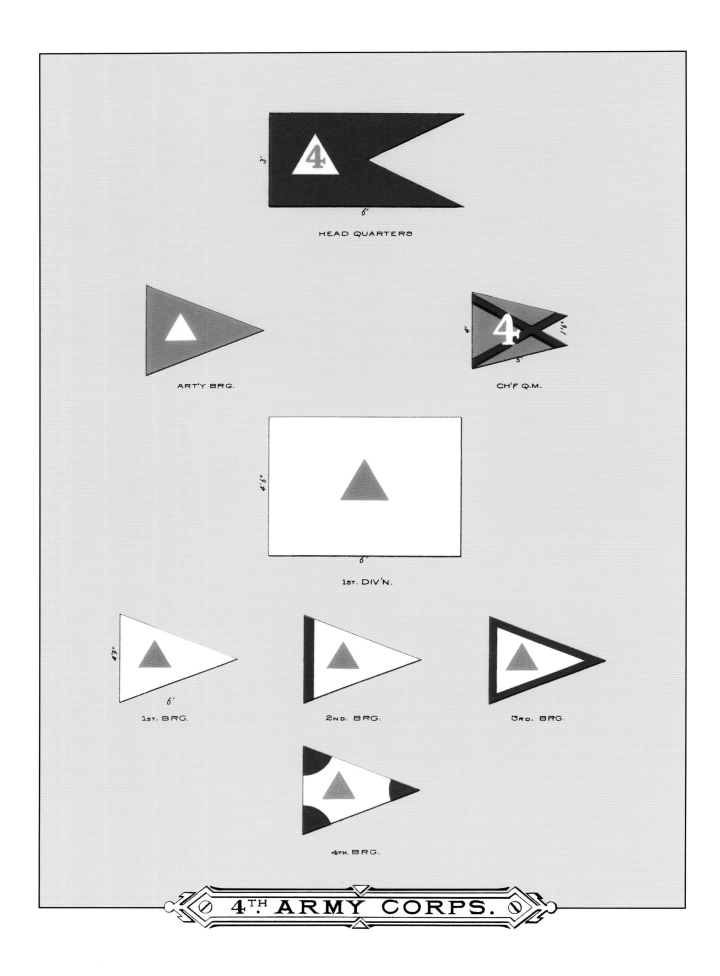

HEAD QUARTERS

ART'Y BRG.

CH'F Q.M.

1ST. DIV'N.

1ST. BRG.

2ND. BRG.

3RD. BRG.

4TH. BRG.

4TH ARMY CORPS.

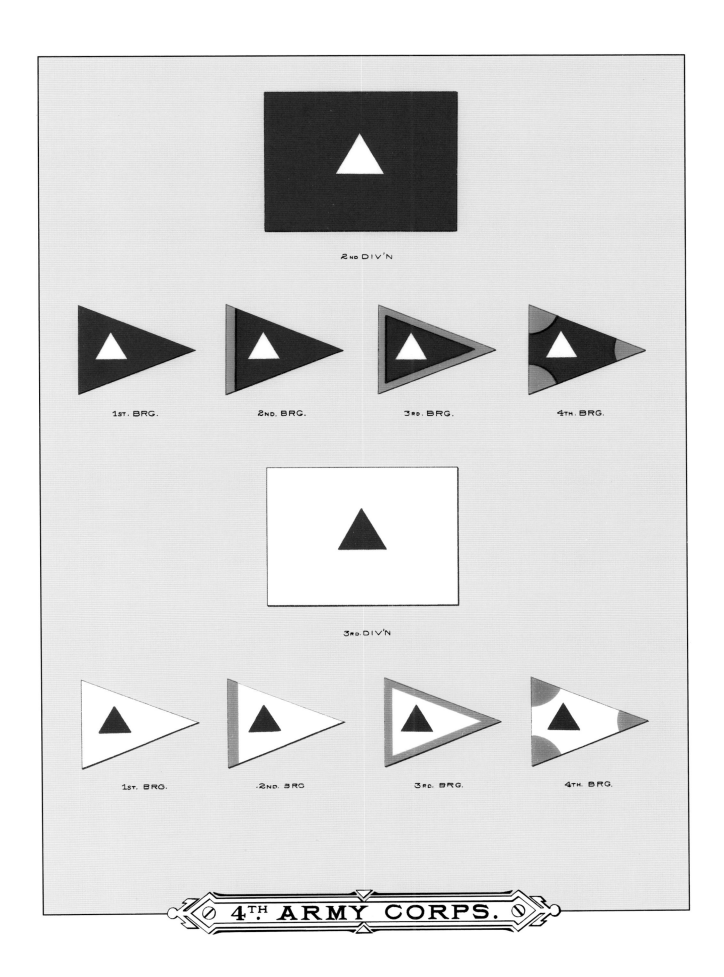

2ND DIV'N

1ST. BRG.　　2ND. BRG.　　3RD. BRG.　　4TH. BRG.

3RD. DIV'N

1ST. BRG.　　.2ND. BRG　　3RD. BRG.　　4TH. BRG.

4TH ARMY CORPS.

FIFTH AL

Created March 3, 1862, by Order of the President of the U. S.   Announced March 13, 1862.   G. O. No. 101, Army of the Po
Corps discontinued G. O. No. 35, Army of the Potomac, J

COMMANDERS.

N. P. BANKS,	Major-General.
F. J. PORTER,	Brigadier-Gene
JOSEPH HOOKER,	Major-General.
D. BUTTERFIELD,	Brigadier-Gene
GEO. G. MEADE,	Major-General.
GEO. SYKES,	"
G. K. WARREN,	"
S. W. CRAWFORD,	Bvt. Major-Gen
CHAS. GRIFFIN,	" "

1st Division—5th Army Corps.

COMMANDERS.		DATE.
A. S. Williams,	Brigadier-General.	March 20, 1862
G. W. Morrell,	"	May, 1862
Chas. Griffin,	"	Oct., 1862; Nov. 16, 1862; Jan., 1863; July 21, 1863; April 3, 1864; Aug. 9, 1864, and Jan. 4, 1865
D. Butterfield,	"	Temporary, November 1, 1862
James Barnes,	Col. 18th Mass. Vols.	December, 1862
"	Brigadier-General.	May, 1863
J. B. Sweitzer,	Col. 62d Pa. Vols.	Oct. 24, 1863, and Dec. 31, 1863
J. J. Bartlett,	Brigadier-General.	Nov. 6, 1863; Feb. 3, 1864; July 21, 1864; Dec. 23, 1864, and April 1, 1865.
J. L. Chamberlain,	"	April 19, 1865

2d Division—5th Army Corps.

Discontinued March, 1864.
Reorganized March, 1864.   (Composed of Troops transferred from 1st Army Corps.)
Discontinued June 5, 1864.   (Troops transferred to other Divisions.)   Reorganized June 6, 1864.

COMMANDERS.		DATE.
James Shields,	Brigadier-General.	March 13, 1862
Geo. Sykes,	"	May 18, 1862
"	Major-General.	January, 1863
G. K. Warren,	Brigadier-General.	Temporary, December, 1862
R. B. Ayres,	"	June 28, 1863, and June 6, 1864
"	Bvt. Major-General.	January, 1865
H. Baxter,	Brigadier-General.	March, 1864
J. C. Robinson,	"	April, 1864
H. H. Lockwood,	"	May 30, 1864
J. Gwyn,	Col. 118th Pa. Vols.	December, 1864

1st Brigade—1st Division.

Discontinued and 4th Brigade, 1st Division, termed
1st Brigade, 1st Division, April, 1864.
Transferred to 2d Division and called 1st Division,
1st Brigade, 2d Division, June 5, 1864.
Reorganized June 6, 1864.   Formerly 3d Brig., 4th Div.

COMMANDERS.		DATE.
D. Donnelly,	Col. 28th N.Y. Vols.	March 20, 1862
J. H. Martindale,	Brigadier-General.	May 18, "
Jas. Barnes,	Col. 18th Mass. Vols.	July 10, "
"	Brigadier-General.	Jan., 1863
"	"	Aug. 18, "
C. A. Johnson,	Col. 25th N.Y. Vols.	Dec, 1862
W. S. Tilton,	" 22d Mass. "	May, 1863
"	" 22d " "	Nov. 19, "
"	" 22d " "	June 18, 1864
Thos. Sherwin, Jr., Lt.-Col. 22d Mass. Vols.		Sept., 1863
J. Hayes,	Col. 18th Mass. Vols.	Oct., "
R. B. Ayres,	Brigadier-General.	April, 1864
J. L. Chamberlain,	"	June 6, 1864
"	"	Nov. 19, "
"	"	Feb. 27, 1865
W. A. Throop, Lt.-Col. 1st Mich. Vols.		Aug. 22, 1864
H. G. Sickel,	" 198th Pa. "	Sept. 24, "
"	" 198th " "	Jan. 15, 1865
J. Gwyn,	" 118th " "	Nov. 7, 1864
A. L. Pearson,	" 155th " "	April 10, 1865

2d Brigade—1st Division.

Organized in May, 1862.
(No Returns on File.)

COMMANDERS.		DATE.
J. J. Abercrombie,	Brigadier-General.	March 14, 1862
Chas. Griffin,	"	June, 1862
"	"	Nov. 1, "
J. B. Sweitzer,	Col. 62d Pa. Vols.	Oct., "
"	" 62d " "	Nov. 16, "
"	" 62d " "	April, 1863
"	" 62d " "	Nov., "
"	" 62d " "	Feb. 3, 1864
Jas. McQuade,	" 14th N.Y. "	March, 1863
P. R. Guiney,	" 9th Mass. "	Oct. 24, "
"	" 9th " "	Jan. 1, 1864
Jas. C. Hull,	Lt.-" 62d Pa. "	Dec. 18, 1863
E. M. Gregory,	" 91st " "	July 3, 1864
"	" 91st " "	Feb. 25, 1865
A. L. Burr,	" 189th N.Y. "	Jan. 23, "

1st Brigade—2d Division.

This Brigade was organized in pursuance of G. O. No. 125,
A. of P., May 18, 1862.
There are no Brigade Returns of the 2d Division when
commanded by Gen. Shields.
Consolidated with 3d Brigade, and termed 4th Brigade,
1st Division, March, 1864.
Reorganized March, 1864.
Transferred to 3d Division, and termed 1st Brigade,
3d Division, June 5, 1864.
Reorganized June 6, 1864 (formerly 1st Brig., 1st Div.)

COMMANDERS.		DATE.
R. C. Buchanan,	Lt. Col. 4th U.S. Inf.	March 18, 1862
R. S. Smith,	Maj. 12th " "	Jan. 27, 1863
R. B. Ayres,	Brigadier-General.	April 21, "
H. Day,	Col. 6th U.S. Inf.	June 28, "
G. K. Giddings,	Maj. 14th " "	Aug. 22, "
S. Burbank,	Col. 2d " "	Sept. 23, "
L. B. Bruen,	Maj. 12th " "	Jan., 1864
S. H. Leonard,	Col. 13th Mass. Vols.	March, "
P. Lyle,	" 90th Pa. "	May 6, "
J. Hayes,	Brigadier-General.	June, "
"	"	April 3, 1865
C. P. Stone,	Col. 14th U.S. Inf.	Aug. 22, 1864
F. Winthrop,	" 5th N.Y. Vols.	Sept., "
"	" 5th " "	March 12, 1865
M. Wiedrich,	Lt.-" 15th N.Y. Hy. Art.	Feb. 16, "

2d Brigade—2d Division.

Organized G. O. No. 125, A. of P., May 18,
No Brigade Returns from Division when comm
by Gen. Shields.
Discontinued September 23, 1863.
Reorganized March 23, 1864.
Transferred to 3d Division, and termed 2d Br
3d Division, June 5, 1864.
Reorganized June 6, 1864.   Formerly 3d Brig.,

COMMANDERS.		D
Wm. Chapman,	Lt.-Col. 3d U.S. Inf.	May
Chas. S. Lovell,	Maj. 10th " "	Oct.,
"	" 10th " "	Dec.
Geo. L. Andrews,	" 17th " "	Nov.,
D. L. Floyd-Jones,	" 11th " "	Feb.,
S. Burbank,	Col. 2d " "	March
R. Coulter,	" 11th Pa. Vols.	March
H. Baxter,	Brigadier-General.	April
J. L. Bates,	Col. 12th Mass. Vols.	May
N. T. Dushane,	" 1st Md. "	June,
S. A. Graham,	{ Purnell Legion, Md. Vols. }	Aug.
A. W. Denison,	Col. 8th Md. Vols.	Oct.
"	" 8th " "	Feb.
"	" 8th " "	May
R. N. Bowerman,	" 4th " "	Jan.
D. L. Stanton,	" 1st " "	April

3d Brigade—1st Division.

COMMANDERS.		DATE.
G. H. Gordon,	Col. 2d Mass. Vols	March 14, 1862
D. Butterfield,	Brigadier-General.	May 18, "
T. B. W. Stockton,	Col. 16th Mich. Vols.	Sept., "
"	" 16th " "	Jan., 1863
H. A. Weeks,	" 12th N.Y. "	Dec., 1862
S. Vincent,	" 83d Pa. "	May 20, 1863
J. C. Rice,	" 44th N.Y. "	July 3, "
J. L. Chamberlain,	" 20th Me. "	Aug. 26, "
"	Brigadier-General.	April 11, 1865
J. Hayes,	Col. 18th Mass. Vols.	Nov. 19, 1863
J. J. Bartlett,	Brigadier-General.	April 3, 1864
"	"	Aug. 9, "
"	"	Oct. 1, "
"	"	March 7, 1865
N. E. Welch,	Col. 16th Mich. Vols.	July 20, 1864
Jas. Gwyn,	" 118th Pa. "	Aug. 17, "
A. L. Pearson,	" 155th " "	Dec. 23, "
J. C. Edmonds,	" 32d Mass. "	April 25, 1865
E. Spear,	" 20th Me. "	June 29, "

4th Brigade—1st Division.

Organized March, 1864.
Formed by consolidation of 1st and 3d Brigades,
2d Division.
Termed 1st Brigade, 1st Division, April, 1864.

COMMANDER.		DATE.
R. B. Ayres,	Brigadier-General.	March, 1864

3d Brigade—2d Division.

Organized G. O. No. 125, A. of P., May 18, 1862.
No Brigade Returns from Division when commanded by Gen. Shields.
Consolidated with 1st Brigade, and termed 4th Brigade, 1st Division, March, 1864.   Reorganized March,
Designated 2d Brigade, 2d Division, June 6, 1864.   Reorganized June 6, 1864.   Discontinued August, 18
Reorganized August, 1864.   Formerly 2d Brigade, 4th Division.

COMMANDERS.		DATE.
G. K. Warren,	Col. 5th N.Y. Vols.	March 13, 1862
P. H. O'Rorke,	" 140th " "	Feb., 1863
S. H. Weed,	Brigadier-General.	June, "
K. Garrard,	"	July, "
E. M. Gregory,	Col. 91st Pa. Vols.	Dec. 5, "
Geo. Ryan,	" 140th N.Y. "	Feb. 15, 1864
"	" 140th " "	Jan., "
D. T. Jenkins,	" 146th " "	March 23, "
N. T. Dushane,	" 1st Md. "	May 23, "
"	" 1st " "	April, "
A. W. Denison,	" 8th " "	May 8, "
R. N. Bowerman,	" 4th " "	June, "
J. H. Kitching,	" 6th N.Y. Hy. Art.	Aug., "
J. W. Hoffman,	" 56th Pa. Vols.	Sept. 14, "
A. H. Grimshaw,	" 4th Del. "	Nov. 20, "
J. Gwyn,	" 118th Pa. "	Feb. 2, 1865
"	" 118th " "	Dec., 1864
Wm. Sargent,	" 210th " "	

MY CORPS.

Discontinued G. O. No. 34.   A. G. O. April 4, 1862.   Reorganized G. O. No. 125, Army of the Potomac, May 18, 1862.
and Troops designated 3d Division, Provisional Corps.

DATE.

March 20, 1862.
May 18, 1862.
November 10, 1862.
November 16, 1862.
December 25, 1862, and February, 1863.
January, 1863, and June 28, 1863.
March 23, 1864, and January, 1865.
Temporary, January, 1865.
April 1, 1865.

3d Division—5th Army Corps.

Joined 5th Corps from Department of Rappahannock, June 18, 1862.
Transferred to other Corps, August, 1862.   Reorganized September 18, 1862.
Dissolved May, 1863.   Reorganized June 28, 1863.

COMMANDERS.		DATE.
G. A. McCall,	Brigadier-General.	June 18, 1862
T. Seymour,	"	" 30, "
A. A. Humphreys,	"	September 18, 1862, and February, 1863
E. M. Gregory,	Col. 91st Pa. Vols.	January 27, 1863
S. W. Crawford,	Brigadier-General.	June 28, and Nov. 1, 1863, and May 1, 1864
"	Bvt. Major-General.	January, 1865
W. McCandless,	Col. 2d Pa. "Reserved."	August 28, 1863, and February 20, 1864
F. Winthrop,	Bvt. Brigadier-General.	January, 1865

4th Division—5th Army Corps.

Organized March, 1864.   (Composed of Troops transferred from 1st Army Corps.)
Discontinued August, 1864.   (Troops transferred to remaining Divisions.)

COMMANDERS.		DATE.
J. S. Wadsworth,	Brigadier-General.	March 27, 1864
L. Cutler,	"	May 6, "

1st Brigade—3d Division.

Corps from Department of the Rappahannock,
June 18, 1862.
Discontinued May, 1864.
...zed June 5, 1864.   Formerly 1st Brig., 2d Div.
Discontinued September, 1864.
Reorganized September, 1864.

COMMANDERS.		DATE.
...nolds,	Brigadier-General.	June, 1862
...lair,	Col. 6th Ia. "Res."	" 27, "
...r,	Brigadier-General.	Sept., "
"		March 28, 1863
...we,	Lt.-Col. 126th Pa. Vols.	Jan., "
...gory,	" 91st " "	Feb., "
...andless,	" 2d " "Res."	June 28, "
"	" 2d " "	Nov. 1, "
	" 2d " "	May 1, 1864
...ley,	" 1st " "	Aug., 1863
	" 1st " "	Feb. 20, 1864
...e,	" 90th " Vols.	June, "
...Coy,	" 107th " "	Aug. 27, "
...g,	Brigadier-General.	Sept., "
"		Jan. 18, 1865
...rrow,	Col. 24th Mich. Vols.	Dec. 23, 1864
	" 24th " "	April 28, 1865
...ellogg,	" 6th Wis. "	Feb. 14, "

2d Brigade—3d Division.

Joined 5th Corps from Department of the Rappahannock,
June 18, 1862.
No 2d Brigade until reorganized June 5, 1864.

COMMANDERS.		DATE.
Geo. G. Meade,	Brigadier-General.	June, 1862
A. L. Magilton,	Col. 4th Pa. "Res."	" 30, "
P. H. Allabach,	" 131st " Vols.	Sept., "
"	" 131st " "	March 7, 1863
J. B. Clark,	" 123d " "	Feb., "
H. Baxter,	Brigadier-General.	June, 1864
"	"	Aug. 29, "
Chas. Wheelock,	Col. 97th N. Y. Vols.	Aug. 7, "

1st Brigade—4th Division.

Discontinued August, 1864.
Troops transferred to remaining Divisions.

COMMANDERS.		DATE.
L. Cutler,	Brigadier-General.	March 27, 1864
W. W. Robison,	Col. 7th Wis. Vols.	May 7, "
E. S. Bragg,	" 6th " "	June 7, "

2d Brigade—4th Division.

Discontinued August, 1864.
Troops transferred to remaining Divisions.

COMMANDERS.		DATE.
J. C. Rice,	Brigadier-General.	March 27, 1864
E. B. Fowler,	Col. 14th N. Y. S. M.	May 10, "
J. W. Hoffman,	" 56th Pa. Vols.	" 21, "

3d Brigade—3d Division.

Joined 5th Corps from Department of the Rappahannock, June 18, 1862.
Not reported until June, 1863.   Discontinued May, 1864.   Reorganized May, 1864.
Consolidated with 1st Brigade, 3d Division, August 21, 1864.
Reorganized August 24, 1864.   Formerly 1st Brigade, 4th Division.
Reorganized September, 1864.

COMMANDERS.		DATE.
T. Seymour,	Brigadier-General.	June, 1862
C. F. Jackson,	Col. 9th Pa. "Res."	" 30, "
J. W. Fisher,	" 5th " "	June 28, 1863
"	" 5th " "	Dec. 4, "
M. D. Hardin,	" 12th " "	Sept., "
W. R. Hartshorne,	Maj. 12th " "	May, 1864
"	Col. 190th " Vols.	July 26, "
James Carle,	" 191st " "	June 6, "
E. S. Bragg,	Brigadier-General.	Aug. "
J. W. Hoffman,	Col. 56th Pa. Vols.	Sept. 13, "
"	" 56th " "	Feb. 10, 1865
H. A. Morrow,	" 24th Mich. "	Jan. 25, "
R. Coulter,	" 11th Pa. "	March 15, "
A. R. Root,	" 94th N. Y. "	May 13, "

3d Brigade—4th Division.

Transferred to 1st Division, June, 1864.

COMMANDERS.		DATE.
Roy Stone	Col. 149th Pa. Vols.	March 27, 1864
E. S. Bragg,	" 6th Wis. "	May 6, "

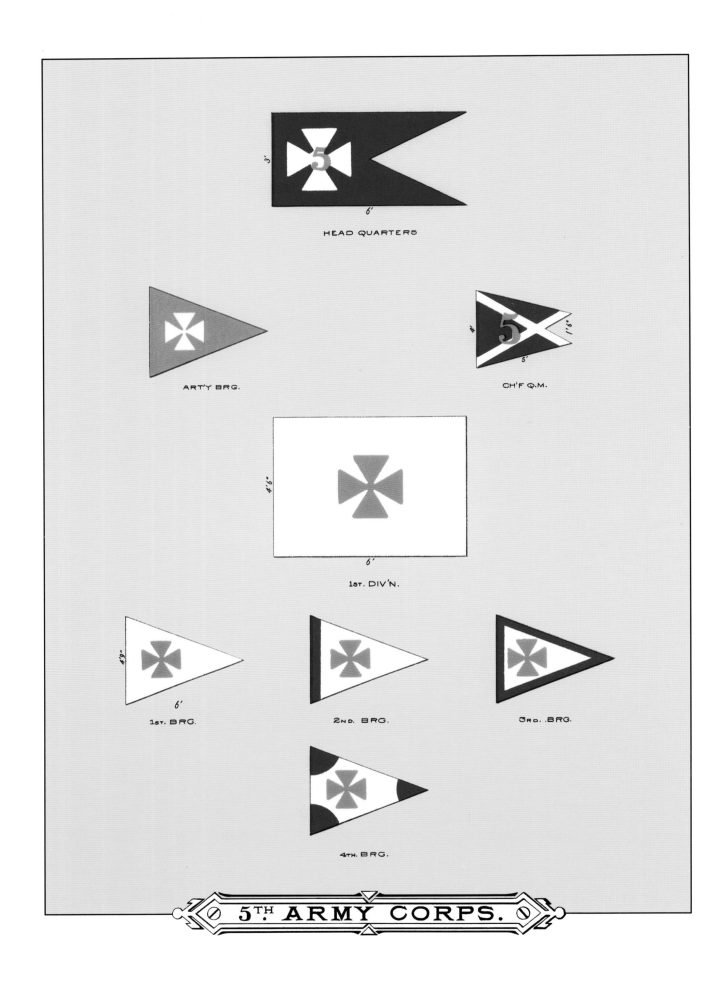

HEAD QUARTERS

ART'Y BRG.

CH'F Q.M.

1ST. DIV'N.

1ST. BRG.

2ND. BRG.

3RD. BRG.

4TH. BRG.

5TH ARMY CORPS.

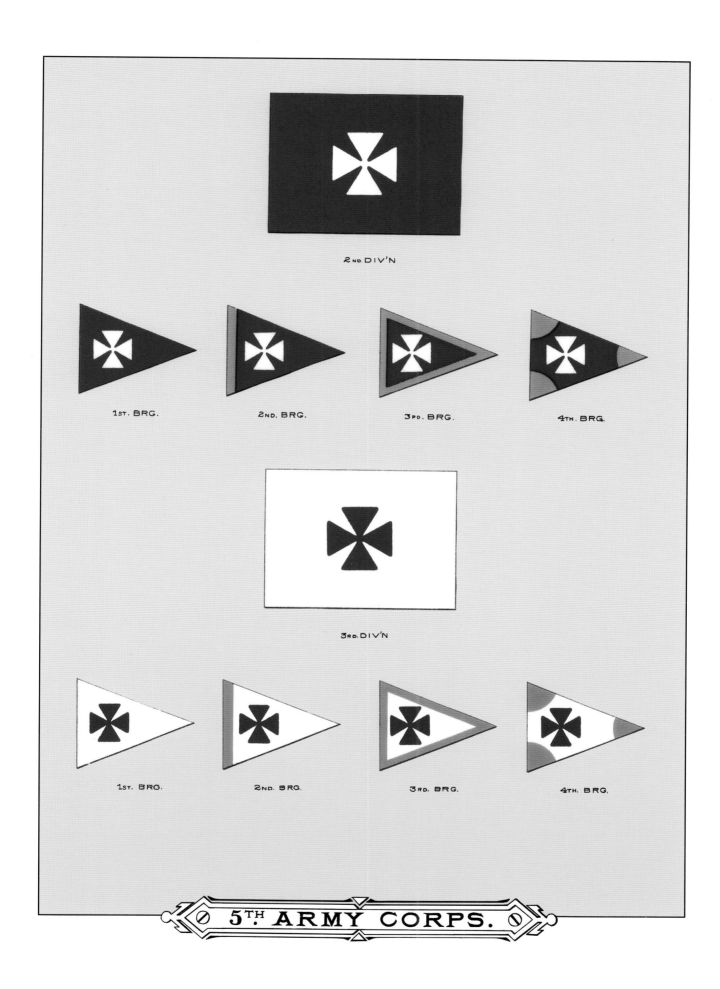

2ND. DIV'N

1ST. BRG. 2ND. BRG. 3RD. BRG. 4TH. BRG.

3RD. DIV'N

1ST. BRG. 2ND. BRG. 3RD. BRG. 4TH. BRG.

5TH ARMY CORPS.

SIXTH A[RMY]

Created G. O. No. 125, Army of the Potomac, May 18, 1862.

COMMANDERS.

WM. B. FRANKLIN,	Brigadier-G[eneral]
WM. F. SMITH,	Major-Gene[ral]
JOHN SEDGWICK,	"
H. G. WRIGHT,	"
GEO. W. GETTY,	Bvt. Major-[General]

1st Division—6th Army Corps.

COMMANDERS.

		DATE.
W. W. Slocum,	Brigadier-General.	May 18, 1862
W. T. H. Brooks,	"	October 22, 1862
H. G. Wright,	"	May 23, 1863, and April 23, 1864
D. A. Russell,	"	December 16, 1863, and May 9, 1864
A. T. A. Torbert,	"	March, 1864
F. Wheaton,	"	September 19, 1864

2d D[ivision]

COMMANDERS.

Wm. F. Smith,	Brigadier-
A. P. Howe,	"
Thos. H. Neill,	"
H. L. Eustis,	"
G. W. Getty,	"
"	Bvt. Majo[r]
L. A. Grant,	Brigadier-

1st Brigade—1st Division.

COMMANDERS.

		DATE.
G. W. Taylor,	Brigadier-General.	May 18, 1862
A. T. A. Torbert,	Col. 1st N. Y. Vols.	Aug. 29, "
"	Brigadier-General.	Feb. 8, 1863
"	"	June, "
H. W. Brown,	Col. 3d N. J. Vols.	Dec., 1862
"	" 3d " "	March, 1864
Wm. H. Penrose,	" 15th " "	April, 1863
"	" 15th " "	May 9, 1864
"	" 15th " "	Feb. 26, 1865
B. Hufty,	Lt.-" 4th " "	Oct. 19, 1864
E. L. Campbell,	" " 15th " "	Jan., 1865

2d Brigade—1st Division.

COMMANDERS.

		DATE.
J. J. Bartlett,	Col. 27th N. Y. Vols.	May 18, 1862
"	Brigadier-General.	Dec., "
"	"	Aug. 5, 1863
H. L. Cake,	Col. 96th Pa. Vols.	Nov., 1862
E. Upton,	" 121st N. Y. "	July 4, 1863
"	" 121st " "	Nov., "
J. E. Hamblin,	" 65th " "	Sept. 19, 1864
"	" 65th " "	March 17, 1865
E. Olcott,	Lt.-" 121st " "	Oct. 19, 1864
R. S. Mackenzie,	" 2d Conn. Hy. Art.	Nov., "
"	Brigadier-General.	Feb. 6, 1865
J. Hubbard,	Col. 2d Conn. Hy. Art.	Jan. 23, "

1st Brigade—2d Division.

Discontinued March, 1863.
Reorganized March, 1864 (formerly 3d Brigade, 3d Div[ision])

COMMANDERS.

W. S. Hancock,	Brigadier-General.	M
A. Cobb,	Col. 5th Wis. Vols.	Se
C. E. Pratt,	Brigadier-General.	
R. F. Taylor,	Col. 33d N. Y. Vols.	Ja
F. Wheaton,	Brigadier-General.	M
J. M. Warner,	Col. 11th Vt. Vols.	Se
"	Brigadier-General.	M
C. W. Eckman,	Col. 93d Pa. Vols.	A

3d Brigade—1st Division.

COMMANDERS.

		DATE.
J. Newton,	Brigadier-General.	May 18, 1862
R. Mattheson,	Col. 32d N. Y. Vols.	July, "
E. H. Stoughton,	" 4th Vt.	Oct. "
G. W. Town,	" 95th Pa.	Nov., "
"	" 95th "	Feb. 23, 1863
D. A. Russell,	Brigadier-General.	Dec. 10, 1862
"	"	March, 1863
"	"	Dec., "
"	"	April 5, 1864
P. E. Ellmaker,	Col. 119th Pa. Vols.	Nov. 20, 1863
G. Clarke,	Lt.-" 119th " "	Dec. 16, "
"	" 119th " "	June 12, 1864
Thos. S. Allen,	" 5th Wis. "	Jan., "
"	" 5th " "	Oct. 31, "
"	" 5th " "	Dec. 21, "
H. Burnham,	" 6th Me. "	Feb., "
H. L. Eustis,	Brigadier-General.	May 9, "
O. Edwards,	Col. 37th Mass. Vols.	July 17, "
"	" 37th " "	March 17, 1865
Isaac C. Bassett,	" 82d Pa. "	Nov. 30, 1864
"	" 82d " "	Jan. 9, 1865
J. E. Hamblin,	" 65th N. Y. "	" 31, "
Jas. R. Neiler,	Lt.-" 82d Pa. "	June, "

4th Brigade—1st Division.

Organized April 18, 1864. Discontinued July 6, 1864.

COMMANDERS.

		DATE.
A. Shaler,	Brigadier-General.	April 18, 1864
Nelson Cross,	Col. 67th N. Y. Vols.	May 6, "
J. E. Hamblin,	" 65th " "	June, "

3d Brigade—2d Division.

COMMANDERS.

J. W. Davidson,	Brigadier-General.	M
J. W. Corning,	Lt.-Col. 33d N. Y. Vols.	Ju
E. Von Vegesack,	" 20th " " "	Au
F. L. Vinton,	Brigadier-General.	Se
Thos. H. Neill,	"	De
"	"	Ju
"	"	Ma
D. D. Bidwell,	Col. 49th N. Y. Vols.	Ma
"	" 49th " " "	Fe
"	" 49th " " "	M
E. C. Mason,	" 7th Me. "	Ja
T. W. Hyde,	" 1st " "	O

Ligh[t]

Organized Janu[ary]

COMMANDER.

C. E. Pratt,	Brigadi[er]

IY CORPS.

Discontinued G. O. No. 35, Army of the Potomac, June 28, 1865.

DATE.
May 18, 1862.
November 16, 1862.
February 4, 1863.
May 9, 1864, and February 11, 1865.
Temporary, January, 1865.

Corps.

DATE.
May 18, 1862
November 16, 1862
January 4, and May 6, 1864
February 21, 1864
March, 1864; June 28, 1864, and January, 1865
February 11, 1865
December, 1864, and January, 1865

2d Brigade—2d Division.

COMMANDERS.		DATE.
Brooks,	Brigadier-General.	May 18, 1862
g,	Col. 2d Vt. Vols.	Oct. 22, "
t,	" 5th " "	Feb., 1863
	" 5th " "	Jan., 1864
	Brigadier-General.	Oct., "
	"	Jan., 1865
	"	Feb. 11, "
	"	March 7, "
er,	Col. 3d Vt. Vols.	Dec., 1863
er,	" 4th " "	Sept. 18, 1864
	" 4th " "	Jan., 1865
	" 4th " "	Feb. 20, "
sdon,	Lt.- " 11th " "	Dec., 1864

4th Brigade—2d Division.

Organized March, 1864 (formerly 2d Brigade, 3d Division.)
Discontinued July 6, 1864.

COMMANDERS.		DATE.
is,	Brigadier-General.	March, 1864
s,	Col. 37th Mass. Vols.	May 9, "

3d Division—6th Army Corps.

Joined 6th Army Corps, September 13, 1862, designated 3d Division.
Discontinued January, 1864, leaving only the 2d Brigade, and 2d Brigade transferred to the 2d Division, January, 1864.
Reorganized March, 1864 (formerly 3d Division, 3d Corps.)

COMMANDERS.		DATE.
D. N. Couch,	Major-General.	September, 1862
J. Newton,	Brigadier-General.	October, 1862, and February, 1863
C. Devens, Jr.,	"	December, 1862
J. J. Bartlett,	"	July 3, 1863
H. D. Terry,	"	August 4, 1863
Henry Prince,	"	March 25, 1864
J. B. Ricketts,	"	April 4, 1864, and April 15, 1865
T. Seymour,	"	October 28, 1864

1st Brigade—3d Division.

Changed to 2d Brigade, 3d Division, October, 1862.
Formerly 3d Brigade, 3d Division.
Discontinued January, 1864. Reorganized March, 1864.

COMMANDERS.		DATE.
Chas. Devens, Jr.,	Brigadier-General.	Sept. 13, 1862
J. Cochrane,	"	Oct., "
A. Shaler,	Col. 65th N. Y. Vols.	March, 1863
"	Brigadier-General.	June, "
S. Titus,	Col. 122d N. Y. Vols.	May, "
J. E. Hamblin,	" 65th " "	Dec. 30, "
W. H. Morris,	Brigadier-General.	March 26, 1864
W. S. Truex,	Col. 14th N. J. Vols.	May 13, "
"	" 14th " "	Nov., "
Wm. Emmerson,	" 151st N. Y. "	July, "
T. Seymour,	Brigadier-General.	April 17, 1865

2d Brigade—3d Division.

Changed to 3d Brigade, 3d Division, October, 1862.
Formerly 1st Brigade, 3d Division.
Transferred temporarily to 2d Division, January, 1864.
Transferred permanently to 2d Division, March, 1864.
Reorganized March, 1864.

COMMANDERS.		DATE.
A. P. Howe,	Brigadier-General.	Sept. 13, 1862
Chas. Devens, Jr.,	"	Oct., "
"	"	Feb., 1863
H. L. Eustis,	Col. 10th Mass. Vols.	Dec., 1862
"	" 10th " "	May 3, 1863
O. Edwards,	" 37th " "	Feb. 21, 1864
D. A. Russell,	Brigadier-General.	March 26, "
B. F. Smith,	Col. 126th Ohio Vols.	April 7, "
"	" 126th " "	Dec. 29, "
J. F. Staunton,	" 67th Pa. "	July 6, "
J. W. Keifer,	" 110th Ohio "	Aug. 26, "
"	" 110th " "	Feb. 8, 1865

3d Brigade—3d Division.

Changed to 1st Brigade, 3d Division, October, 1862. Formerly 2d Brigade, 3d Division.
Discontinued January, 1864.

COMMANDERS.		DATE.
J. Cochrane,	Brigadier-General.	September 13, 1862
A. P. Howe,	"	October, "
Thos. A. Rowley,	Col. 102d Pa. Vols.	November, "
F. Wheaton,	Brigadier-General.	December 15, "

y Corps.

ed May, 1863.

DATE.
January 26, 1863

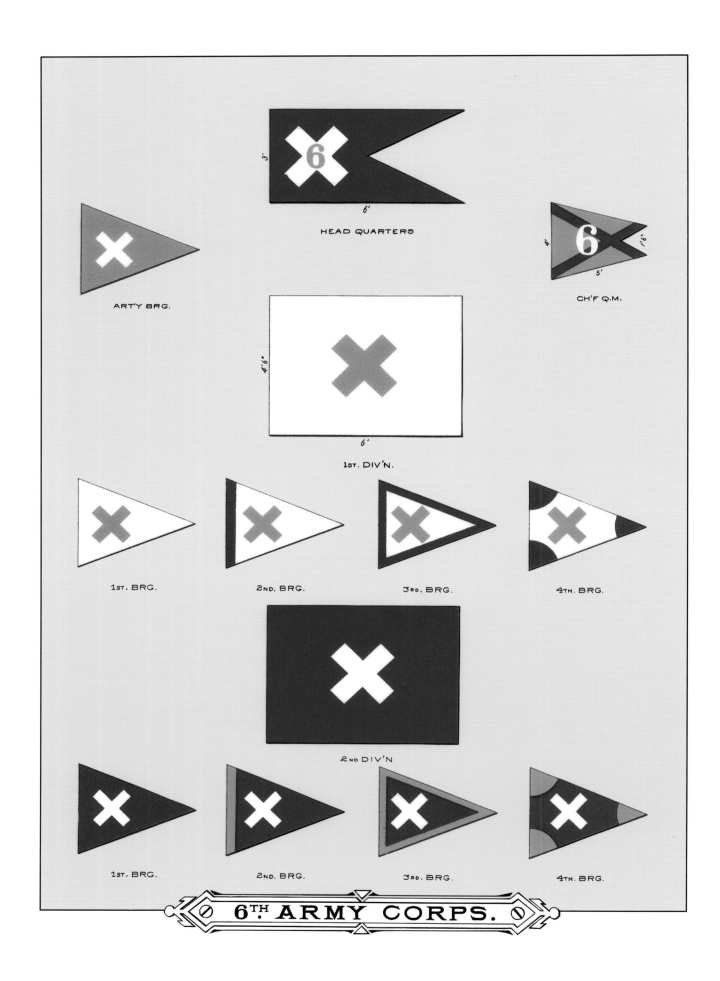

HEAD QUARTERS

ART'Y BRG.

CH'F Q.M.

1ST. DIV'N.

1ST. BRG.

2ND. BRG.

3RD. BRG.

4TH. BRG.

2ND DIV'N

1ST. BRG.

2ND. BRG.

3RD. BRG.

4TH. BRG.

6TH ARMY CORPS.

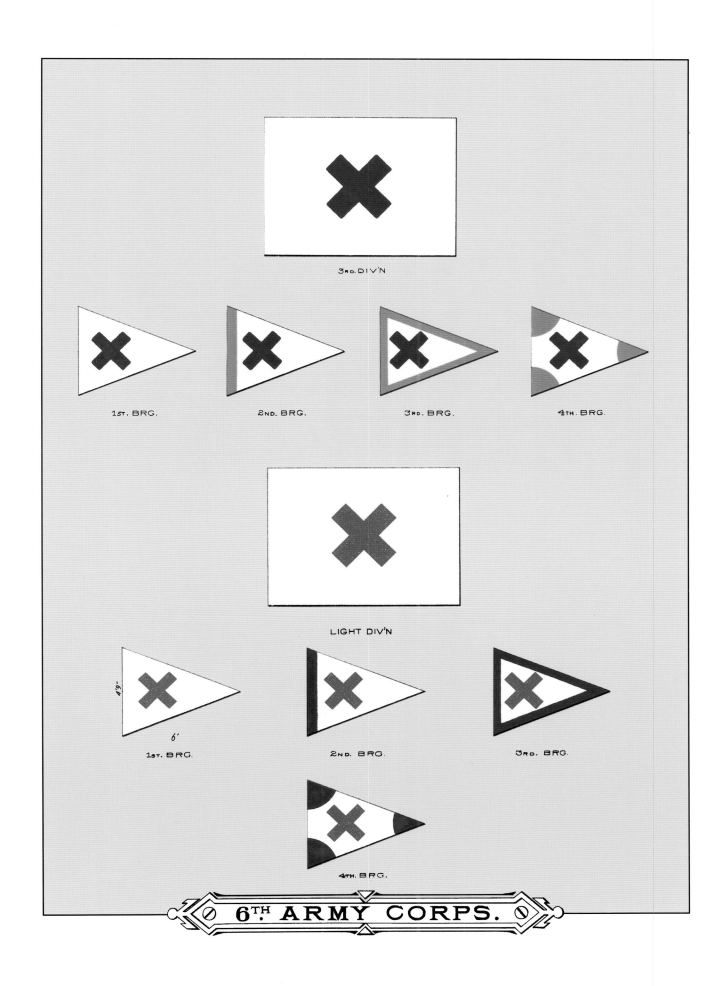

3RD. DIV'N

1ST. BRG.   2ND. BRG.   3RD. BRG.   4TH. BRG.

LIGHT DIV'N

4'9"

6'

1ST. BRG.   2ND. BRG.   3RD. BRG.

4TH. BRG.

6TH ARMY CORPS.

Created G. O. No. 84. A. G. O. July 22, 1862.   Discontinued G. O. No. 262. A. G. O. August 1, 1863.

COMMANDI

JOHN A. DIX,
H. M. NAGLEE,
FREDK. STEELE,
J. J. REYNOLDS,

Division at Suffolk, Va.—7th Army Corps.

Transferred to Army of the Potomac, September, 1862. Reorganized September, 1862.
Discontinued, called 1st Division, 7th Corps, April, 1863.

COMMANDERS.		DATE.
J. K. F. Mansfield,	Brigadier-General.	July, 1862
John J. Peck,	Major-General.	September 22, 1862, and January 2, 1863
M. Corcoran,	Brigadier-General.	September 30, 1862

1st D

Organized A

COMMANDER.	
M. Corcoran,	Brigadier

Weber's Brigade—Division at Suffolk, Va.

Transferred to 2d Army Corps, September, 1862.

COMMANDER.		DATE.
Max Weber,	Brigadier-General.	July, 1862

Foster's Provisional Brigade—Division at Suffolk, Va.

Transferred to 1st Division, 7th Corps, April, 1863.

COMMANDER.		DATE.
R. S. Foster,	Col. 13th Ind. Vols.	Sept. 23, 1863

1st Brigade—1st Division.

Formerly Terry's Brigade, Division at Suffolk, Va.
Transferred to 4th Army Corps, June, 1863.

COMMANDER.		
H. D. Terry,	Brigadier-General.	Ap

2d Provisional Brigade—Division at Suffolk, Va.

Termed Terry's Brigade, January, 1863.
Transferred to 1st Division, 7th Corps, April, 1863.

COMMANDERS.		DATE.
Alfred Gibbs,	Col. 130th N. Y. Vols.	Dec. 5, 1862
H. D. Terry,	Brigadier-General.	Jan. 21, 1863

Corcoran's Brigade—Division at Suffolk, Va.

Joined December, 1862.
Transferred to 1st Division, 7th Corps, April, 1863.

COMMANDER.		DATE.
M. Corcoran,	Brigadier-General.	Dec., 1862

Empire Brigade—Division at Suffolk, Va.

Joined October, 1862.
Transferred to Department of North Carolina, December 28, 1862.

COMMANDER.		DATE.
F. B. Spinola,	Brigadier-General.	Oct., 1862

Reserve Brigade—Division at Suffolk, Va.

Organized April 24, 1863.
Designation changed to Wistar's Brigade, June, 1863.

COMMANDERS.		DATE.
D. W. Wardrop,	Col. 99 h N. Y. Vols.	April 24, 1863
J. J. Wistar,	Brigadier-General.	May 13, "

3d

Formerly Corcoran
Transferred to Dep

COMMANDER.	
M. Murphy,	

Brigade at Norf

COMMANDER.	
E. L. Viele,	Brigadie

7th Army Corps as reorganized

District of Eastern Arkansas—7th Army Corps.

COMMANDERS.		DATE.
N. B. Buford,	Brigadier-General.	January, 1864, and September 28, 1864
Wm. Crooks,	Col. 6th Minn. Vols.	Temporary, August 6, 1864
A. McD. McCook,	Brigadier-General.	March 9, 1865
J. M. Thayer,	"	May 25, 1865
C. Bentzoni,	Col. 56th U. S. C. T.	June 12, 1865

District of North-E

Designation changed to Ind

COMMANDER.	
R. R. Livingston,	Col. 1st N

MY CORPS.

d G. O. No. 14. A. G. O. January 6, 1864. Finally discontinued G. O. No. 131. A. G. O. August 1, 1865.

	DATE.
General.	July 22, 1862.
er-General.	" 25, 1863.
General.	January 20, 1864.
	December 22, "

y Corps.

ed July, 1863.

	DATE.
	April 9, 1863

2d Division—7th Army Corps.

Formerly 3d Division, 9th Corps. Joined 7th Corps, March, 1863.

COMMANDER.		DATE.
Geo. W. Getty,	Brigadier-General.	March, 1863

2d Brigade—1st Division.

rmerly Foster's Provisional Brigade, Division at Suffolk, Va.
Transferred to Department of the South, July, 1863.

COMMANDER.		DATE.
er,	Col. 13th Ind. Vols.	April 30, 1863

1st Brigade—2d Division.

Joined Corps, March, 1863.
Transferred to Department of the South, July, 1863.

COMMANDERS.		DATE.
H. S. Fairchild,	Col. 89th N. Y. Vols.	March, 1863
R. C. Hawkins,	" 9th " "	April, "
W. R. Pease,	" 117th " "	May, "
S. M. Alvord,	" 3d " "	June, "

2d Brigade—2d Division.

Joined Corps, March, 1863.

COMMANDER.		DATE.
Edw. Harland,	Col. 8th Conn. Vols.	March, 1863

sion.

Suffolk, Va.
, July, 1863.

	DATE.
	April 9, 1863

3d Brigade—2d Division.

Joined Corps, March, 1863.

COMMANDERS.		DATE.
A. H. Dutton,	Col. 21st Conn. Vols.	March, 1863
W. H. P. Steere,	" 4th R. I. "	July 29, '

rmy Corps.

	DATE.
	July, 1862

. O. No. 14. A. G. O. January 6, 1864.

s—7th Army Corps.

ay, 1864. Discontinued June, 1864.

	DATE.
	January, 1864

District of the Frontier—7th Army Corps.

Designation changed to Frontier Division, December, 1864. Discontinued February, 1865.

COMMANDERS.		DATE.
W. R. Judson,	Col. 6th Kan. Cav.	January 7, 1864, and March 24, 1864
John M. Thayer,	Brigadier-General.	February, 1864; May 19, 1864, and January, 1865
John Edwards,	"	December, 1864

1st Brigade—District of the Frontier.

Designation changed to Indian Brigade, District of the Frontier, Feb., 1864.
Reorganized March 21, 1864. Formerly 2d Brigade, District of the Frontier.
Designation changed to 1st Brigade, Frontier Division, December, 1864.
Transferred to 3d Division, 7th Corps, February, 1865.

COMMANDERS.		DATE.
W. A. Phillips,	Col. 3d Indian Home Guards.	Jan., 1864
John Edwards,	" 18th Iowa Vols.	March 21, "
"	Brigadier-General.	Jan. 16, 1865
C. W. Adams,	Col. 12th Kan. Vols.	Dec. 3, 1864

2d Brigade—District of the Frontier.

Designation changed to 1st Brigade, District of the Frontier, March, 1864.
Reorganized March, 1864.
Designation changed to 2d Brigade, Frontier Division, December, 1864.
Discontinued January 16, 1865.
Reorganized January, 1865. Formerly 3d Brigade, Frontier Division.

COMMANDERS.		DATE.
John Edwards,	Col. 18th Iowa Vols.	Jan., 1864
C. W. Adams,	" 12th Kans. "	March, "
J. M. Williams,	" 1st " Col'd Vols.	May 7, "
W. R. Judson,	" 6th " Cav.	Jan., 1865

3d Brigade—District of the Frontier.

Discontinued March, 1864. Reorganized May, 1864.
Designation changed to 3d Brigade, Frontier Division, December, 1864.
Designation changed to 2d Brigade, Frontier Division, January, 1865.

COMMANDERS.		DATE.
T. M. Bowen,	Col. 13th Kans. Vols.	Jan., 1864
E. Lynde,	" 9th " Cav.	May 18, "
W. R. Judson,	" 6th " "	July 3, "
"	" 6th " "	Dec.,

Indian Brigade—District of the Frontier.

Formerly 1st Brigade, District of the Frontier.
Designation changed to Indian Brigade, Frontier Division, Dec., 1864.
Transferred to 3d Division, 7th Corps, February, 1865.

COMMANDERS.		DATE.
Wm. A. Phillips,	Col. 3d Indian Home Guards.	Feb., 1864
"	" 3d " " "	Dec. 17, "
Stephen H. Wattles,	" 1st " " "	July 30, "

1st Division—7th Army Corps.

Organized May 11, 1864. Formerly 3d Division, 7th Corps.

COMMANDERS.		DATE.
Fredk. Salomon,	Brigadier-General.	May 11, 1864, and Sept. 23, 1864
Cyrus Bussey,	"	July 25, 1864

2d Division—7th Army Corps.

COMMANDERS.		DATE.
E. A. Carr,	Brigadier-General.	January, 186
Nathan Kimball,	"	February 13, "
J. R. West,	"	April 25, "
C. C. Andrews,	"	June 16, "
A. Shaler,	"	December 28, "

1st Brigade—1st Division.

Formerly 1st Brigade, 3d Division.

COMMANDERS.			DATE.
Chas. E. Salomon,	Col.	9th Wis. Vols.	May, 1864
C. H. Mackey,	"	33d Iowa "	Nov. 28, "
A. Dengler,	Lt.- "	43d Ills. "	Feb. 18, 1865
"	" "	43d " "	June 24, "
T. M. Bowen,	"	13th Kans. "	March 22, "

2d Brigade—1st Division.

Formerly 3d Brigade, 3d Division.
Discontinued February, 1865.
Reorganized February, 1865.
Formerly Colored Brigade, 7th Corps.

COMMANDERS.			DATE.
A. Engelman,	Col.	43d Ills. Vols.	May, 1864
Jno. A. Garrett,	"	40th Iowa "	Nov. 10, "
J. M. Williams,	"	79th U. S. C. T.	Feb. 6, 1865
J. G. Hudson,	"	60th " "	July, "

1st Brigade—2d Division.

Organized May 13, 1864.

COMMANDERS.			DATE.
Wm. H. Graves,	Col.	12th Mich. Vols.	May 13, 1864
"	"	12th " "	Jan., 1865
A. B. Morrison,	"	57th U. S. C. T.	Sept., 1864
H. Mattson,	"	3d Minn. Vols.	Oct., "
F. M. Drake,	Lt.- "	36th Iowa "	June 11, 1865

2d Brigade—2d Division.

Discontinued March, 1864.
Reorganized May, 1864.

COMMANDERS.		
A. Engelman,	Col.	43d Ills. Vols. Jan
C. C. Andrews,	Brigadier-General.	May
Oliver Wood,	Col.	22d Ohio Vols. June
Homer Thrall,	Lt.- "	22d " " Aug
M. L. Stevenson,	"	2d Ark. " Sep
Jas. M. True,	"	62d Ills. " Nov
L. C. True,	Lt.- "	62d " " Apr
"	" "	62d " " July
John Edwards,	Brigadier-General.	May
L. W. Beal,	Lt.-Col.	126th Ills. Vols. June

3d Brigade—1st Division.

Organized May 13, 1864.
Transferred to Cavalry Division, September, 1864.

COMMANDERS.		DATE.
J. A. Leman,	Maj. 3d Mo. Cav.	May 13, 1864
Cyrus Bussey,	Brigadier-General.	" 25, "
J. F. Ritter,	Col. 1st Mo. Cav.	July 29, "

3d Brigade—2d Division.

Transferred to Cavalry Division, September 15, 1864.

COMMANDERS.		DATE.
G. M. Mitchell,	Col. 54th Ills. Vols.	January, 1864
Henry Yates,	Lt.- " 106th Ills. "	February, "
Washington F. Geiger,	" 8th Mo. Cav.	May 15, "

Separate Dismounted Cavalry Brigade.

Organized March 18, 1865.

COMMANDERS.		DATE.
W. F. Geiger,	Col. 8th Mo. Cav.	March, 1865
J. H. Reed,	Lt.- " 8th " "	April, "
P. Clayton,	Brigadier-General.	May 30, "
"	"	July, "
M. H. Brawner,	Lt.-Col. 1st Mo. Cav.	June, "

Cavalry Brigade—"Post of Little Rock."

Organized February, 1865. Discontinued June, 1865.

COMMANDER.		DATE.
M. M. Trumbull,	Col. 9th Iowa Cav.	Feb., 1865

Independent C

Discontinued Octob

COMMANDER.	
P. Clayton,	Col. 5th Kan

REORGANIZED—Continued.

3d Division—7th Army Corps.

Changed to 1st Division, 7th Corps, May 11, 1864.
Reorganized February 1, 1865.

COMMANDERS.		DATE.
Fredk. Salomon,	Brigadier-General.	January, 1864
Cyrus Bussey,	"	February 6, 1865

Cavalry Division—7th Army Corps.

Discontinued May, 1864. Reorganized September 15, 1864.
Discontinued March, 1865.

COMMANDERS.		DATE.
J. M. Davidson,	Brigadier-General.	January, 1864
Eugene A. Carr,	"	February 13, "
J. R. West,	"	September 15, "

1st Brigade—3d Division.

ged to 2d Brigade, 3d Division, March, 1864.
Formerly 2d Brigade, 3d Division.

COMMANDERS.		DATE.
McLean,	Col. 43d Ind. Vols.	Jan., 1864
e,	Brigadier-General.	March, "
mon,	Col. 9th Wis. Vols.	April 30, "
ards,	Brigadier-General.	Feb., 1865
arrett,	Col. 40th Iowa Vols.	May 7, "
nson,	" 1st Ark. "	June, 1865

2d Brigade—3d Division.

Changed to 1st Brigade, 3d Division, March, 1864.
Formerly 1st Brigade, 3d Division.
No 2d Brigade after reorganization of Division.

COMMANDERS.		DATE.
Jas. M. Lewis,	Col. 28th Wis. Vols.	Jan., 1864
S. A. Rice,	Brigadier-General.	Feb. 1, "
Wm. E. McLean,	Col. 43d Ind. Vols.	March, "

1st Brigade—Cavalry Division.

Dropped from Cavalry Division, April, 1865.
Troops left for another command.

COMMANDERS.		DATE.
J. F. Ritter,	Col. 1st Mo. Cav.	Jan. 6, 1864
Albert Erskine,	" 13th Ills. "	Sept. 19, "
M. H. Brawner,	Maj. 7th Mo. "	Jan. 24, 1865
J. K. Mizner,	Col. 3d Mich. "	Feb., "

2d Brigade—Cavalry Division.

Formerly 3d Brigade, 1st Division.
Changed to " Dismounted Separate Cavalry Brigade,"
March 18, 1865.

COMMANDERS.		DATE.
W. F. Geiger,	Col. 8th Mo. Cav.	Jan., 1864
"	" 8th " "	Feb., 1865
J. F. Ritter,	" 1st " "	Sept. 19, 1864
Wm. Thompson,	" 1st Iowa "	Nov. 6, "
Cyrus Bussey,	Brigadier-General.	Dec. 1, "

3d Brigade—3d Division.

Organized March, 1864. Transferred to District of South Kansas, May, 1865.
Known as the Indian Brigade prior to March, 1865.

COMMANDERS.		DATE.
A. Engelman,	Col. 43d Ills. Vols.	March, 1864
Wm. A. Phillips,	" 3d Indian Home Guards.	February, 1865

3d Brigade—Cavalry Division.

Formerly 3d Brigade, 2d Division.
Discontinued February, 1865.

COMMANDERS.		DATE.
Daniel Anderson,	Col. 1st Iowa Cav.	Jan., 1864
W. F. Geiger,	" 8th Mo. "	Sept. 19, "

4th Brigade—Cavalry Division.

Organized September, 1864.
Discontinued February, 1865.

COMMANDERS.		DATE.
A. H. Ryan,	Col. 3d Ark. Cav.	Sept. 9, 1864
John K. Mizner,	" 3d Mich. "	Oct. 31, "

Colored Brigade.

Organized January, 1865. Formerly 2d Brigade, Frontier Division.
Transferred to 1st Division, February, 1865.

	COMMANDER.		DATE.
DATE.			
an., 1864	J. M. Williams,	Col. 1st Kans. Col'd Vols.	Jan., 1865

District of South Kansas.

Organized April 22, 1865.

COMMANDERS.		DATE.
James G. Blunt,	Major-General.	May 8, 1865
John A. Garrett,	Col. 40th Iowa Vols.	June, "

Cavalry Brigade—District of South Kansas.

Organized May, 1865.

COMMANDERS.		DATE.
A. N. Duffie,	Brigadier-General.	May, 1865
John A. Garrett,	Col. 40th Iowa Vols.	June, "

Indian Brigade—District of South Kansas.

Formerly 3d Brigade, 3d Division.
Discontinued May 31, 1865.

COMMANDERS.		DATE.
Wm. A. Phillips,	Col. 3d Ind. Vols.	May, 1865
John Ritchie,	Bvt. Brigadier-Genl.	May 16, "

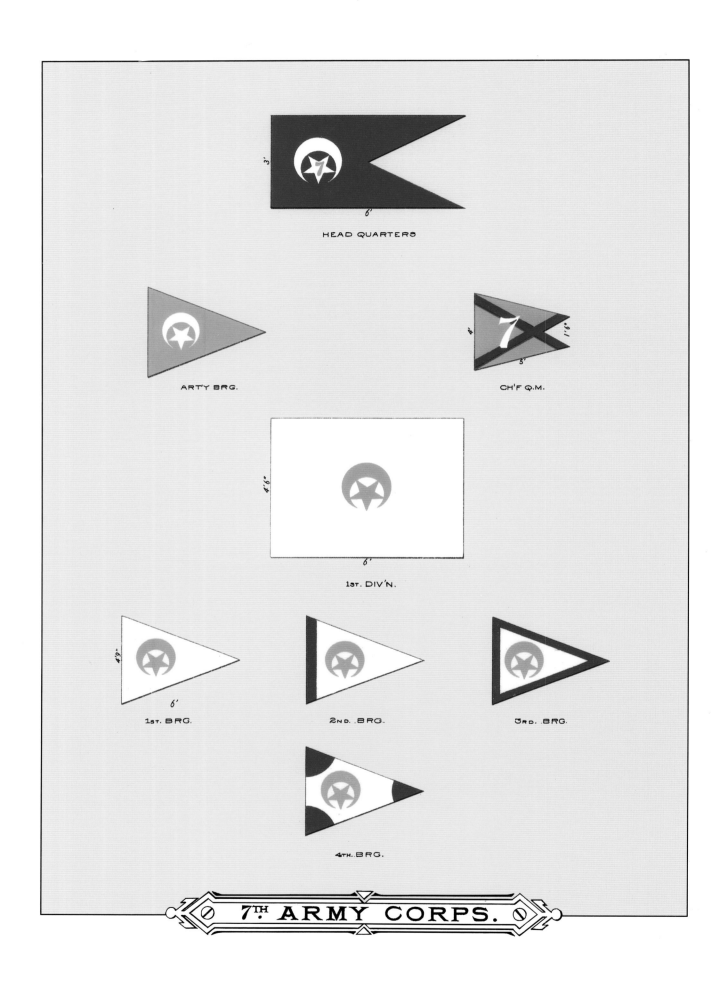

HEAD QUARTERS

ART'Y BRG.

CH'F Q.M.

1st. DIV'N.

1st. BRG.

2nd. BRG.

3rd. BRG.

4th. BRG.

7TH ARMY CORPS.

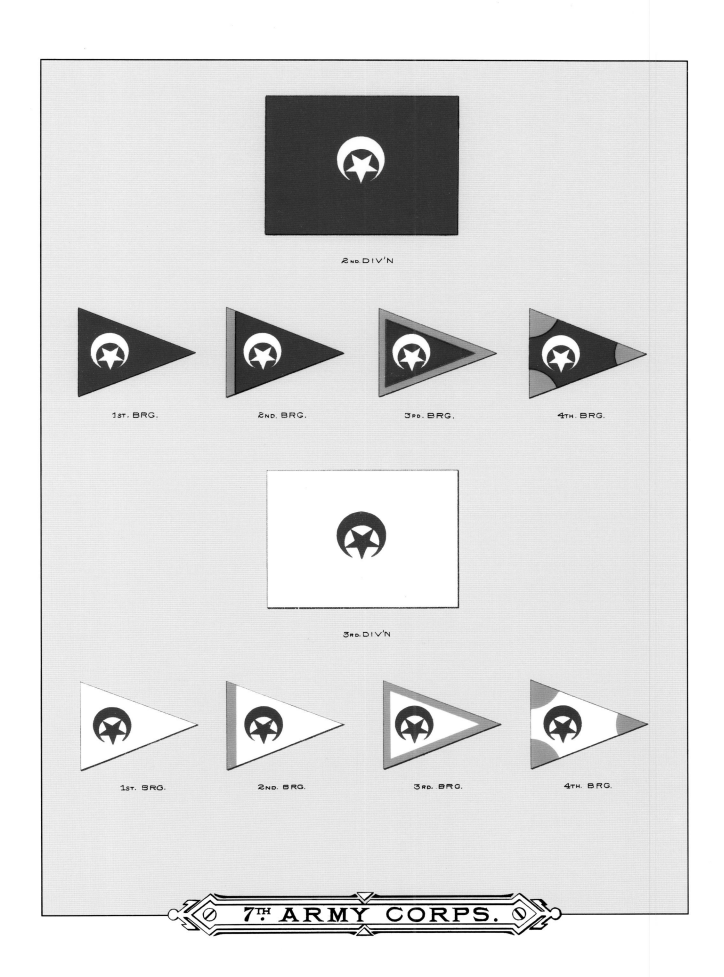

2ND. DIV'N

1ST. BRG. 2ND. BRG. 3RD. BRG. 4TH. BRG.

3RD. DIV'N

1ST. BRG. 2ND. BRG. 3RD. BRG. 4TH. BRG.

7TH ARMY CORPS.

EIGHTH A[RMY CORPS.]

TROOPS IN THE M[IDDLE DEPARTMENT.]

Designated 8th Army Corps, G. O. No. 84. A. G. O. July 22, [1862.]

COMMANDERS.

JOHN E. WOOL,	Major-General.
R. C. SCHENCK,	"
H. H. LOCKWOOD,	Brigadier-General[.]
L. WALLACE,	Major-General.
W. W. MORRIS,	Bvt. Brigadier-Ge[neral.]

Railroad District.

Discontinued September, 1862.

COMMANDER.		DATE.
B. F. Kelly,	Brigadier-General.	July 22, 1862

District of "Eastern Shore," Maryland.

Discontinued January 5, 1863, and designated 1st Separate Brigade.
Recreated December 13, 1864.
Consolidated with District of Delaware, March, 1865, and termed " District of Delaware and Eastern Shore."

COMMANDERS.		DATE.
H. H. Lockwood,	Brigadier-General.	July 22, 1862
John R. Kenly,	"	Dec. 13, 1864

District of Delaware.

Organized July, 1863. Discontinued May, 1864.
Reorganized August 20, 1864.
Consolidated with District of Eastern Shore of Maryland, March [1865.]

COMMANDERS.		DA[TE.]
D. Tyler,	Brigadier-General.	July
Henry B. Judd,	Maj. U. S. A.	Jan. 1
J. R. Kenly,	Brigadier-General.	April
S. M. Bowman,	Col. 84th Pa. Vols.	Aug. 2

Railroad Brigade.

Discontinued September, 1862.

COMMANDER.		DATE.
D. S. Miles.	Col. 2d U. S. Inf.	July 22, 1862

First Separate Brigade.

Organized January 5, 1863.
Discontinued June, 1863. Troops transferred to Army of the Potomac.
Reorganized October, 1863. Discontinued July 31, 1865.

COMMANDERS.		DATE.
H. H. Lockwood,	Brigadier-General.	January 5, and October 28, 1863
E. B. Tyler,	"	Dec. 18, 1863, and Mar. and Dec., 1864
Samuel A. Graham,	Col. "Purnell Legion," Md.Vols.	February, 1863
J. R. Kenly,	Brigadier-General.	Nov. 18, 1864, and June 5, 1865

Second Separate Brigade.

Organized January 5, 1863. Discontinued July 29, 1865.

COMMANDERS.		DATE.
W. W. Morris,	Bvt. Brigadier-General.	Jan. 5, 1863 ; May 10, 1864, and Apri[l]
P. A. Porter,	Col. 8th N. Y. Art.	January 20, 1863
D. Macauley,	" 11th Ind. Vols.	January, 1865

1st Division—8th Army Corps.

Organized March, 1863.
Transferred to Department of West Virginia, June, 1863.

COMMANDER.		DATE.
B. F. Kelly,	Brigadier-General.	April 1, 1863

2d Division—8th Army Corps.

Organized February, 1863. (Formerly Milroy's Division.)
Transferred to Army of the Potomac, June, 1863.

COMMANDER.		DATE.
R. H. Milroy,	Brigadier-General.	February, 1863

1st Brigade—1st Division.

Organized March, 1863. (Formerly Md. Brigade.)

COMMANDER.		DATE.
J. R. Kenly,	Brigadier-General.	March, 1863

4th Brigade—1st Division.

Organized March, 1863.

COMMANDER.		DATE.
J. M. Campbell,	Col. 54th Pa. Vols.	March 27, 1863

1st Brigade—2d Division.

Organized March, 1863.

COMMANDER.		DATE.
W. L. Elliott,	Brigadier-General.	March 5, 1863

2d Brigade—2d Division.

Organized March, 1863.

COMMANDERS.		DA[TE.]
Geo. Hay,	Col. 87th Pa. Vols.	March
W. G. Ely,	" 18th Conn. "	May

2d Brigade—1st Division.

Organized March, 1863.

COMMANDER.		DATE.
W. H. Morris,	Brigadier-General.	March, 1863

5th Brigade—1st Division.

Organized March, 1863.

COMMANDER.		DATE.
J. A. Mulligan,	Col. 23d Ills. Vols.	March 27, 1863

3d Brigade—1st Division.

Organized March, 1863.

COMMANDER.		DATE.
B. F. Smith,	Col. 126th Ohio Vols.	March 27, 1863

6th Brigade—1st Division.

Organized March, 1863.

COMMANDER.		DATE.
N. Wilkinson,	Col. 6th Va. Vols.	March 27, 1863

3d Brigade—2d Division.

Organized March, 1863.

COMMANDER.		DATE.
A. T. McReynolds,	Col. 1st N. Y. Cav.	March 27, 1863

MY CORPS.

DLE DEPARTMENT

Discontinued G. O. No. 131.   A. G. O. August 1, 1865.

DATE.	
July 22, 1862.	
December 22, 1862.	
" 5, 1863.	
March 12, 1864, and April 19, 1865.	
January 30, 1865.	

Defences of Baltimore.

Discontinued January 5, 1863, and designated 2d Separate Brigade.
Recreated June, 1863.
Discontinued October, 1863, and designated 3d Separate Brigade.

COMMANDERS.		DATE.
. Morris,	Col. 2d U. S. Art.	July 22, 1862
Tyler,	Brigadier-General.	June 29, 1863

Defences of the Upper Potomac.

Created January, 1863.
Discontinued February, 1863.

COMMANDER.		DATE.
B. F. Kelly,	Brigadier-General.	Jan., 1863

Maryland Brigade—Defences of the Upper Potomac.

Organized December, 1862.
Designation changed to 1st Brigade, 1st Division, March, 1863.

COMMANDER.		DATE.
J. R. Kenly,	Brigadier-General.	Dec., 1862

District of Delaware and the "Eastern Shore."

Organized March, 1865.
Discontinued July, 1865.

COMMANDERS.		DATE.
J. R. Kenly,	Brigadier-General.	March, 1865
J. M. Wilson,	Col. 155th Ind. Vols.	June, "

Third Separate Brigade.

Organized February, 1863.   Discontinued June, 1863.   (Troops transferred to Army of the Potomac.)
Reorganized July, 1863.   Discontinued August, 1863.
Reorganized October, 1863.   (Formerly " Defences of Baltimore.")   Discontinued December, 1863.
Reorganized March, 1864.   Discontinued July 31, 1865.

COMMANDERS.		DATE.
H. S. Briggs,	Brigadier-General.	February 14, 1863
Samuel A. Graham,	Col. "Purnell Legion," Md. Vols.	July, 1863
E. B. Tyler,	Brigadier-General.	October, 1863
H. H. Lockwood,	"	March 24, and July 20, 1864
J. R. Kenly,	"	May 16, 1864

Fourth Separate Brigade.

Organized March, 1863.
Transferred to Department of West Virginia, June, 1863.

COMMANDERS.		DATE.
B. S. Roberts,	Brigadier-General.	March, 1863
W. W. Averill,	"	May 23, "

3d Division, or "District of Kanawha"—8th Army Corps.

Transferred from Department of Ohio, March, 1863.
Transferred to Department of West Virginia, June, 1863.

COMMANDER.		DATE.
E. P. Scammon,	Brigadier-General.	March, 1863

Milroy's Division—8th Army Corps.

Organized January, 1863.
Designation changed to 2d Division, 8th Corps, February, 1863.

COMMANDER.		DATE.
R. H. Milroy,	Brigadier-General.	January, 1863

1st Brigade—3d Division.

COMMANDER.	DATE.
ayes,	Col. 23d Ohio Vols.	March, 1863

2d Brigade—3d Division.

COMMANDER.	DATE.
C. B. White,	Col. 12th Ohio Vols.	March, 1863

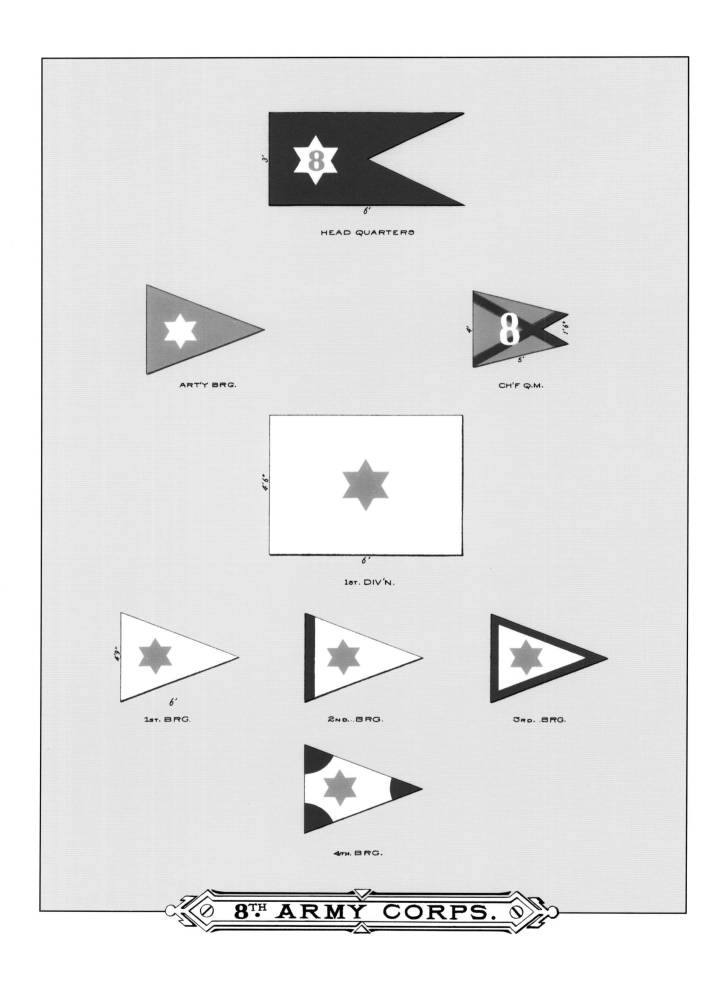

HEAD QUARTERS

ART'Y BRG.

CH'F Q.M.

1ST. DIV'N.

1ST. BRG.

2ND. BRG.

3RD. BRG.

4TH. BRG.

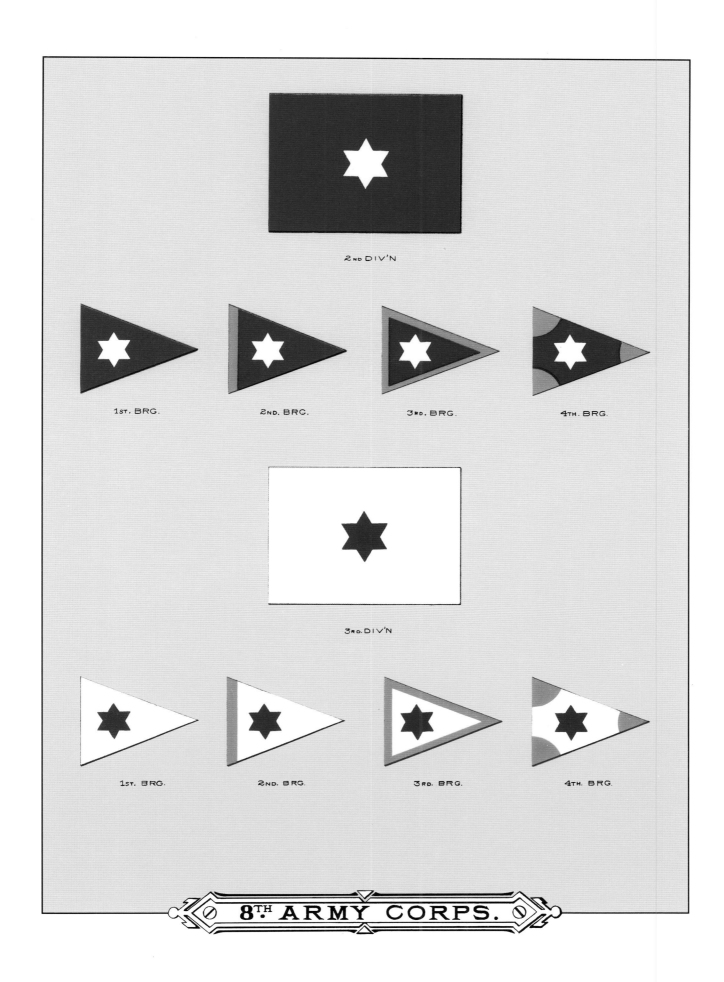

2ND DIV'N

1ST. BRG.   2ND. BRG.   3RD. BRG.   4TH. BRG.

3RD. DIV'N

1ST. BRG.   2ND. BRG.   3RD. BRG.   4TH. BRG.

8TH ARMY CORPS.

Created G. O. No. 84.   A. G. O. July 22, 186

COMMANDERS.

A. E. BURNSIDE,	Major-General.
O. B. WILCOX,	Brigadier-General.
JOHN SEDGWICK,	Major-General.
WM. F. SMITH,	"
J. G. PARKE,	"
R. B. POTTER,	Brigadier-General.

1st Division—9th Army Corps.

Discontinued September 1, 1864.
Reorganized September 13, 1864. (Formerly 3d Division, 9th Corps.)

COMMANDERS.		DATE.
I. I. Stevens,	Brigadier-General.	July 22, 1862
B. C. Christ,	Col. 50th Pa. Vols.	September 1, 1862
O. B. Wilcox,	Brigadier-General.	{ Sept. 8, 1862 ; Feb., 1863 ; Sept. 13, 1864 ; Feb. 2, 1865, and March 7, 1865 }
Wm. M. Fenton,	Col. 8th Mich. Vols.	October 16, 1862
Daniel Leasure,	" 100th Pa. "	October 26, 1862, and May 10, 1864
W. W. Burns,	Brigadier-General.	November, 1862
Thos. Welsh,	"	April 11, 1863
E. Ferrero,	"	August 18, 1863
T. G. Stevenson,	"	April 19, 1864
T. L. Crittenden,	Major-General.	May 12, 1864
J. H. Ledlie,	Brigadier-General.	June 9, 1864
J. White,	"	August 6, 1864
J. F. Hartranft,	"	" 28, "
N. B. McLaughlin,	Col. 57th Mass. Vols.	Dec. 30, 1864, and Feb. 25, and July 15, 1865
W. F. Bartlett,	Brigadier-General.	June 20, 1865

2d Division—9th Army Corps.

No Return of Division on File until December, 1862.

COMMANDERS.		DATE.
J. L. Reno,	Major-General.	July 22, 1862
S. D. Sturgis,	Brigadier-General.	October, 1862, and March, 1863
E. Ferrero,	"	February, 1863
J. F. Hartranft,	Col. 51st Pa. Vols.	May, 1863, and November 16, 1863
R. B. Potter,	Brigadier-General.	June 5, 1863 ; May 1, 1864, and Jan
S. G. Griffin,	Col. 6th N. H. Vols.	August, 1863, and April, 1864
"	Brigadier-General.	Dec. 22, 1864 ; April 2, 1865, and May
J. K. Sigfried,	Col. 48th Pa. Vols.	October, 1863
O. B. Wilcox,	Brigadier-General.	January 26, 1864
Z. R. Bliss,	Col. 7th R. I. Vols.	March 16, 1864
J. J. Bartlett,	Brigadier-General.	April 20, 1865

1st Brigade—1st Division.

Organized September 24, 1862.
Discontinued September 1, 1864.
Reorganized Sept. 13, 1864. (Formerly 1st Brig., 3d Div.)

COMMANDERS.			DATE.
W. M. Fenton,	Col. 8th Mich. Vols.	Sept.	24, 1862
"	" 8th " "	Oct.	26, "
"	" 8th " "	Dec.	15, "
W. H. Withington,	" 17th " "	Oct.	16, "
O. M. Poe,	" 2d " "	Nov.	15, "
"	" 2d " "	Feb.,	1863
D. Morrison,	" 79th N. Y. "	April	10, "
"	" 79th " "	June,	"
H. Bowman,	" 36th Mass. "	"	
S. Carruth,	" 35th " "	April,	1864
J. H. Ledlie,	Brigadier-General.	May,	"
J. P. Gould,	Col. 59th Mass. Vols.	June	9, "
W. F. Bartlett,	Brigadier-General.	July	21, "
J. H. Barnes,	Lt.-Col. 29th Mass. Vols.	"	30, "
B. C. Christ,	" 50th Pa. "	Sept.	13, "
S. Harriman,	" 37th Wis. "	"	30, "
"	" 37th " "	Dec.	17, "
J. F. Hartranft,	Brigadier-General.	Oct.	25, "
Jas. Bintliff,	Col. 38th Wis. Vols.	Nov.	28, "
John Green,	Lt.- " 37th " "	July,	1865

2d Brigade—1st Division.

Organized September, 1862.
Transferred to 2d Division and termed 3d Brigade,
2d Division, June, 1863.
Reorganized August, 1863. (Formerly 3d Brig., 2d Div.)
Discontinued September 1, 1864.
Reorganized Sept. 13, 1864. (Formerly 2d Brig., 3d Div.)

COMMANDERS.			DATE.
B. C. Christ,	Col. 50th Pa. Vols.	Sept.,	1862
"	" 50th " "	Dec.,	"
"	" 50th " "	March,	1863
"	" 50th " "	Sept.,	"
W. H. Withington,	" 17th Mich. "	Nov.,	1862
G. W. Mindel,	" 27th N. J. "	Jan.,	1863
Wm. M. Fenton,	" 8th Mich. "	Feb.,	"
E. W. Pierce,	" 29th Mass. "	Aug.,	"
"	" 29th " "	Jan.,	1864
"	" 29th " "	June	4, "
Jos. H. Barnes,	Lt.- " 29th " "	March,	"
D. Leasure,	" 100th Pa. "	April,	"
J. M. Sudsburg,	" 3d Md. "	May	10, "
G. P. Robinson,	Lt.- " 3d " "	July	31, "
Wm. Humphrey,	" 2d Mich. "	Sept.	13, "
J. F. Hartranft,	Brigadier-General.	"	30, "
W. C. Newberry,	Lt.-Col. 24th N. Y. Cav.	Oct.	9, "
B. M. Cutcheon,	" 20th Mich. Vols.	"	16, "
R. Ely,	" 8th " "	March 10, 1865
W. H. Telford,	" 50th Pa. "	June	11, "
S. R. Schwenck,	Lt.- " 50th " "	July	1, "

1st Brigade—2d Division.

Organized September, 1862.
Discontinued January, 1864.
Reorganized March, 1864.

COMMANDERS.			DATE.
Jas. Nagle,	Brigadier-General.	Sept.,	1862
"	"	March,	1863
S. G. Griffin,	Col. 6th N. H. Vols.	Feb.,	"
"	" 6th " "	May	21, "
Z. R. Bliss,	" 7th R. I.	Aug.	30, "
"	" 7th " "	July	25, 1864
J. K. Sigfried,	" 48th Pa.	Sept.	30, 1863
"	" 48th " "	Nov.	16, "
"	" 48th " "	April,	1864
T. B. Allard,	" 2d Md.	Oct.,	1863
H. B. Titus,	" 9th N. H.	March,	1864
J. I. Curtin,	" 45th Pa.	May	7, "
"	" 45th " "	Aug.	21, "
"	" 45th " "	Feb.	11, 1865
H. Pleasants,	Lt.- " 45th " "	June	19, 1864
S. Carruth,	" 35th Mass. "	Jan.	23, 1865
"	" 35th " "	May	4, "
J. F. Brannon,	" 48th Pa.	June	9, "

2d Brigade—2d Division.

Organized September, 1862.

COMMANDERS.			D
E. Ferrero,	Brigadier-General.	Sept.	
"	"	March	
"	"	June	
J. F. Hartranft,	Col. 51st Pa. Vols.	Feb.	
"	" 51st " "	April	
W. Harriman,	" 11th N. H. "	May.	
E. Schall,	Lt.- " 51st Pa. "	Aug.	
M. N. Collins,	" 11th N. H. "	Dec.	
H. B. Titus,	" 35th Mass. "	Feb.,	
H. B. Titus,	" 9th N. H. "	April	
"	" 9th " "	Dec.	
"	" 9th " "	May	
S. G. Griffin,	" 6th " "	"	
"	Brigadier-General.	Feb.	
"	"	April	
S. M. Weld,	Col. 56th Mass. Vols.	June	

3d Brigade—1st Division.

Organized September, 1862. Discontinued January, 1864.
Reorganized September, 1864. (Formerly 1st Brigade of *Old* 1st Division)

COMMANDERS.			DATE.
Thos. Welsh,	Col. 45th Pa. Vols.	Sept.,	1862
"	" 45th " "	Jan.	27, 1863
Dan'l Leasure,	" 100th " "	Nov.,	1862
"	" 100th " "	Feb.,	1863
"	" 100th " "	Sept.,	"
Cornelius Byington,	Maj. 2d Mich. "	Aug.,	"
Wm. Humphrey,	Col. 2d " "	Nov.,	"
J. H. Barnes,	Lt.- " 29th Mass. "	Sept.,	1864
N. B. McLaughlin,	" 57th " "	" 15, "
"	" 57th " "	Feb.	2, 1865
"	" 57th " "	March	7, "
"	" 57th " "	May	11, "
G. P. Robinson,	Lt.- " 3d Md. "	Dec.	30, 1864
"	" 3d " "	Feb.	25, 1865
"	" 3d " "	March 25, "
J. Bintleff,	" 38th Wis. "	April	3, "
E. G. Marshall,	" 14th N. Y. Hy. Art.	" 24, "

3d Brigade—2d Division.

Organized June, 1863. (Formerly 2d Brig., 1st Div.) Transferred to 3d Brig., 1st Div., August, 186
Reorganized October, 1863. Transferred to Department of the Ohio, January, 1864.

COMMANDERS.			DATE.
B. C. Christ,	Col. 50th Pa. Vols.	June,	1863
Wilson C. Lemert,	" 86th Ohio "	Oct.,	"

Provisional Brigade—1st Division.

Organized May, 1864. Discontinued June, 1864.

COMMANDER.		DATE.
E. G. Marshall,	Col. 14th N. Y. Hy. Art.	May,	1864

Provisional Br

Organized Nov. 28, 1864. Discontinued Dec

COMMAND
J. F. Hartranft,	Brigadie

MY CORPS.

tinued G. O. No. 131.   A. G. O. August 1, 1865.

DATE.

22, 1862; March 17, 1863, and April 13, 1864.
, 1862; April 11, 1863; Jan. 18, 1864; March 16, 1864; }
31, 1864; January 24, 1865, and June 17, 1865.   }
ary 16, 1863.
ruary 5, 1863.
ch 19, 1863; June 5, 1863; Jan. 26, 1864; Aug. 15, 1864; }
12, 1865; Feb. 2, 1865, and July 2, 1865.   }
ust 21, 1863.

3d Division—9th Army Corps.

No Return of Division on file from July to December, 1862.
Transferred to Department of Virginia, March, 1863. Reorganized April, 1864.
Designation changed to 1st Division, September 13, 1864.
Reorganized September 13, 1864. (Formerly 4th Division, 9th Corps.)
Transferred to Department of Virginia, November 26, 1864.
Reorganized December 15, 1864. (Formerly Provisional Brigade, 9th Corps.)

COMMANDERS.		DATE.
G. Parke,	Major-General.	July 22, 1862
W. Getty,	Brigadier-General.	November, 1862
B. Wilcox,	"	April 19, 1864
Ferrero,	"	September 13, 1864, and October 25, 1864
F. Hartranft,	"	October 9, 1864, and December 15, 1864
Curtin,	Col. 45th Pa. Vols.	May 3, 1865

4th Division—9th Army Corps.

Organized April 18, 1864.
Discontinued September 13, 1864, and designated 3d Division, 9th Corps.

COMMANDER.		DATE.
E. Ferrero,	Brigadier-General.	April 18, 1864

1st Brigade—3d Division.

First Return on File, December, 1862.
Discontinued May, 1865.

COMMANDERS.		DATE.
wkins,	Col. 9th N.Y.Vols.	Dec., 1862
	" 9th " "	Feb., 1863
child,	" 89th " "	Jan., "
ranft,	" 51st Pa. "	April 20, 1864
ist,	" 50th " "	Aug. 28, "
arns,	" 39th U.S.C.T.	Sept., "
	" 30th " "	Oct., "
ven,	" 200th Pa. Vols.	Dec. 15, "
	" 200th " "	March 7, 1865
almont,	" 208th " "	Feb. 11, "
	" 208th " "	April 3, "
McCall,Lt.-	" 200th " "	March 25, "

2d Brigade—3d Division.

First Return on File, December, 1862.
Discontinued May, 1865.

COMMANDERS.		DATE.
E. Harland,	Col. 8th Conn.Vols.	Nov. 30, 1862
B. C. Christ,	" 50th Pa. "	April, 1864
W. Humphrey,	" 2d Mich. "	June 19, "
C. S. Russell,	" 28th U.S.C.T.	Sept. 13, "
H. G. Thomas,	" 19th " "	Oct., "
J. A. Matthews,	" 205th Pa. Vols.	Dec. 15, "
	" 205th " "	Feb. 21, 1865
R. C. Cox,	" 207th " "	" 1, "

1st Brigade—4th Division.

Organized May 4, 1864.

COMMANDER.		DATE.
J. K. Sigfried,	Col. 48th Pa. Vols.	May 4, 1864

2d Brigade—4th Division.

Organized May 4, 1864.

COMMANDERS.		DATE.
H. G. Thomas,	Col. 19th U.S.C.T.	May 4, 1864
C. S. Russell,	" 28th " "	Sept. 7, "

3d Brigade—3d Division.

Organized January, 1863.

COMMANDERS.		DATE.
A. F. Stevens,	Col. 13th N. H. Vols.	Jan., 1863
A. H. Dutton,	" 21st Conn. "	Feb., "

---

ttached to either Division.)

into two Brigades and termed 3d Div., 9th Corps.

DATE.
Nov. 28, 1864

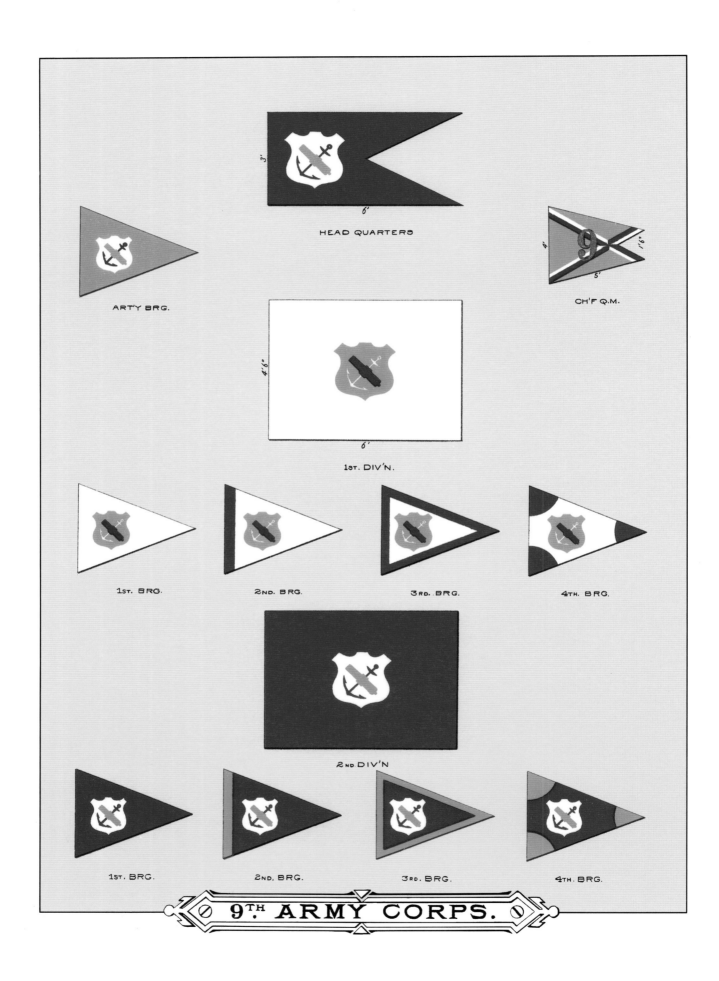

HEAD QUARTERS

ART'Y BRG.

CH'F Q.M.

1st. DIV'N.

1st. BRG.

2nd. BRG.

3rd. BRG.

4th. BRG.

2nd. DIV'N

1st. BRG.

2nd. BRG.

3rd. BRG.

4th. BRG.

9TH ARMY CORPS.

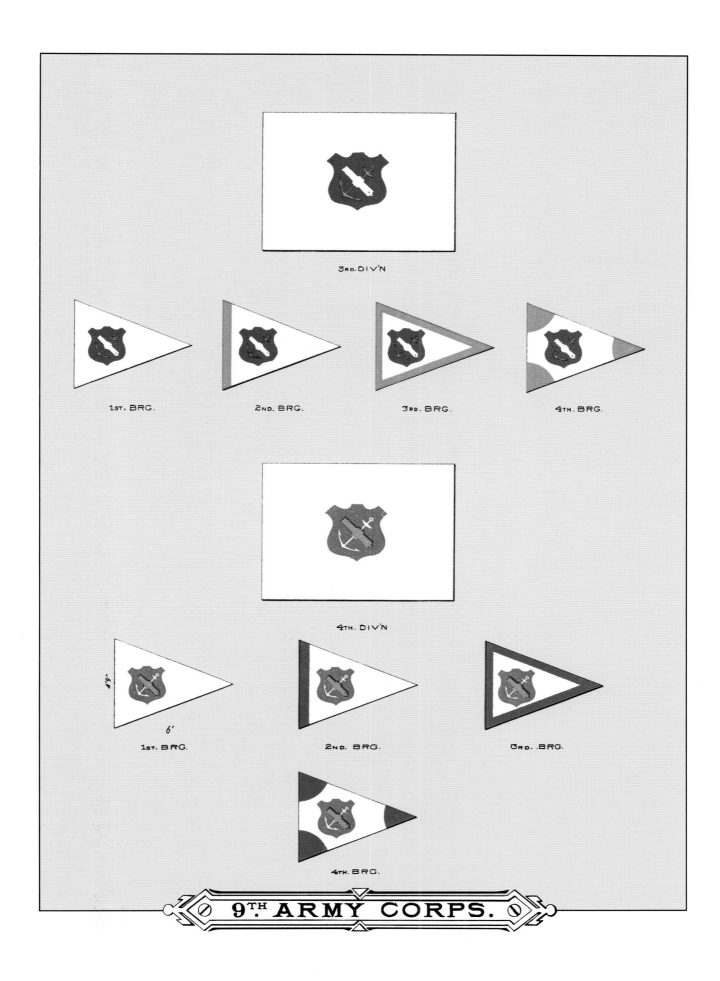

3RD. DIV'N

1ST. BRG.

2ND. BRG.

3RD. BRG.

4TH. BRG.

4TH. DIV'N

1ST. BRG.

2ND. BRG.

3RD. .BRG.

4TH. BRG.

9TH ARMY CORPS.

TENTH A.

Created G. O. No. 123. A. G. O. September 3, 1862. Reorganized April, 1864. Discontinued G. O. No. 297. A. G. O. December 3, 1864.

Finally discontinued G.

COMMANDERS.

O. M. MITCHELL,	Major-General.
J. M. BRANNAN,	Brigadier-General.
DAVID HUNTER,	Major-General.
Q. A. GILLMORE,	"
"	"
A. H. TERRY,	Brigadier-General.
"	Bvt. Major-General.
"	Major-General.
W. T. H. BROOKS,	Brigadier-General.
D. B. BIRNEY,	Major-General.
A. AMES,	Bvt. Major-General.

U. S. Forces—Beaufort, S. C.

Command changed to U. S. Forces, Port Royal Island, November, 1862.

COMMANDERS.		DATE.
J. M. Brannan,	Brigadier-General.	Sept., 1862
J. L. Chatfield,	Col. 6th Conn. Vols.	Oct. 1, "
T. H. Good,	" 47th Pa. " " "

U. S. Forces—Port Royal Island.

Command transferred to Department of the South, April, 1864.

COMMANDERS.		DATE.
T. H. Good,	Col. 47th Pa. Vols.	Nov., 1862
T. Seymour,	Brigadier-General.	Dec. 26, "
R. Saxton,	"	Feb. 19, 1863
"	"	July, "
W. W. H. Davis,	Col. 104th Pa. Vols.	May 27, "

U. S. Forces—Hilton Head, S. C.

Termed Hilton Head District, January, 1864.

COMMANDERS.	
N. W. Brown,	Col. 3d R. I. Heavy Artillery.
Jas. L. Frazer,	" 47th N. Y. Vols.
A. H. Terry,	Brigadier-General.
J. L. Chatfield,	Col. 6th Conn. Vols.
E. Metcalf,	" 3d R. I. Heavy Artillery.
D. C. Strawbridge,	" 76th Pa. Vols.
W. B. Barton,	" 48th N. Y. "
T. Seymour,	Brigadier-General.

Barton's Brigade.
U. S. Forces—Hilton Head, S. C.

Organized December, 1863.

COMMANDER.		DATE.
W. B. Barton,	Col. 48th N. Y. Vols.	Dec., 1863

U. S.

COMMA J. B. Howell, Col. 85

U. S. Forces—Folly Island, S. C.

Transferred to U. S. Forces, Morris Island, S. C., July, 1863.

COMMANDERS.		DATE.
Israel Vogdes,	Brigadier-General.	April 8, 1863
W. W. H. Davis,	Col. 104th Pa. Vols.	July 19, "

U. S. Forces—"North End" of Folly

Termed Vogdes' Division, U. S. Forces, Folly Island, S. C.

COMMANDERS.	
Israel Vogdes,	Brigadier-General.
R. S. Foster,	"

1st Brigade—U. S. Forces.
Folly Island, S. C.

Organized June, 1863. Discontinued July, 1863.

COMMANDER.		DATE.
H. S. Putnam,	Col. 7th N. H. Vols.	June, 1863

2d Brigade—U. S. Forces.
Folly Island, S. C.

Organized June, 1863. Discontinued July, 1863.

COMMANDER.		DATE.
J. B. Howell,	Col. 85th Pa. Vols.	June, 1863

1st or Foster's Brigade—U. S. Forces.
"North End" of Folly Island, S. C.

COMMANDERS.		DATE.
R. S. Foster,	Brigadier-General.	Aug. 31, 1863
J. C. Drake,	Col. 112th N. Y. Vols.	Dec. 16, "

2d or Alford's Brigade—U. S. F
"North End" of Folly Island,

Termed 2d Brigade, Vogdes' Division, U. S. Folly Island, S. C., January, 1864, not kn as 2d Brigade subsequent to that time.

COMMANDERS	
S. M. Alford,	Col. 3d N. Y. Vols. Aug.
"	" 3d " " Nov.
H. S. Fairchild,	" 89th " " Oct.

U. S. Forces—Morris Island, S. C.

Designation changed to U. S. Forces, Morris Island, Northern District, January, 1864.

COMMANDERS.		DATE.
A. H. Terry,	Brigadier-General.	July 19, 1863
"	"	November 10, "
T. Seymour,	"	October, "

1st Brigade—U. S. Forces.
Morris Island, S. C.

COMMANDERS.		DATE.
Israel Vogdes,	Brigadier-General.	July 19, 1863
H. R. Guss,	Col. 97th Pa. Vols.	Aug. 2, "
H. M. Plaisted,	" 11th Me. "	Oct. 11, "
T. G. Stevenson,	Brigadier-General.	Nov. 23, "

2d Brigade—U. S. Forces.
Morris Island, S. C.

Transferred to Gen. G. H. Gordon's command, October, 1863.
Reorganized November, 1863. (Formerly 5th Brigade.)

COMMANDERS.		DATE.
J. B. Howell,	Col. 85th Pa. Vols.	July 19, 1863
Thos. O. Osborne,	" 39th Ills. "	Sept. 19, "
W. W. H. Davis,	" 104th Pa. "	Nov. 23, "
"	" 104th " "	Dec., "
G. B. Dandy,	" 100th N. Y. "	Dec., "

3d Brigade—U. S. Forces.
Morris Island, S. C.

Discontinued November, 1863.
Reorganized November 23, 1863. (Formerly 4th Brigade.)
Transferred to Hilton Head District, January, 1864.

COMMANDERS.		DATE.
T. G. Stevenson,	Brigadier-General.	July 19, 1863
"	"	Oct., "
J. R. Hawley,	Col. 7th Conn. Vols.	Sept., "
J. Montgomery,	" 2d S. C. Col. Vols.	Nov. 23, "

4th Brigade—U. S. Forces.
Morris Island, S.

Designation changed to 3d Brigade, November, 1863.

COMMANDER.		D
J. Montgomery,	Col. 2d S. C. Col. Vols.	Aug.

MY CORPS.

ized G. O. No. 49. A. G. O. March 27, 1865." To include all troops in North Carolina, not belonging to Corps in Gen. W. T. Sherman's command."

G. O. August 1, 1865.

DATE.
September 3, 1862.
October 27, "
January 20, 1863.
June 3, "
May, 1864.
April, "
October 10, "
March 27, 1865.
June 19, 1864.
July 21, "
May 12, 1865.

Hilton Head District.

Formerly U. S. Forces, Hilton Head, S. C. Organized January, 1864.
Transferred to Department of the South, April, 1864.

COMMANDERS.		DATE.
Truman Seymour,	Brigadier-General.	January, 1864
J. B. Howell,	Col. 85th Pa. Vols.	February 5, "

DATE.
ber, 1862
"
"
12, 1863
6, "
6, "
er 9, "
er 6, "

lead, S. C.

1863.

Barton's Brigade—Hilton Head District.

Organized January, 1864.
Transferred to District of Florida, February, 1864

DATE.	COMMANDER.		DATE.
Dec., 1863	W. B. Barton,	Col. 48th N. Y. Vols.	Jan., 1864

Howell's Brigade—Hilton Head District.

Organized January, 1864.
Transferred to Department of the South, April, 1864.

COMMANDERS.		DATE.
J. B. Howell,	Col. 85th Pa. Vols.	Jan., 1864
R. Duryea,	" 6th Conn. Vols.	Feb. 6, "

Montgomery's Brigade—Hilton Head District.

Organized January, 1864.
Joined District from Morris Island, January 31, 1864.
Transferred to District of Florida, February, 1864.

COMMANDER.		DATE.
J. Montgomery,	Col. 2d S. C. Vols.	Jan. 31, 1864

U. S. Forces—"South End" of Folly Island, S. C.

Discontinued January 15, 1864, and termed U. S. Forces, Folly Island, S. C.

COMMANDERS.		DATE.
G. H. Gordon,	Brigadier-General.	August 31, 1863
"	"	November, "
A. Schemmelfinnig,	"	October "

DATE.
August 16, 1863
ry, January, 1864

African Brigade—U S. Forces. orth End" of Folly Island, S. C.

COMMANDERS.	DATE.
d,	Brigadier-General.	Aug. 31, 1863
eecher,	Col. 1st N.C.Col.Vols. Oct., "
	" 1st " " " Dec. 14, "
tlefield,	" 4th S. C. " " Nov. 6, "

1st Brigade—U. S. Forces. "South End" of Folly Island, S. C.

Termed 1st Brigade, U. S. Forces, Folly Island, S. C., January 15, 1864.

COMMANDERS.		DATE.
A. Schemmelfinnig,	Brigadier-General.	Aug. 31, 1863
L. Von Gilsa,	Col. 41st N. Y. Vols.	Oct., "
"	" 41st " "	Jan. 13, 1864
Wm. Gurney,	" 127th " "	Dec., 1863

2d Brigade—U. S. Forces. "South End" of Folly Island, S. C.

Termed 2d Brigade, U. S. Forces, Folly Island, S. C., January 15, 1864.

COMMANDERS.		DATE.
A. Ames,	Brigadier-General.	Aug. 31, 1863
W. H. Noble,	Col. 17th Conn. Vols.	Nov. 27, "

3d Brigade—U. S. Forces. "South End" of Folly Island, S. C.

Formerly 2d Brigade, U. S. Forces, Morris Island, S. C.
Transferred to U. S. Forces, Hilton Head, S. C., December, 1863.

COMMANDER.		DATE.
J. B. Howell,	Col. 85th Pa. Vols.	Oct. 31, 1863

U. S. Forces—Seabrook Island, S. C.

Organized April, 1863.
Transferred to U. S. Forces, Morris Island, S. C., July, 1863.

COMMANDER.		DATE.
T. G. Stevenson,	Brigadier-General.	April, 1863

U. S. Forces—St. Helena Island, S. C.

Organized June 10, 1863.
Transferred to U. S Forces, Morris Island, S. C., July, 1863.
Reorganized December, 1863.
Transferred to District of Florida, February, 1864.

COMMANDERS.		DATE.
G. C. Strong,	Brigadier-General.	June 13, 1863
J. R. Hawley,	Col. 7th Conn. Vols.	Dec., "

Brigade—U. S. Forces. Morris Island, S. C.

ansferred from Folly Island, August, 1863.
Changed to 2d Brigade, November, 1863.

COMMANDER.	DATE.
. Davis,	Col. 104th Pa. Vols.	Aug. 31, 1863

N

Organized January 15, 1864. T

COMMANDERS.

A. H. Terry,   Brigadier-G

A. Schemmelfinnig,   "

U. S. Forces—Folly Island, S. C.—Northern District.

Organized January 15, 1864. (Formerly U. S. Forces—North and South end Folly Island.)
Transferred to Department of the South, April, 1864.

COMMANDERS.   **DATE.**

G. H. Gordon,	Brigadier-General.	January,	1864
Adelbert Ames,	"	" 28,	"
A. Schemmelfinnig,	"	February,	"

Vogdes' Division—

Organized January 15, 1864. (Formerly U. S

COMMANDER.

R. S. Foster,   Brigadier-

1st Brigade—U. S. Forces—Folly Island, S. C.

Transferred to Department of the South, April, 1864.

COMMANDER.   **DATE.**

| L. Von Gilsa, | Col. 41st N. Y. Vols. | Jan., | 1864 |

2d Brigade—U. S. Forces—Folly Island, S. C.

Transferred to District of Florida, February, 1864.
Reorganized Feb., 1864. (Formerly 2d Brig., Vogdes' Div.)
Transferred to Department of the South, April, 1864.

COMMANDERS.   **DATE.**

W. H. Noble,	Col. 17th Conn. Vols.	Jan.,	1864
"	" 17th " "	" 29,	"
A. Ames,	Brigadier-General.	" 23,	"
S. M. Alford,	Col. 3d N. Y. Vols.	Feb.,	"
W. Heine,	" 103d " "	March,	"

1st Brigade—Vogdes' Division.

Transferred to District of Florida,
February, 1864.

COMMANDER.   **DATE.**

| J. C. Drake, | Col. 112th N. Y. Vols. | Jan., | 1864 |

2d Bri

Designation c
Fol

COMM

S. M. Alford,

D

Organized February 16, 1864. Designated 4th

COMMANDERS.

T. Seymour,   Brigadier-G

J. P. Hatch,   "

1st Division—District of Florida.

Discontinued April, 1864.

COMMANDER.   **DATE.**

| A. Ames, | Brigadier-General. | February 25, 1864 |

1st Brigade—1st Division.

Discontinued April, 1864.

COMMANDER.   **DATE.**

| Wm. H. Noble, | Col. 17th Conn. Vols. | Feb. 25, 1864 |

2d Brigade—1st Division.

Discontinued April, 1864.

COMMANDER.   **DATE.**

| J. R. Hawley, | Col. 7th Conn. Vols. | Feb., 1864 |

3d Brigade—1st Division.

Discontinued April, 1864.

COMMANDERS.   DA

| M. S. Littlefield, | Col. 21st U. S. C. T. | Feb. |
| E. N. Hallowell, | " 54th Mass. Vols. | " |

Barton's Brigade—District of Florida.

Discontinued April, 1864.

COMMANDER.   DAT

| W. B. Barton, | Col. 48th N. Y. Vols. | Feb. 29, |

PS—Continued.

ment of the South, April, 1864.

DATE.
January 17, 1864
February, "

—Folly Island, S. C.

Folly Island.) Discontinued February, 1864.

DATE.
January 15, 1864

U. S. Forces—Morris Island, S. C.—Northern District.

Organized January 15, 1864.
Transferred to Department of the South, April, 1864.

COMMANDER.		DATE.
W. W. H. Davis,	Col. 104th Pa. Vols.	January 17, 1864

Division.

le, U. S. Forces, 1864.

DATE.
s. Jan., 1864

3d Brigade—Vogdes' Division.

Transferred to District of Florida, February, 1864.

COMMANDER.		DATE.
Jas. C. Beecher,	Col. 1st N. C. Col. Vols.	Jan., 1864

1st Brigade—U. S. Forces—Morris Island, S. C.

Transferred to Department of the South, April, 1864.

COMMANDERS.		DATE.
H. M. Plaisted,	Col. 11th Me. Vols.	Jan. 22, 1864
W. P. Spofford,	Lt.- " 11th " "	March, "

2d Brigade—U. S. Forces—Morris Island, S. C.

Transferred to Department of the South, April, 1864.

COMMANDERS.		DATE.
Henry M. Hoyt,	Col. 52d Pa. Vols.	Jan. 17, 1864
T. D. Hart,	Lt.- " 104th " "	Feb. 12, "

---

ida.

Department of the South, April, 1864.

DATE.
February, 1864
March 24, "

2d Division—District of Florida.

Discontinued April, 1864.

COMMANDERS.		DATE.
J. C. Drake,	Col. 112th N. Y. Vols.	February 23, 1864
R. S. Foster,	Brigadier-General.	" 28, "

1st Brigade—2d Division.

Transferred to and formed part of the 4th Separate Brigade, Department South, April, 1864.
Discontinued April, 1864.

COMMANDERS.		DATE.
rake,	Col. 112th N. Y. Vols.	Feb. 25, 1864
obbs,	" 13th Ind. "	March, "

2d Brigade—2d Division.

Transferred to and formed part of the 4th Separate Brigade, Department South, April, 1864.
Discontinued April, 1864.

COMMANDER.		DATE.
B. C. Tilghman,	Col. 3d U. S. C. T	Feb. 25, 1864

3d Brigade—2d Division.

Transferred to Department of the South, March, 1864.

COMMANDER.		DATE.
Jas. Montgomery,	Col. 2d S. C. C. T.	Feb. 25, 1864

Light Brigade—District of Florida.

Discontinued April, 1864.

COMMANDER.		DATE.
. Henry,	Col. 40th Mass. Vols.	Feb. 29, 1864

1st Division—10th Army Corps.

COMMANDERS.		DATE.
R. S. Foster,	Brigadier-General.	April, 1864
A. H. Terry,	"	May 4, "
A. Ames,	"	October 10, "

2d I

COMMANDERS.	
S. M. Alford,	Col. 3d N
J. W. Turner,	Brigadier-
R. S. Foster,	

1st Brigade—1st Division.

COMMANDERS.		DATE.
F. B. Pond,	Col. 62d Ohio Vols.	April 27, 1864
"	" 62d " "	July 28, "
"	" 62d " "	Sept. 14, "
J. B. Howell,	" 85th Pa. "	May 2, "
"	" 85th " "	August, "
A. C. Voris,	" 67th Ohio "	October, "

2d Brigade—1st Division.

COMMANDERS.		DATE.
H. M. Plaisted,	Col. 11th Me. Vols.	April, 1864
J. R. Hawley,	" 7th Conn. "	May, "
"	Brigadier-General.	Oct. 13, "
J. C. Abbott,	Col. 7th N. H. Vols.	Sept. 12, "

1st Brigade—2d Division.

COMMANDERS.		
G. V. Henry,	Col. 40th Mass. Vols.	Ap
S. M. Alford,	" 3d N. Y. "	Ma
N. M. Curtis,	" 142d " "	Jun
"	" 142d " "	No
A. M. Barney,	Lt.- " 142d " "	Oct

3d Brigade—1st Division.

COMMANDERS.		DATE.
J. R. Hawley,	Col. 7th Conn. Vols.	April, 1864
H. M. Plaisted,	" 11th Me. "	May, "
"	" 11th " "	Aug. 24, "
R. S. Foster,	Brigadier-General.	June 23, "
G. B. Dandy,	Col. 100th N. Y. Vols.	Nov. 2, "

3d

COMMANDERS.	
Louis Bell,	Col. 4th
"	" 4th
F. A. Osborn,	" 24th

Tenth Army Corps, as Reorganized

To embrace all Troops in North Carolina, not be

COMMANDERS.	
A. H. TERRY,	Major-Gener
A. AMES,	Bvt. Major-C

1st Division—10th Army Corps.

Discontinued July, 1865.

COMMANDER.		DATE.
H. W. Birge,	Bvt. Major-General.	March 27, 1865

2d I

COMMANDERS.	
A. Ames,	Bvt. Major-C
R. Daggett,	Col. 117th N
J. S. Little,	" 76th P
W. B. Coan,	" 48th N

1st Brigade—1st Division.

Discontinued July, 1865.

COMMANDER.		DATE.
H. Graham,	Col. 22d Iowa Vols.	March 27, 1865

2d Brigade—1st Division.

Discontinued July, 1865.

COMMANDER.		DATE.
J. C. Abbott,	Col. 7th N. H. Vols.	March 27, 1865

1st Brigade—2d Division.

Discontinued June, 1865.
Reorganized July, 1865. (Formerly 3d Brigade.)

COMMANDERS.		
N. M. Curtis,	Brigadier-General.	Ma
R. Daggett,	Col. 117th N. Y. Vols.	Apr
A. M. Barney,	" 142d " "	Ma
F. W. Parker,	" 4th N. H. "	July

3d Brigade—1st Division.

Discontinued July, 1865.

COMMANDER.		DATE.
N. W. Day,	Col. 131st N. Y. Vols.	March 27, 1865

3d

De

COMMANDERS.	
G. F. Granger,	Col. 9th
A. Alden,	" 169th

my Corps.

	DATE.
	April, 1864
	May, "
	August 23, "

3d Division—10th Army Corps.

Discontinued September, 1864. Reorganized October 5, 1864.

COMMANDERS.		DATE.
A. Ames,	Brigadier-General.	April 26, 1864
O. S. Ferry,	"	June, "
Wm. Birney,	"	August 27, "
"	"	October 5, "

2d Brigade—2d Division.

COMMANDERS.		DATE.
rton,	Col. 48th N. Y. Vols.	April, 1864
"	" 48th " "	Aug. 28, "
an,	Lt.- " 48th " "	July 2, "
packer,	" 97th Pa. "	Sept. 16, "

1st Brigade—3d Division.

COMMANDERS.		DATE.
Richard White,	Col. 55th Pa. Vols.	April 26, 1864
H. R. Guss,	" 97th " "	May, "
G. Marston,	Brigadier-General.	June, "
Jas. Shaw, Jr.,	Col. 7th U. S. C. T.	Aug., "
"	" 7th " "	Oct. 26, "
W. Birney,	Brigadier-General.	Sept., "
A. C. Voris,	Col. 67th Ohio Vols.	Oct. 6, "

2d Brigade—3d Division.

Discontinued September, 1864. Reorganized October 6, 1864.

COMMANDERS.		DATE.
J. D. Rust,	Col. 8th Maine Vols.	April 28, 1864
J. C. Drake,	" 112th N. Y. "	May, "
J. B. Armstrong,	" 134th Ohio "	June 22, "
J. H. Holman,	" 1st U. S. C. T.	Aug., "
Ulysses Doubleday,	" 45th " "	Oct. 8, "
"	" 45th " "	Nov. 6, "
E. Wright,	" 10th " "	Oct. 29, "

sion.

	DATE.
	June 20, 1864
	Sept. 23, "
	Aug. 12, "

g to Corps in GEN. W. T. SHERMAN'S Command.

DATE.
March 27, 1865.
May 12, "

my Corps.

DATE.
March 27, 1865
May 13, "
June 8, "
July 18, "

3d Division—10th Army Corps.

COMMANDERS.		DATE.
C. J. Paine,	Brigadier-General.	March 27, 1865
D. Bates,	Col. 30th U. S. C. T.	July, "

2d Brigade—2d Division.

COMMANDERS.		DATE.
Little,	Col. 76th Pa. Vols.	April 5, 1865
an,	" 48th N. Y. "	June 9, "
cDonald,	" 47th " "	July 19, "

1st Brigade—3d Division.

COMMANDERS.		DATE.
D. Bates,	Col. 30th U. S. C. T.	March 27, 1865
Wm. H. Revere, Jr.,	" 107th " "	July, "

2d Brigade—3d Division.

COMMANDERS.		DATE.
S. A. Duncan,	Col. 4th U. S. C. T.	March 27, 186
O. P. Stearns,	" 39th " "	July 14, "

sion.

1st Brigade.

DATE.
March 27, 1865
June 12, "

3d Brigade—3d Division.

COMMANDERS.		DATE.
J. H. Holman,	Col. 1st U. S. C. T.	March, 1865
A. M. Blackman,	" 27th " "	April 22, "
N. Goff, Jr.,	" 37th " "	May, "
"	" 37th " "	July, "
A. G. Chamberlin,	Lt.- " 37th " "	June, "

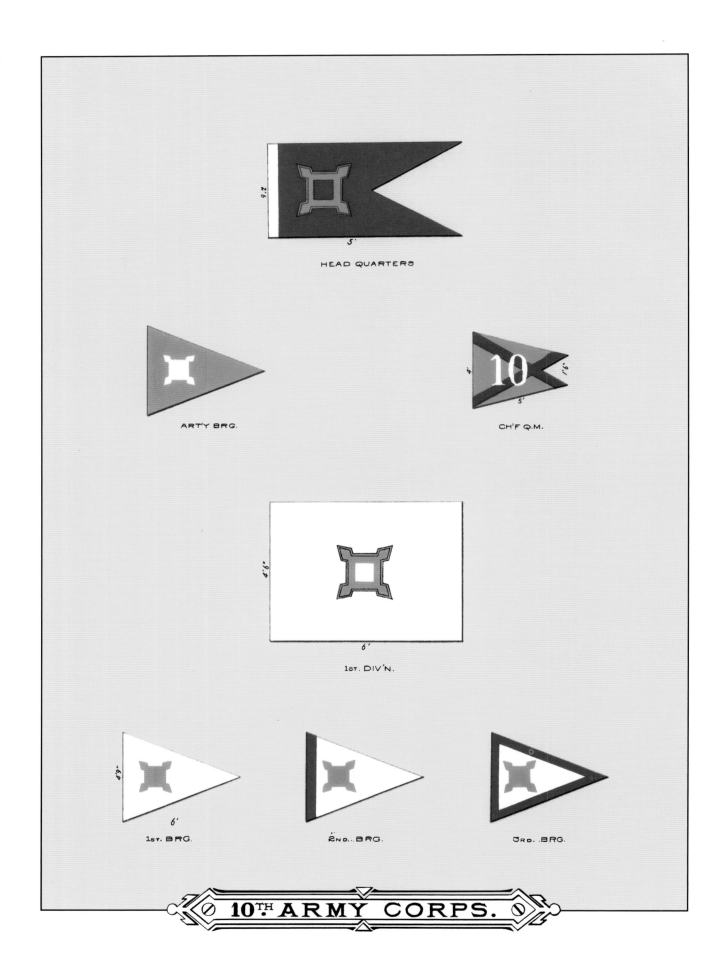

HEAD QUARTERS

ART'Y BRG.

CH'F Q.M.

1st. DIV'N.

1st. BRG.

2ND. BRG.

3RD. BRG.

10TH ARMY CORPS.

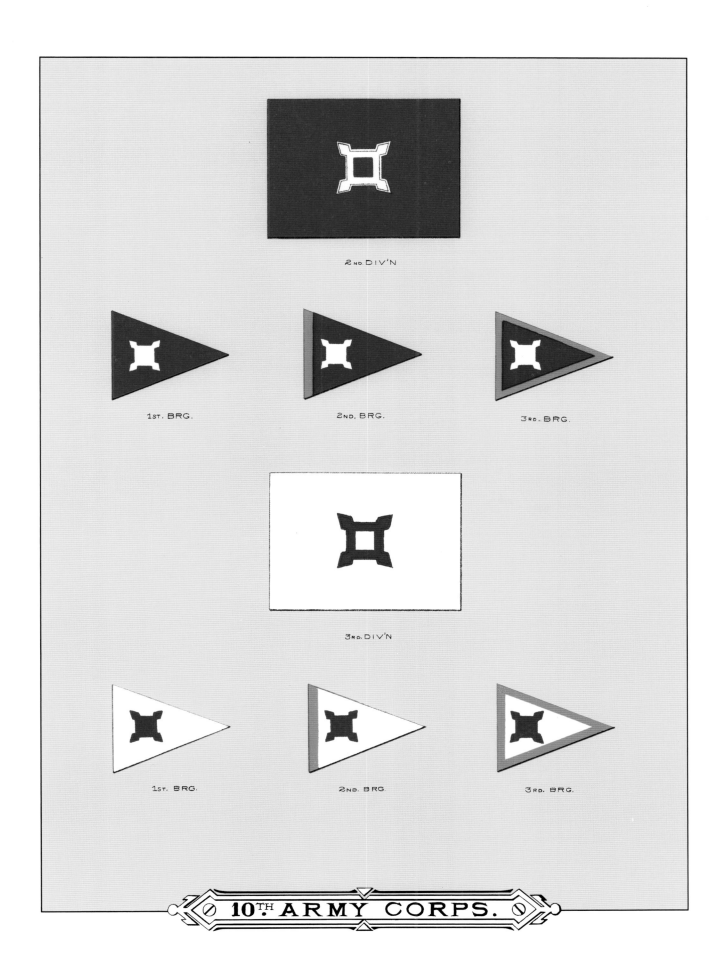

2ND. DIV'N

1ST. BRG.   2ND. BRG.   3RD. BRG.

3RD. DIV'N

1ST. BRG.   2ND. BRG.   3RD. BRG.

10TH ARMY CORPS.

ELEVENTH

Created G. O. No. 129. A. G. O. September 12, 1862.   Consolidated with the 12th Army

COMMANDERS.

F. SIGEL,	Major-Gene
J. H. STAHEL,	Brigadier-G
A. VON STEINWEHR,	"
C. SCHURZ,	Major-Gene
O. O. HOWARD,	"

1st Division—11th Army Corps.

Discontinued August, 1863.   Reorganized January 2, 1864.

COMMANDERS.		DATE.
J. H. Stahel,	Brigadier-General.	September, 1862
"	"	February 5, 1863
N. C. McLean,	"	January 10, "
"	"	March 10, "
C. Devens, Jr.,	"	April, "
F. C. Barlow,	"	May 24, "
A. Ames,	"	July 1, "
A. Schemmelfinnig,	"	" 14, "
G. H. Gordon,	"	" 17, "
W. T. Ward.	"	January 12, 1864

2d Division—11th Army Corps.

No " Returns " prior to October, 1862.

COMMANDERS.	
A. Von Steinwehr,	Brigadier-General.
"	"
"	"
A. Buschbeck,	Col. 27th Pa. Vols.
"	" 27th "
"	" 27th "

1st Brigade—1st Division.

COMMANDERS.		DATE.
L. Von Gilsa,	Col. 41st N. Y. Vols.	Sept., 1862
"	" 41st " "	Feb., 1863
"	" 41st " "	May, "
G. Van Arnsburg,	" 45th " "	Jan. 12, "
G. Bourry,	" 68th " "	May 25, "
A. Schemmelfinnig,	Brigadier-General.	July 17, "
B. Harrison,	Col. 70th Ind. Vols.	Jan. 9, 1864

2d Brigade—1st Division.

COMMANDERS.		DATE.
N. C. McLean,	Col. 75th Ohio Vols.	Sept., 1862
"	Brigadier-General.	Feb. 5, 1863
"		April, "
J. C. Lee,	Col. 55th Ohio Vols.	Jan. 10, "
"	" 55th " "	March 10, "
A. Ames,	Brigadier-General.	May 24, "
"	"	July 14, "
P. P. Brown,	Col. 57th N. Y. Vols.	July, "
A. L. Harris,	" 75th Ohio "	" "
W. H. Noble,	" 17th Conn. "	" "
John Coburn,	" 33d Ind. "	Jan. 1864
J. P. Baird,	" 85th " "	March 25, "

1st Brigade—2d Division.

No Brigade " Returns " on file prior to October, 1862.

COMMANDERS.		DATE.
A. Buschbeck,	Col. 27th Pa. Vols.	Oct. 31, 1862
"	" 27th " "	March, 1863
"	" 27th " "	July, "
"	" 27th " "	March 3, 1864
G. A. Muhleck,	" 73d " "	Nov., 1862
C. Soest,	" 29th N. Y. "	Feb., 1863
C. R. Coster,	" 134th " "	June, "
G. W. Mindel,	" 33d N. J. "	Nov. 28 "
P. H. Jones,	" 154th N. Y. "	Jan. 30, 1864
D. B. Allen,	Lt.- " 154th " "	Feb. 25, "

2d

COMMA		
O. Smith,	Col. 73d	
"	" 73	
F. C. Barlow,	Brigad	
J. Wood,	Col. 136th	

ARMY CORPS.

lled 20th Corps. G. O. No. 144. A. G. O. April 4, 1864.   Discontinued April 18, 1864.

DATE.
September, 1862, and February 5, 1863.
December, 1862.
February, 1863.
March 29, 1863, and January 21, 1864.
April 2, 1863, and February 25, 1864.

3d Division—11th Army Corps.

COMMANDERS.		DATE.
Carl Schurz,	Brigadier-General.	September, 1862
"	Major-General.	April 2, 1863
A. Schemmelfinnig,	Brigadier-General.	March 29, "
S. J. McGroarty,	Col. 61st Ohio Vols.	January 21, 1864
H. Tyndale,	Brigadier-General.	February 15, "

DATE.
er 31, 1862
h, 1863
" "
h 3, 1864
1863
28, "
mber 28, "

vision.

5, 1862.

DATE.
Oct. 25, 1862
May 24, 1863
April 17, "
Jan. 3, 1864

1st Brigade—3d Division.

COMMANDERS.		DATE.
A. Schemmelfinnig,	Brigadier-General.	Sept., 1862
"	"	April 2, 1863
G. Bourry,	Col. 68th N. Y. Vols.	March 29, "
H. Tyndale,	Brigadier-General.	July 13, "
"	"	Oct., "
G. Van Arnsburg,	Col. 45th N. Y. Vols.	Aug. 30, "
F. Hecker,	" 82d Ills. "	Sept. 19, "
S. J. McGroarty,	" 61st Ohio "	Jan. 10, 1864
H. Broughton,	" 143d N. Y. "	Jan. 22, "
C. H. Fox,	" 101st Ills. "	Feb. 15, "
J. S. Robinson,	" 82d Ohio "	March 13, "

2d Brigade—3d Division.

COMMANDERS.		DATE.
W. Krzyzonowski,	Col. 58th N. Y. Vols.	Sept., 1862
"	" 58th " "	March 7, 1864
J. I. Lockman,	" 119th " "	Jan. 8, "

3d Brigade—3d Division.

Organized October 19, 1863. Discontinued March 24, 1864.

COMMANDERS.		DATE.
F. Hecker,	Col. 82d Ills. Vols.	Oct. 19, 1863
S. J. McGroarty,	" 61st Ohio "	Feb. 21, 1864

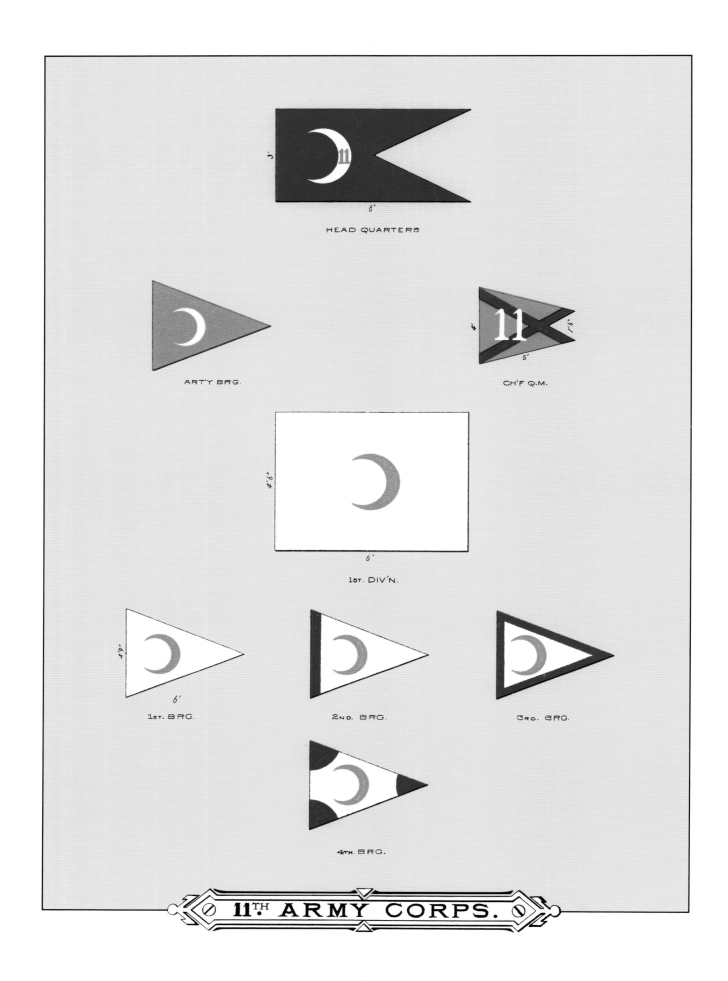

HEAD QUARTERS

ART'Y BRG.

CH'F Q.M.

1ST. DIV'N.

1ST. BRG.

2ND. BRG.

3RD. BRG.

4TH. BRG.

11TH ARMY CORPS.

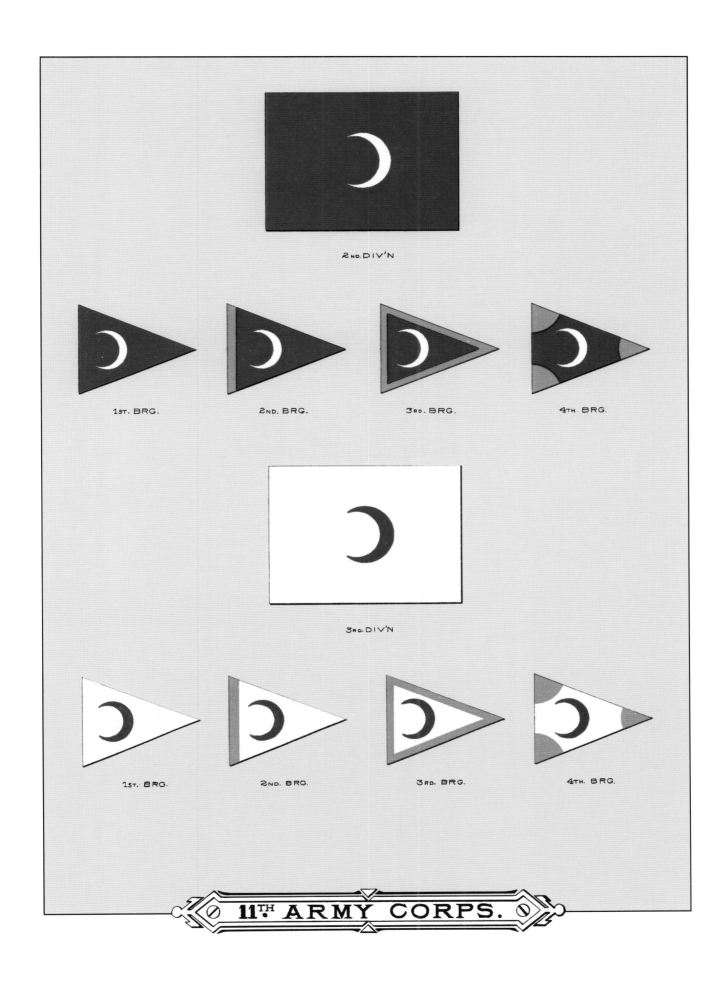

2ND. DIV'N

1ST. BRG.   2ND. BRG.   3RD. BRG.   4TH. BRG.

3RD. DIV'N

1ST. BRG.   2ND. BRG.   3RD. BRG.   4TH. BRG.

11TH ARMY CORPS.

SECOND A[...]

ARMY O[...]

Created by order of the President of the U. S., June 26, 1862.

	COMMANDER.
	N. P. BANKS, Major-Ge[...]

1ST DIVISION—2D ARMY CORPS—ARMY OF VIRGINIA.

COMMANDER.		DATE.
A. S. Williams,	Brigadier-General.	June, 1862.

1st Brigade—1st Division.	2d Brigade—1st Division.	3d Brigade—1st Division.
	Discontinued August, 1862, and troops transferred to 2d Div., 2d Army Corps, and termed 1st Brigade, 2d Division.	
COMMANDER. DATE.	COMMANDER. DATE.	COMMANDER. DATE.
S. W. Crawford, Brigadier-General. June, 1862	John W. Geary, Brigadier-General. July, 1862	Geo. H. Gordon, Brigadier-General. July, 1862

MY CORPS,

VIRGINIA.

ation changed to 12th Army Corps, G. O. No. 129.   A. G. O. September 12, 1862.

DATE.	
June 26, 1862.	

2D DIVISION—2D ARMY CORPS—ARMY OF VIRGINIA.

COMMANDERS.		DATE.
C. C. Augur,	Brigadier-General.	July, 1862.
G. S. Greene,	"	August, 1862.

1st Brigade—2d Division.

Designation changed to 2d Brigade, 2d Division, August, 1862.
Reorganized August, 1862 (formerly 2d Brigade, 1st Division.)

COMMANDERS.		DATE.	
ames Cooper,	Brigadier-General.	July,	1862
Henry Prince,	"	July	16, "
ohn W. Geary,	"	Aug.,	"
Chas. Candy,	Col. 66th Ohio Vols.	"	9, "

2d Brigade—2d Division.

Designation changed to 3d Brigade, 2d Division, August, 1862.
Reorganized August, 1862 (formerly 1st Brigade, 2d Division.)

COMMANDERS.		DATE.	
John P. Slough,	Brigadier-General.	June,	1862
Jas. A. Tait,	Col. 1st D. C. Vols.	July	1, "
Danl. Ullman,	" 78th N. Y.	"	10, "
Geo. S. Greene,	Brigadier-General.	"	16, "
Henry Prince,	"	Aug.,	"
D. P. DeWitt,	Col. 3d Md. Vols.	"	9, "
T. B. Van Buren,	Col. 102d N. Y. Vols.	"	12, "

3d Brigade—2d Division.

Formerly 2d Brigade, 2d Division.

COMMANDER.		DATE.	
G. S. Greene,	Brigadier-General.	Aug.,	1862

TWELFTH

Created G. O. No. 129. A. G. O. September 12, 1862. Discontinued April 18, 186

	COMMANDERS.	
A. S. WILLIAMS,		Brigadier-Ge
H. W. SLOCUM,		Major-Gener

1ST DIVISION—12TH ARMY CORPS.

COMMANDERS.		DATE.
G. H. Gordon,	Brigadier-General.	September 18, 1862.
A. S. Williams,	"	October 20, 1862.
"	"	September 13, 1863.
"	"	January 30, 1864.
J. F. Knipe,	"	August 31, 1863.
"	"	December 22, 1863.

1st Brigade—1st Division.

COMMANDERS.		DATE.
S. W. Crawford,	Brigadier-General.	Sept., 1862
J. F. Knipe,	Col. 46th Pa. Vols.	Sept. 18, "
"	Brigadier-General.	July 26, 1863
"	"	Sept. 13, "
"	"	Jan. 30, 1864
"	"	March, "
S. Ross,	Col. 20th Conn. Vols.	Aug. 30, 1863
"	" 20th " "	Dec. 22, "
"	" 20th " "	Feb. 2, 1864
A. L. McDougall,	" 123d N. Y. "	May 18, 1863

2d Brigade—1st Division.

Organized October 3, 1862. Discontinued May, 1863.

COMMANDERS.		DATE.
Thos. L. Kane,	Brigadier-General.	Oct. 3, 1862
N. J. Jackson,	"	March 21, 1863
S. Ross,	Col. 20th Conn. Vols.	" 29, "

3d Brigade—1st Division.

Discontinued October, 1862. Reorganized December 9, 1862.

COMMANDERS		DATE.
T. H. Ruger,	Col. 3d Wis. Vols.	Sept. 18, 1862
"	" 3d " "	Feb., 1863
"	" 3d " "	Sept. 16, "
G. H. Gordon,	Brigadier-General.	Oct., 1862
J. K. Murphy,	Col. 29th Pa. Vols.	Dec. 9, "
E. A. Carman,	" 13th N. Y. "	Aug. 16, 1863

..MY CORPS.

..dated with 11th Corps and designated 20th Corps, G. O. No. 144.   A. G. O. April 4, 1864.

DATE.	
September 18, 1862, and August 31, 1863.	
October 20, 1862, and September 13, 1863.	

2D DIVISION—12TH ARMY CORPS.

COMMANDERS.		DATE.
J. W. Geary,	Brigadier-General.	September, 1862.
"	"	February 17, 1864.
D. Ireland,	Col. 137th N. Y. Vols.	January 27, "
C. Candy,	" 66th Ohio "	February 9, "

1st Brigade—2d Division.			2d Brigade—2d Division.			3d Brigade—2d Division.		
COMMANDERS.		DATE.	COMMANDERS.		DATE.	COMMANDERS.		DATE.
C. Candy,	Col. 66th Ohio Vols.	Sept., 1862	T. B. Van Buren,	Col. 102d N. Y. Vols.	Sept., 1862	G. S. Greene,	Brigadier-General.	Sept., 1862
"	" 66th " "	Dec. 30, "	H. J. Steinrook,	" 109th Pa. "	" 15, "	D. Ireland,	Col. 137th N. Y. Vols.	Oct. 29, 1863
"	" 66th " "	March, 1863	J. C. Lane,	Lt.- " 102d N. Y. "	" 20, "	"	" 137th " "	Feb. 9, 1864
"	" 66th " "	Feb. 18, 1864	N. J. Jackson,	Brigadier-General.	Oct. 28, "	K. S. Van Voorhees, Lt.- " 137th " "		Jan. 27, "
T. H. Ruger,	" 3d Wis. "	Oct., 1862	"	"	Jan., 1863			
W. R. Creighton,	" 7th Ohio "	Feb., 1863	J. M. Sudsberg,	Col. 3d Md. Vols.	Dec. 22, 1862			
A. Pardee, Jr., Lt.- " 147th Pa. "		Aug. 16, "	T. L. Kane,	Brigadier-General.	March 21, 1863			
"	" 147th " "	Jan. 18, 1864	C. A. Cobham, Jr.,	Col. 111th Pa. Vols.	May 7, "			
H. Patrick,	" 5th Ohio "	Nov. 30, 1863	"	" 111th " "	March 9, 1864			
			L. W. Ralston,	Lt.- " 109th " "	Dec. 27, 1863			
			B. Jelleff,	Capt. 5th Ohio Vols.	Jan. 24, 1864			
			W. F. Stevens,	" 29th " "	Feb. 4, "			

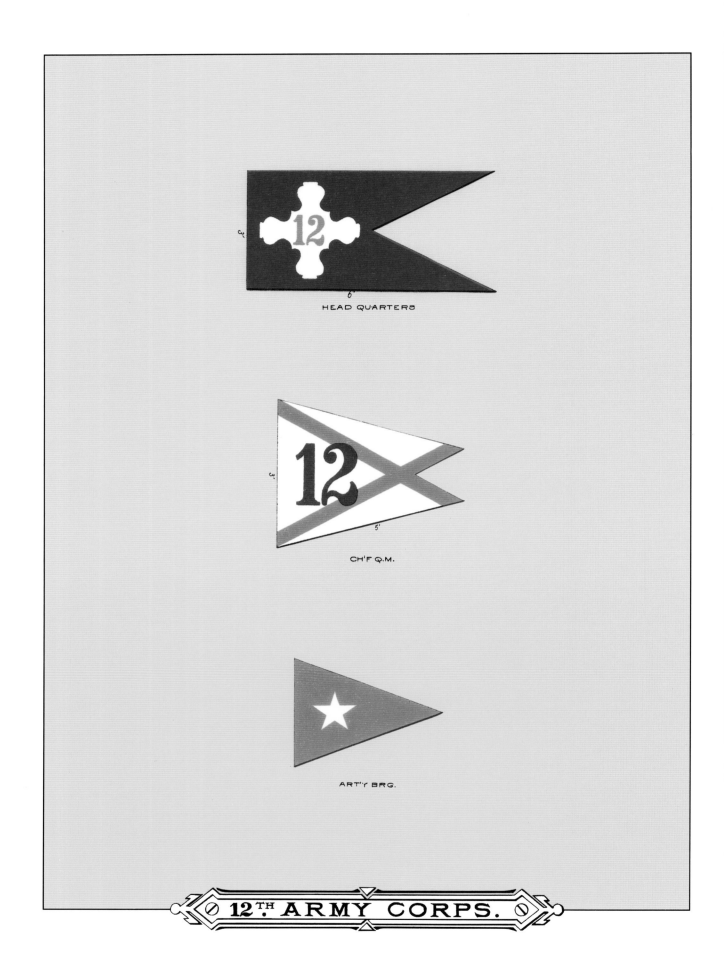

HEAD QUARTERS

CH'F Q.M.

ART'Y BRG.

12TH ARMY CORPS.

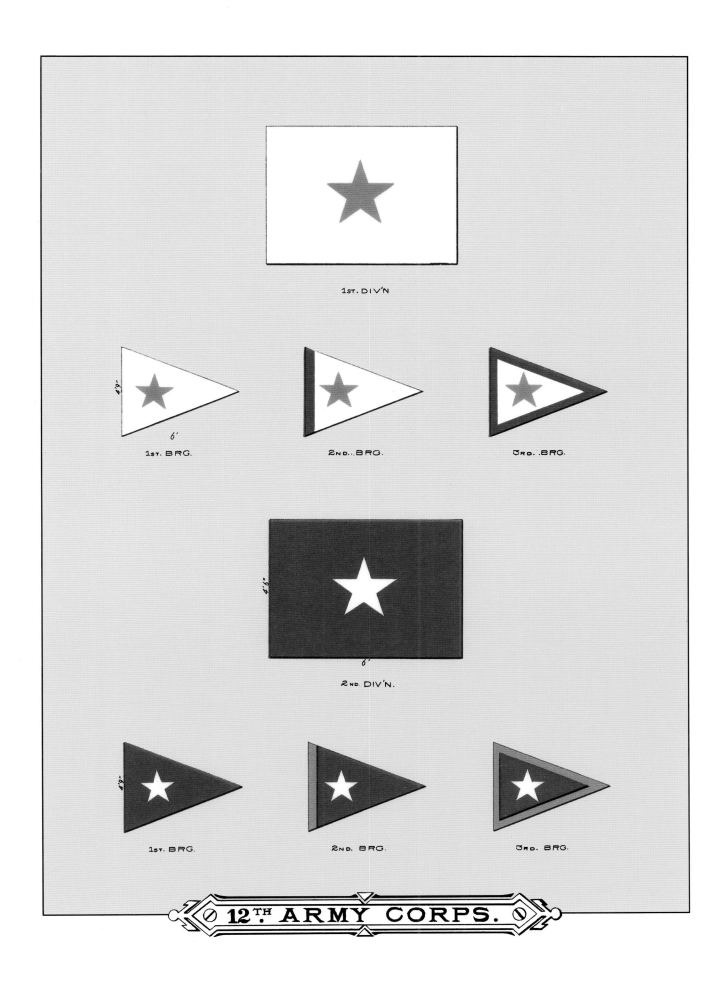

1ST. DIV'N

1ST. BRG.

2ND. BRG.

3RD. BRG.

2ND. DIV'N.

1ST. BRG.

2ND. BRG.

3RD. BRG.

12TH ARMY CORPS.

THIRTEENTH

Created G. O. No. 168. A. G. O. October 24, 1862.   Reorganized G. O. No. 210. A. G. O. December 18, 1862.

Finally discontinued (

COMMANDERS.

U. S. GRANT,	Major-Gene
J. A. McCLERNAND,	"
E. O. C. ORD,	"
C. C. WASHBURN,	"
N. J. T. DANA,	"
W. P. BENTON,	Brigadier-G
GORDON GRANGER,	Major-Gene

District of Memphis.

Discontinued. Corps reorganized December 18, 1862.

COMMANDER.		DATE.
W. T. Sherman,	Major-General.	November, 1862

1st Brigade—District of Memphis.	2d Brigade—District of Memphis.	3d Brigade—District of Memphis.	4th Brigade—District of Mem
Discontinued December 18, 1862.	Transferred to 1st Division, Right Wing, Dec., 1862.	Transferred to 1st Division, Right Wing, Dec., 1862.	Discontinued December 18, 1862.
COMMANDER **DATE.**	**COMMANDER.** **DATE.**	**COMMANDER.** **DATE.**	**COMMANDER.**
M. L. Smith, Brigadier-General. Nov., 1862	J. W. Denver, Brigadier-General. Nov., 1862	Not given on Returns.	D. Stuart, Col. 55th Ills. Vols. No

D

I

COMMAN
S. A. Hurlbut, Ma

RIGHT WING—13TH ARMY CORPS.

Discontinued. Corps reorganized December 18, 1862.

COMMANDER.		DATE.
J. B. McPherson,	Brigadier-General.	November, 1862

1st Division—Right Wing.	3d Division—Right Wing.	4th Division—Right Wing.
Discontinued December 18, 1862.	Discontinued December 18, 1862.	Discontinued December 18, 1862.
COMMANDER. **DATE.**	**COMMANDER.** **DATE.**	**COMMANDERS.**
J. W. Denver, Brigadier-General. Dec. 9, 1862	John A. Logan, Brigadier-General. Nov., 1862	T. J. McKean, Brigadier-General. Nov J. G. Lauman, " Dec.

1st Brigade—1st Division—Right Wing.	1st Brigade—3d Division—Right Wing.	1st Brigade—4th Division—Right Wing
COMMANDER. **DATE.**	**COMMANDERS.** **DATE.**	**COMMANDER.**
John A. McDowell, Col. 6th Iowa Vols. Dec., 1862	C. C. Marsh, Col. 20th Ills. Vols. Nov., 1862 John E. Smith, Brigadier-General. Dec., "	J. C. Pugh, Col. 41st Ills. Vols. Dec

2d Brigade—1st Division—Right Wing.	2d Brigade—3d Division—Right Wing.	2d Brigade—4th Division—Right Wing
COMMANDER. **DATE.**	**COMMANDER.** **DATE.**	**COMMANDER.**
J. R. Cockerell, Col. 70th Ohio Vols. Dec., 1862	M. D. Leggett, Col. 78th Ohio Vols. Nov., 1862	Cyrus Hall, Col. 14th Ills. Vols. Dec

	4th Brigade—3d Division—Right Wing.	3d Brigade—4th Division—Right Wing
	COMMANDER. **DATE.**	**COMMANDER.**
	J. D. Stevenson, Col. 7th Mo. Vols. Nov., 1862	A. K. Johnson, Col. 28th Ills. Vols. Dec

1st Cavalry Brigade—Right Wing.

Organized December, 1862.

COMMANDER.		DATE.
B. H. Grierson,	Col. 6th Ills. Cav.	December, 1862

Cavalry

Transferred to De

COMMAN
J. J. Mudd, Col.

ARMY CORPS.

No. 210.   A. G. O. June 11, 1864.   Reorganized G. O. No. 20, Military Division of West Mississippi, February 18, 1865.

G. O. July 20, 1865.

DATE.
October 24, 1862.
December 18, 1862, and February 23, 1864.
June 19, 1863; Sept. 15, 1863, and Jan. 9, 1864.
August, 1863, and October 20, 1863.
October 26, 1863.
June, 1864.
February 18, 1865.

District of Corinth.

Discontinued.   Corps reorganized December 18, 1862.

COMMANDER.		DATE.
G. M. Dodge,	Brigadier-General.	November, 1862

rigade—District of Memphis.	1st Brigade—District of Corinth.	2d Brigade—District of Corinth.	3d Brigade—District of Corinth.
Discontinued December 18, 1862.	Discontinued December 18, 1862.	Discontinued December 18, 1862.	Discontinued December 18, 1862.

COMMANDER.	DATE.	COMMANDER.	DATE.	COMMANDER.	DATE.	COMMANDER.	DATE.
nd, Col. 72d Ohio Vols.	Nov., 1862	T. W. Sweeney, Col. 52d Ills. Vols.	Nov., 1862	A. Mersy, Col. 9th Ills. Vols.	Nov., 1862	M. M. Bane, Col. 50th Ills. Vols.	Nov., 1862

, 1862.

DATE.
November, 1862

LEFT WING—13TH ARMY CORPS.

Discontinued.   Corps reorganized December 18, 1862.

COMMANDER.		DATE.
S. Hamilton,	Major-General.	November, 1862

Stanley's Division—Left Wing.	Quinby's Division—Left Wing.	McArthur's Division—Left Wing.
Discontinued December 18, 1862.	Discontinued December 18, 1862.	Discontinued December 18, 1862.

COMMANDER.	DATE.	COMMANDER.	DATE.	COMMANDER.	DATE.
anley, Brigadier-General.	Nov., 1862	Isaac F. Quinby, Brigadier-General.	Nov., 1862	J. McArthur, Brigadier-General.	Nov., 1862

st Brigade—Stanley's Division—Left Wing.	1st Brigade—Quinby's Division—Left Wing.	1st Brigade—McArthur's Division—Left Wing.

COMMANDER.	DATE.	COMMANDER.	DATE.	COMMANDER.	DATE.
er, Col. 27th Ohio Vols.	Nov., 1862	John B. Sanborn, Col. 4th Minn. Vols.	Nov., 1862	G. W. Deitzler, Col. 1st Kans. Vols.	Nov., 1862

d Brigade—Stanley's Division—Left Wing.	2d Brigade—Quinby's Division—Left Wing.	2d Brigade—McArthur's Division—Left Wing.

COMMANDER.	DATE.	COMMANDER.	DATE.	COMMANDER.	DATE.
mis, Col. 26th Ills. Vols.	Nov., 1862	E. R. Eckley, Col. 80th Ohio Vols.	Nov. 21, 1862	G. Bouck, Col. 18th Wis. Vols.	Nov., 1862

	3d Brigade—Quinby's Division—Left Wing.	3d Brigade—McArthur's Division—Left Wing.

		COMMANDER.	DATE.	COMMANDER.	DATE.
		G. B. Boomer, Col. 26th Mo. Vols.	Nov., 1862	M. M. Crocker, Col. 13th Iowa Vols.	Nov., 1862

my Corps.

3.
ptember 14, 1863.

DATE.
August, 1863

1st Division—13th Army Corps.

Organized July, 1863. (Formerly 9th and 14th Divisions.)

COMMANDERS.		DATE.
C. C. Washburn,	Brigadier-General.	June 30, 1863
"	Major-General.	September 15, 1863, and November, 1863
W. P. Benton,	Brigadier-General.	August, 1863, and December, 1863
M. K. Lawler,	"	October 20, 1863, and May 23, 1864
F. H. Warren,	"	February, 1864, and April 1, 1864
N. J. T. Dana,	Major-General.	March 11, 1864
J. C. Veatch,	Brigadier-General.	February 27, 1865
E. S. Dennis,	"	May, 1865

1st Brigade—1st Division.

COMMANDERS.		DATE.
W. P. Benton,	Brigadier-General.	July, 1863
D. Shunk,	Col. 8th Ind. Vols.	Aug. "
"	" 8th " "	Feb., 1864
H. D. Washburn,	" 18th " "	Oct., 1863
"	" 18th " "	April 1, 1864
F. H. Warren,	Brigadier-General.	Dec., 1863
"	"	March 11, 1864
G. W. K. Bailey,	Col. 99th Ills. Vols.	May, "
J. R. Slack,	Brigadier-General.	Feb., 1865
J. A. McLaughlin,	Lt.-Col. 47th Ind. Vols.	May 26, "

2d Brigade—1st Division.

COMMANDERS.		DATE.
W. M. Stone,	Col. 22d Iowa Vols.	July, 1863
S. L. Glasgow,	" 23d " "	Aug. 13, "
C. L. Harris,	" 11th Wis.	Sept. 16, "
S. Merrill,	" 21st Iowa "	Feb. 11, 1864
M. K. Lawler,	Brigadier-General.	March 10, "
"	"	April, "
L. A. Sheldon,	Col. 42d Ohio Vols.	March 27, "
J. Keigwin,	" 49th Ind.	May 23, "
E. S. Dennis,	Brigadier-General.	Feb., 1865
B. Dornblaser,	Col. 46th Ills. Vols.	May 25, "

3d Brigade—1st Division.

Discontinued March, 1864.
Reorganized February 18, 1865.
Transferred from Corps, May, 1865.

COMMANDERS.		DATE.
J. Keigwin,	Col. 49th Ind. Vols.	July, 1863
"	" 49th " "	Dec. 23, "
T. W. Bennett,	" 69th " "	Aug., "
M. K. Lawler,	Brigadier-General.	Sept. 23, "
"	"	Nov., "
"	"	Feb. 28, 1864
L. A. Sheldon,	Col. 42d Ohio Vols.	Oct., 1863
L. Kent,	" 29th Ills. "	Feb., 1865
"	" 29th " "	April, "
W. B. Kinsey,	Lt.-" 161st N. Y. "	March, "

4th Brigade—1st Division.

Discontinued September, 1863.

COMMANDER.		DATE.
D. W. Lindsey,	Col. 22d Ky. Vols.	July, 1863

Provisional Brigade—1st Division.

Organized March, 1864. Discontinued April, 1864.

COMMANDER.		DATE.
J. C. Cobb,	Col. 2d Eng. "Corps de Afrique."	March 8, 1864

4th Division—13th Army Corps.

Formerly 4th Division, 16th Corps. Organized July 28, 1863. Transferred to 17th Army Corps, August 17, 1863.
Reorganized August, 1863. (Formerly Old 10th Division.) Not reported subsequent to June, 1864.

COMMANDERS.		DATE.
M. M. Crocker,	Brigadier-General.	July 28, 1863
M. K. Lawler,	"	August 15, 1863
S. G. Burbridge,	"	September 18, 1863
W. J. Landrum,	Col. 19th Ky. Vols.	December 8, 1863, and March 15, 1864
T. E. G. Ransom,	Brigadier-General.	February 9, 1864
F. W. Moore,	Col. 83d Ohio Vols.	May 29, 1864

1st Brigade—4th Division.

COMMANDERS.		DATE.
J. C. Pugh,	Col. 41st Ills. Vols.	July, 1863
R. Owen,	" 60th Ind. "	Aug. 31, "
W. J. Landrum,	" 19th Ky. "	Nov. 21, "
"	" 19th " "	Jan. 9, 1864
J. Cowan,	Lt.-" 19th " "	Dec. 10, 1863
"	" 19th " "	March 15, 1864
F. Emerson,	" 67th Ind. "	March 27, "
F. A. Sears,	Maj. 67th " "	April 8, "
F. W. Moore,	Col. 83d Ohio "	" 28, "
D. P. Grier,	" 77th Ills. "	May 30, "

2d Brigade—4th Division.

COMMANDERS.		DATE.
C. Hall,	Col. 14th Ills. Vols.	July, 1863
W. J. Landrum,	" 19th Ky. "	Aug., "
"	" 19th " "	Oct. 6, "
J. Cowan,	Lt.-" 19th " "	Aug. 24, "
D. P. Grier,	" 77th Ills. "	Nov. 21, "
M. V. Hotchkiss,	Maj. 77th " "	Dec. 5, "
H. Rust, Jr.,	Col. 13th Me. "	Jan. 27, 1864
J. W. Vance,	" 96th Ohio "	March 14, "
A. H. Brown,	Lt.-" 96th " "	April 9, "
J. R. Parker,	" 48th " "	" 19, "
G. W. Clark,	" 64th Iowa "	May 11, "

3d Brigade—4th Division.

Not reported subsequent to August, 1863.

COMMANDER.		DATE.
A. K. Johnson,	Col 28th Ills. Vols.	July, 1863

12th Division—13th Army Corps.

Organized February, 1863. Designation changed to 3d Division, 13th Corps, August, 1863.

COMMANDERS.		DATE.
W. A. Gorman,	Brigadier-General.	February, 1863
A. P. Hovey,	"	" "
A. L. Lee,	"	July 26, "

1st Brigade—12th Division.

COMMANDERS.		DATE.
A. P. Hovey,	Brigadier-General.	Feb., 1863
G. F. McGinnis,	"	" "
W. T. Spicely,	Col. 24th Ind. Vols.	July, "

2d Brigade—12th Division.

COMMANDERS.		DATE.
G. F. McGinnis,	Brigadier-General.	Feb., 1863
P. Kinney,	Col. 56th Ohio Vols.	" "
J. R. Slack,	" 47th Ind. "	April 9, "

(Right column — partially cut off)

COMM	
F. J. Herron,	
N. J. T. Dana,	
C. C. Andrews,	

1st Brigade—2d Division.

COMMANDERS.		
Wm. Vandever,	Brigadier-General.	Au
"	"	Oc
Wm. McE. Dye,	Col. 20th Iowa Vols.	Au
"	" 20th " "	Ap
J. G. Clark,	" 26th Ind. "	No
J. C. Black,	" 37th Ills. "	
J. O. Hudnutt,	Lt.-" 38th Iowa "	Fe
S. L. Glasgow,	" 23d " "	
"	" 23d " "	Ma
H. Bertram,	" 20th Wis. "	Ma
J. McNulta,	" 94th Ills. "	Ju

(Section)

C
COMM
P. J. Osterhaus,

1st Brigade—9th Division

COMMANDERS.		
Wm. Vandever,	Brigadier-General.	Ja
T. T. Garrard,	Col. 3d Ky. Vols.	Fe
J. Keigwin,	" 49th Ind. "	Ma

13th D

Organized February, 1863. Discont

COMMANDERS.	
L. F. Ross,	Brigadie
F. Salomon,	

1st Brigade—13th Division.

COMMANDERS.		
F. Salomon,	Brigadier-General.	Feb
S. A. Foster,	Col. 35th Mo. Vols.	May
W. E. McLean,	" 43d Ind. "	June

Corps—Continued.

Division—13th Army Corps.

Joined Corps, August, 1863.

		DATE.
-General.		August, 1863, and January 3, 1864
"		September 28, 1863
dier-General.		March 4, 1865

3d Division—13th Army Corps.

Organized August 14, 1863. (Formerly 12th Division.)

COMMANDERS.		DATE.
A. L. Lee,	Brigadier-General.	August 31, 1863
G. F. McGinnis,	"	Sept. 13, 1863, and May 24, 1864
R. A. Cameron,	"	March 3, 1864
W. P. Benton,	"	February and June, 1865
D. P. Grier,	Col. 77th Ills. Vols.	May 28, 1865

2d Brigade—2d Division.

COMMANDERS.		DATE.
ne,	Brigadier-General.	Aug., 1863
,	Col. 91st Ills. Vols.	" 25, "
)ye,	" 20th Iowa "	Oct., "
,	" 20th Wis. "	Jan., 1864
,	" 94th Ills. "	March 12, "
,	" 94th " "	May 2, "
on,	Brigadier-General.	April 17, "
ely,	Col. 24th Ind. Vols.	March 5, 1865

3d Brigade—2d Division.

Organized December, 1863.
Discontinued January, 1864.
Reorganized February, 1865.

COMMANDERS.		DATE.
T. E. G. Ransom,	Brigadier-General.	Dec., 1863
J. C. Black,	Col. 37th Ills. Vols.	Feb., 1865
F. W. Moore,	" 83d Ohio "	March 5, "

1st Brigade—3d Division.

COMMANDERS.		DATE.
G. F. McGinnis,	Brigadier-General.	Aug., 1863
W. T. Spicely,	Col. 24th Ind. Vols.	Sept. 13, "
R. A. Cameron,	Brigadier-General.	Oct., "
"	"	Feb. 5, 1864
"	"	May 24, "
D. Macauley,	Col. 11th Ind. Vols.	Dec. 6, 1863
A. M. Flory,	Lt.- " 46th " "	March 3, 1864
T. H. Bringhurst,	" 46th " "	April 26, "
D. P. Grier,	" 77th Ills. "	Feb., 1865
H. Orff,	" 35th Wis. "	May 28, "
R. Ritter,	" 28th Ills. "	June, "

2d Brigade—3d Division.

COMMANDERS.		DATE.
J. R. Slack,	Col. 47th Ind. Vols.	Aug. 31, 1863
"	" 47th " "	April, 1864
W. H. Raynor,	" 56th Ohio "	Nov. 21, 1863
H. M. Day,	" 91st Ills. "	Feb., 1865

3d Brigade—3d Division.

Not reported in 3d Division as organized, August, 1863.

COMMANDER.		DATE.
C. Krez,	Col. 27th Wis. Vols.	Feb. 27, 1865

Division—13th Army Corps.

Division and designated 1st Division, 13th Corps, July, 1863.

	DATE.
ier-General.	January 6, 1863

10th Division—13th Army Corps.

Designation changed to 4th Division, 13th Corps, August, 1863.

COMMANDER.		DATE.
A. J. Smith,	Brigadier-General.	December, 1862

2d Brigade—9th Division.

COMMANDERS.		DATE.
dsey,	Col. 22d Ky. Vols.	Dec., 1862
,	" 22d " "	May, 1863
urcy,	" 16th Ohio "	Feb., "
lon,	" 42d " "	"

3d Brigade—9th Division.

Discontinued February 4, 1863.

COMMANDER.		DATE.
J. F. DeCourcy,	Col. 16th Ohio Vols.	Dec., 1862

1st Brigade—10th Division.

COMMANDERS.		DATE.
S. G. Burbridge,	Brigadier-General.	Dec., 1862
R. Owen,	Col. 60th Ind. Vols.	July, 1863

2d Brigade—10th Division.

COMMANDERS.		DATE.
W. J. Landrum,	Col. 19th Ky. Vols.	Dec., 1862
"	" 19th " "	March, 1863
D. P. Grier,	" 77th Ills. "	Feb. 9, "

---

my Corps.

oops transferred to 16th Army Corps.)

	DATE.
	February, 1863
	May, "

14th Division—13th Army Corps.

Organized March, 1863. Consolidated with 9th Division and designated 1st Division, 13th Corps, July, 1863.

COMMANDER.		DATE.
E. A. Carr,	Brigadier-General.	March, 1863

2d Brigade—13th Division.

COMMANDERS.		DATE.
sk,	Brigadier-General.	Feb., 1863
ce,	Col. 33d Iowa Vols.	June, "

1st Brigade—14th Division.

COMMANDERS.		DATE.
W. P. Benton,	Brigadier-General.	March, 1863
H. D. Washburn,	Col. 18th Ind. Vols.	May 31, "
D. Shunk,	" 8th " "	June, "

2d Brigade—14th Division.

COMMANDERS.		DATE.
C. L. Harris,	Col. 11th Wis. Vols.	March, 1863
M. K. Lawler,	Brigadier-General.	May 2, "

FOURTEENTH

Created G. O. No. 168. A. G. O. October 24, 1862.   Reorganized G. O.

	COMMANDERS.	
W. S. ROSECRANS,	Major-Genera
GEO. H. THOMAS,	"
J. M. PALMER,	"
R. W. JOHNSON,	Brigadier-Ge
J. C. DAVIS,	Bvt. Major-G

C

Discontinued G. O. No. 9. A. G. (

COMMANDER

G. H. Thomas, Major-G

1st Division—"Centre."

COMMANDER.		DATE.
S. S. Fry,	Brigadier-General.	Nov., 1862

3d Division—"Centre."

COMMANDER.		DATE.
L. H. Rousseau,	Brigadier-General.	Nov., 1862

7th Division—"Centre."

COMMANDER.		D
R. B. Mitchell,	Brigadier-General.	Dec.,

1st Brigade—1st Division. "Centre."

Commander.	Date.
M. B. Walker, Col. 31st Ohio Vols.	Nov., 1862

2d Brigade—1st Division. "Centre."

Commander.	Date.
J. M. Harlan, Col. 10th Ky. Vols.	Nov., 1862

9th Brigade—3d Division. "Centre."

Commander.	Date.
B. F. Scribner, Col. 38th Ind. Vols.	Nov., 1862

17th Brigade—3d Division. "Centre."

Commander.	Date.
J. G. Jones, Col. 42d Ind. Vols.	Nov., 1862

1st Brigade—7th Division. "Centre."

COMMANDER.		D
J. D. Morgan,	Brigadier-General.	Dec.,

3d Brigade—1st Division—"Centre."

COMMANDER.		DATE.
Jas. B Steedman,	Brigadier-General.	Nov., 1862

28th Brigade—3d Division—"Centre."

COMMANDERS.		DATE.
H. A. Hambright,	Col. 79th Pa. Vols.	Nov., 1862
J. C. Starkweather,	" 1st Wis. "	Dec., "

2d Brigade—7th Division—"Centre."

COMMANDER.		D
D. McCook,	Col. 52d Ohio Vols.	Dec.,

RIGHT WING—14TH ARMY CORPS.

First Return on file December, 1862.   Discontinued and designated 20th Army Corps, G. O. No. 9. A. G. O. January 9, 1863.

COMMANDER.		DATE.
A. McD. McCook,	Major-General.	At Organization.

1st Division—Right Wing.

COMMANDER.		DATE.
Jeff. C. Davis,	Brigadier-General.	Dec., 1862

2d Division—Right Wing.

COMMANDER.		DATE.
R. W. Johnson,	Brigadier-General.	Dec., 1862

3d Division—Right Wing.

COMMANDER.		D
P. H. Sheridan,	Brigadier-General.	Dec.,

1st Brigade—1st Division.

COMMANDER.		DATE.
P. S. Post,	Col. 59th Ills. Vols.	Dec., 1862

1st Brigade—2d Division.

COMMANDER.		DATE.
August Willich,	Brigadier-General.	Dec., 1862

1st Brigade—3d Division.

COMMANDERS.		D
J. W. Sill,	Brigadier-General.	Dec.
N. Grensel,	Col. 36th Ills. Vols.	"

2d Brigade—1st Division.

COMMANDER.		DATE.
W. P. Carlin,	Col. 38th Ills. Vols.	Dec., 1862

2d Brigade—2d Division.

COMMANDERS.		DATE.
H. M. Buckley,	Col. 5th Ky. Vols.	Dec., 1862
P. P. Baldwin,	" 6th Ind. "	" 24, "

2d Brigade—3d Division.

COMMANDER.		D
B. Laibold,	Lt.-Col. 2d Mo. Vols.	D

3d Brigade—1st Division.

COMMANDER.		DATE.
W. E. Woodruff,	Col. 2d Ky. Vols.	Dec., 1862

3d Brigade—2d Division.

COMMANDERS.		DATE.
E. N. Kirk,	Brigadier-General.	Dec., 1862
J. B. Dodge,	Col. 30th Ind. Vols.	" 31, "

3d Brigade—3d Division.

COMMANDERS.		D
G. W. Roberts,	Col. 42d Ills. Vols.	Dec.,
L. P. Bradley,	" 51st " "	"

Cavalry

COMMANDER.	
D. S. Stanley,	Brigadie

1st

COMMANDER.	
R. H. G. Minty,	Col. 4th

Regular

Organized December 18, 1862.   Termed 4

COMMANDER.	
Oliver L. Shepherd,	Lt.-Col. 18th

ARMY CORPS.

G. O. January 9, 1863.   Discontinued G. O. No. 131.   A. G. O. August 1, 1865.

DATE.
October 24, 1862.
January   9, 1863.
October 28, "
August   6, 1864.
"   9, "

RE.

and designated 14th Army Corps.

DATE.
At Organization.

8th Division—"Centre."		12th Division —"Centre."		13th Division—"Centre."	
				Transferred to "Left Wing," 14th Army Corps, December, 1862.	
COMMANDER.	**DATE.**	**COMMANDERS.**	**DATE.**	**COMMANDER.**	**DATE.**
gley, Brigadier-General.	Nov., 1862	E. Dumont, Brigadier-General.	Nov., 1862	J. M. Palmer, Brigadier-General.	Nov., 1862
		J. J. Reynolds, "	Dec., "		

7th Brigade—8th Division. "Centre."		39th Brigade—12th Division. "Centre."		40th Brigade—12th Division. "Centre."		1st Brigade—13th Division. "Centre."	
COMMANDER.	**DATE.**	**Commanders.**	**Date.**	**Commander.**	**Date.**	**COMMANDER.**	**DATE.**
Miller, Col. 29th Ind. Vols.	Nov., 1862	J. R. Scott, Col. 16th Ills. Vols.	Dec., 1862	A. O. Miller, Col. 72d Ind. Vols.	Nov., 1862.	G. W. Roberts, Col. 42d Ill. Vols.	Nov., 1862
		A. B. Moore, Col. 104th Ills. Vols.	Dec., 1862				

29th Brigade—8th Division—"Centre."		Ward's Brigade—12th Division—"Centre."		2d Brigade—13th Division—"Centre."	
COMMANDER.	**DATE.**	**COMMANDER.**	**DATE.**	**COMMANDER.**	**DATE.**
nley, Col. 18th Ohio Vols.	Nov., 1862	W. T. Ward, Brigadier-General.	Nov., 1862	J. D. Morgan, Brigadier-General.	Nov., 1862

LEFT WING—14TH ARMY CORPS.

First Return on file December, 1862.   Discontinued and designated 21st Army Corps G. O. No. 9.   A. G. O. January 9, 1863.

COMMANDER.		**DATE.**
T. L. Crittenden,	Major-General.	At Organization.

1st Division—Left Wing.		2d Division—Left Wing.		3d Division—Left Wing.	
COMMANDER.	**DATE.**	**COMMANDER.**	**DATE.**	**COMMANDER.**	**DATE.**
ood, Brigadier-General.	Dec., 1862	J. M. Palmer, Brigadier-General.	Dec., 1862	H. P. Van Cleve, Brigadier-General.	Dec., 1862

1st Brigade—1st Division.		1st Brigade—2d Division.		1st Brigade—3d Division.	
COMMANDER.	**DATE.**	**COMMANDER.**	**DATE.**	**COMMANDER.**	**DATE.**
ascall, Brigadier-General.	Dec., 1862	C. Cruft, Brigadier-General.	Dec., 1862	S. Beatty, Brigadier-General.	Dec., 1862

2d Brigade—1st Division.		2d Brigade—2d Division.		2d Brigade—3d Division.	
COMMANDER.	**DATE.**	**COMMANDER.**	**DATE.**	**COMMANDER.**	**DATE.**
agner, Col. 15th Ind. Vols.	Dec., 1862	W. B. Hazen, Brigadier-General.	Dec., 1862	J. P. Tyffe, Col. 59th Ohio Vols.	Dec., 1862

3d Brigade—1st Division.		3d Brigade—2d Division.		3d Brigade—3d Division.	
COMMANDER.	**DATE.**	**COMMANDER.**	**DATE.**	**COMMANDER.**	**DATE.**
arker, Col. 65th Ohio Vols.	Dec., 1862	W. Grose, Col. 36th Ind. Vols.	Dec., 1862	S. Mathews, Col. 21st Ind. Vols.	Dec., 1862

Army Corps.

DATE.
December, 1862

ry Division.

DATE.
December   22, 1862

Army Corps.

sion, 14th Army Corps, January 9, 1863.

DATE.
December, 1862

1st Division—14th Army Corps.

COMMANDERS.		DATE.
R. S. Granger,	Brigadier-General.	Jan. 9, 1863
L. H. Rousseau,	Major-General.	March 29, "
"	"	Sept. 21, "
J. H. King,	Brigadier-General.	July 26, "
"	"	June 3, 1864
"	"	Aug. 6, "
A. Baird,	"	" 24, 1863
R. W. Johnson,	"	Nov. 17, 1863
"	"	July 13, 1864
W. P. Carlin,	"	Aug. 17, "
G. P. Buell,	Bvt. "	March 28, 1865
C. C. Walcutt,	"	April 3, "

1st Brigade—1st Division.

COMMANDERS.		DATE.
B. F. Scribner,	Col. 38th Ind. Vols.	Jan. 9, 1863
"	" 38th " "	Dec. 5, "
W. P. Carlin,	Brigadier-General.	Oct. 19, "
"		Jan., 1864
M. C. Taylor,	Col. 15th Ky. Vols.	Aug. 17, "
D. Hapeman,	Lt.- " 104th Ills. "	Sept., "
H. C. Hobart,	" 21st Wis. "	Nov., "
H. A. Hambright,	" 79th Pa. "	June 8, 1865

2d Brigade—1st Division.

Discontinued April, 1863. (Transferred to 2d Division.)
Reorganized April, 1863. (Formerly 3d Brigade, 1st Division.)
Transferred from Corps September, 1864. Reorganized November, 1864.

COMMANDERS.		DATE.
J. Beatty,	Col. 3d Ohio Vols.	Jan. 9, 1863
J. C. Starkweather,	" 1st Wis. "	April, "
"	Brigadier-General.	July 30, "
H. A. Hambright,	Col. 79th Pa. Vols.	June 15, "
"	" 79th " "	Sept. 28, "
M. F. Moore,	" 69th Ohio "	Oct., "
J. H. King,	Brigadier-General.	Nov., "
"	"	July 13, 1864
W. L. Stoughton,	Col. 11th Mich. Vols.	June 13, "
J. R. Edie,	Maj. 15th U. S. Inf.	Aug. 6, "
J. H. Brigham,	Lt.-Col. 69th Ohio Vols.	Nov. 15, "
G. P. Buell,	Bvt. Brigadier-General.	Jan. 17, 1865
"	"	April 4, "
M. H. Fitch,	Lt.-Col. 21st Wis. Vols.	March 28, "

3d Brigade—1st Division.

Discontinued April, 1863 (termed 2d Brigade, 1st Division.)
Reorganized April, 1863 (formerly 4th Brigade, 1st Division.)
Discontinued June 6, 1865.

COMMANDERS.		DATE.
J. C. Starkweather,	Col. 1st Wis. Vols.	Jan. 9, 1863
"	Brigadier-General.	Nov., "
H. A. Hambright,	Col. 79th Pa. Vols.	March 9, "
"	" 79th " "	Jan., 1864
"	" 79th " "	Sept. 12, "
"	" 79th " "	March 28, 1865
R. S. Granger,	Brigadier-General.	April 21, 1863
J. H. King,	"	May 6, "
"	"	Aug. 24, "
S. K. Dawson,	Maj. 19th U. S. Inf.	July 26, "
Wm. Sirwell,	Col. 78th Pa. Vols.	Oct., "
J. M. Neibling,	" 21st Ohio "	March, 1864
B. F. Scribner,	" 38th Ind. "	May, "
M. F. Moore,	" 69th Ohio "	July, "
D. Miles,	Lt.- " 79th Pa. "	Oct. 12, "

4th Brigade—1st Division.

Discontinued April, 1863, and termed 3d Brigade, 1st Division.

COMMANDER.		DATE.
O. L. Shepherd,	Lt.-Col. 18th U. S. Inf.	Jan. 9, 1863

2d Division—14th Army Corps.

COMMANDERS.		DATE.
J. S. Negley,	Major-General.	Jan. 9, 1863
J. C. Davis,	Brigadier-General.	Oct., "
J. D. Morgan,	"	Aug., 1864
R. F. Smith,	Col. 16th Ills. Vols.	June, 1865

1st Brigade—2d Division.

Discontinued April, 1863. (Transferred from Corps.)
Reorganized April, 1863. (Formerly 2d Brigade, 1st Division.)

COMMANDERS.		DATE.
J. G. Speers,	Brigadier-General.	Jan. 9, 1863
J. Beatty,	"	April, "
R. F. Smith,	Col. 16th Ills. Vols.	Oct., "
"	" 16th " "	" 15, 1864
J. D. Morgan,	Brigadier-General.	Nov., 1863
C. M. Lum,	Col. 10th Mich. Vols.	Aug., 1864
Wm. Vandever,	Brigadier-General.	Jan. 18, 1865
G. W. Evans,	Lt.-Col. 60th Ills. Vols.	June, "

2d Brigade—2d Division.

COMMANDERS.		DATE.
A. W. Raffen,	Lt.-Col. 19th Ills. Vols.	Jan. 9, 1863
M. F. Moore,	" 69th Ohio "	Feb , "
T. R. Stanley,	" 18th " "	March, "
"	" 18th " "	Aug. 1, "
W. L. Stoughton,	" 11th Mich. "	June 23, "
J. G. Mitchell,	" 113th Ohio "	Oct., "
"	" 113th " "	Feb., 1864
"	Brigadier-General.	June, 1865
J. Beatty,	"	Nov., 1863
J. S. Pearce,	Lt.-Col. 98th Ohio Vols.	Sept., 1864
Peter Ege,	" 34th Ills. "	June, 1865

3d Brigade—2d Division.

Discontinued June, 1865.

COMMANDERS.		DATE.
J. F. Miller,	Col. 29th Ind. Vols.	Jan. 9, 1863
W. Sirwell,	" 78th Pa. "	June, "
D. McCook,	" 52d Ohio "	Oct., "
"	" 52d " "	Feb., 1864
O. F. Harmon,	" 125th Ills. "	Dec., 1863
"	" 125th " "	June 27, 1864
C. J. Dilworth,	" 85th " "	" 27, "
J. W. Langley,	Lt.- " 125th " "	Sept., "
"	" " 125th " "	March, 1865
R. D. Fearing,	" 92d Ohio "	Jan., "

3d Division—14th Army Corps.

COMMANDERS.		DA
J. B. Steedman,	Brigadier-General.	Jan.
J. M. Schofield,	"	April
J. M. Brannan,	"	May
A. Baird,	"	Oct.
"	"	Nov.,
G. P. Este,	Col. 14th Ohio Vols.	Oct.

1st Brigade—3d Division.

Discontinued July, 1865.

COMMANDERS.		D.
M. B. Walker,	Col. 31st Ohio Vols.	Jan.
"	" 31st " "	July
J. M. Connell,	" 17th " "	"
J. B. Turchin,	Brigadier-General.	Oct.
M. C. Hunter,	Col. 82d Ind. Vols.	Sept.
H. K. Milward,	Lt.- " 18th Ky. "	June,

2d Brigade—3d Division.

Discontinued July, 1865.

COMMANDERS.		D.
J. M. Harlan,	Col. 10th Ky. Vols.	Jan.
C. W. Chapman,	" 74th Ind. "	Marc
"	" 74th " "	Sept
J. B. Steedman,	Brigadier-General.	April
J. T. Croxton,	Col. 4th Ky. Vols.	Aug.
James George,	" 2d Minn. "	Oct.,
F. Van Derveer,	" 35th Ohio "	Nov.
"	" 35th " "	Feb.
G. Kammerling,	" 9th " "	Jan.,
N. Gleason,	" 87th Ind. "	June
"	" 87th " "	April
T. Doan,	Lt.- " 101st " "	Jan.
B. H. Showers,	" " 17th Ohio "	June

3d Brigade—3d Division.

Discontinued June, 1865.

COMMANDERS.		D.
F. Van Derveer,	Col. 35th Ohio Vols.	Jan.
E. H. Phelps,	" 38th " "	Oct.,
W. H. Hayes,	" 10th Ky. "	Nov.
G. P. Este,	" 14th Ohio "	April
"	" 14th " "	Nov.
H. K. Milward,	Lt.- " 18th Ky. "	Oct.
"	" " 18th " "	Marc
G. S. Greene,	Brigadier-General.	April

O. January 9, 1863.————————————————————————

4th Division—14th Army Corps.

Transferred from Corps June, 1863.
ʳganized June, 1863. (Formerly 5th Division, 14th Army Corps.)
Discontinued October 9, 1863.

COMMANDERS.		DATE.	
ᵒrgan,	Brigadier-General.	Jan.	9, 1863
ᵐith,	Col. 16th Ills. Vols.	May,	"
ʸnolds,	Major-General.	June,	"

5th Division—14th Army Corps.

————

Designated 4th Division, June, 1863.

————

COMMANDER.		DATE.	
J. J. Reynolds,	Brigadier-General.	Jan.	9, 1863

Temporary Division—14th Army Corps.

————

Organized June 7, 1865.

————

COMMANDER.		DATE.	
A. S. Williams,	Bvt. Major-General.	June 7, 1865	

1st Brigade—4th Division.

COMMANDERS.		DATE.	
ᵢth,	Col. 16th Ills. Vols.	Jan.	9, 1863
ₘ,	" 10th Mich. "	May,	"
ᵈer,	" 17th Ind. "	June,	"
	" 17th " "	Aug.,	"
ller,	" 72d " "	July,	"

1st Brigade—5th Division.

COMMANDER.		DATE.	
J. T. Wilder,	Col. 17th Ind. Vols.	Jan.	9, 1863

1st Brigade—Temporary Division.

COMMANDER.		DATE.	
J. S. Robinson,	Brigadier-General.	June 8, 1865	

2d Brigade—4th Division.

COMMANDERS.		DATE.	
ᵒk,	Col. 52d Ohio Vols.	Jan.	9, 1863
ll,	" 105th " "	June,	"
ᵇinson,	" 75th Ind. "	July 8,	"
	" 75th " "	Sept. 20,	"
ng,	" 68th " "	Aug. 2,	"

2d Brigade—5th Division.

COMMANDER.		DATE.	
A. S. Hall,	Col. 105th Ohio Vols.	Jan.	9, 1863

2d Brigade—Temporary Division.

COMMANDER.		DATE.	
Wm. Hawley,	Col. 3d Wis. Vols.	June 8, 1865	

3d Brigade—4th Division.

Organized June, 1863.

COMMANDERS.		DATE.	
ᵏ,	Brigadier-General.	June,	1863
ʳchin,	"	July 28,	"

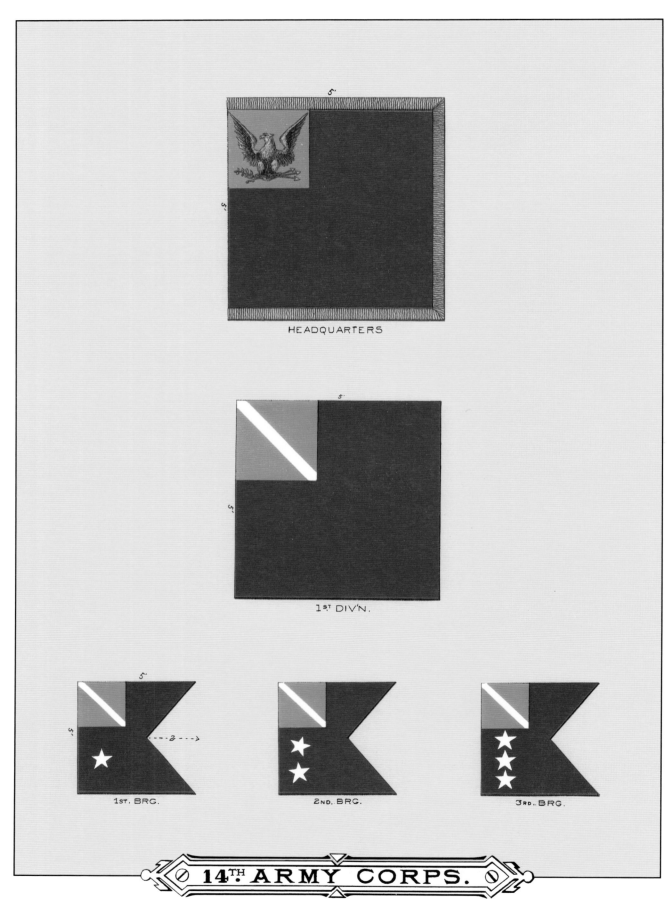

HEADQUARTERS

1ST DIV'N.

1ST. BRG.

2ND. BRG.

3RD. BRG.

14TH ARMY CORPS.

DEPARTMENT OF THE CUMBERLAND.

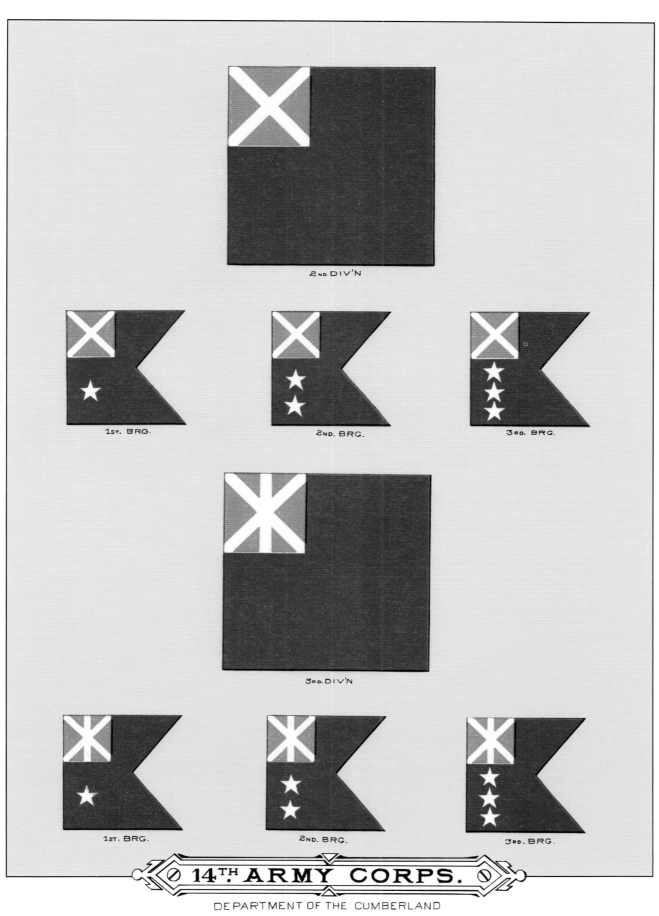

2ND. DIV'N

1ST. BRG. 2ND. BRG. 3RD. BRG.

3RD. DIV'N

1ST. BRG. 2ND. BRG. 3RD. BRG.

14TH ARMY CORPS.

DEPARTMENT OF THE CUMBERLAND

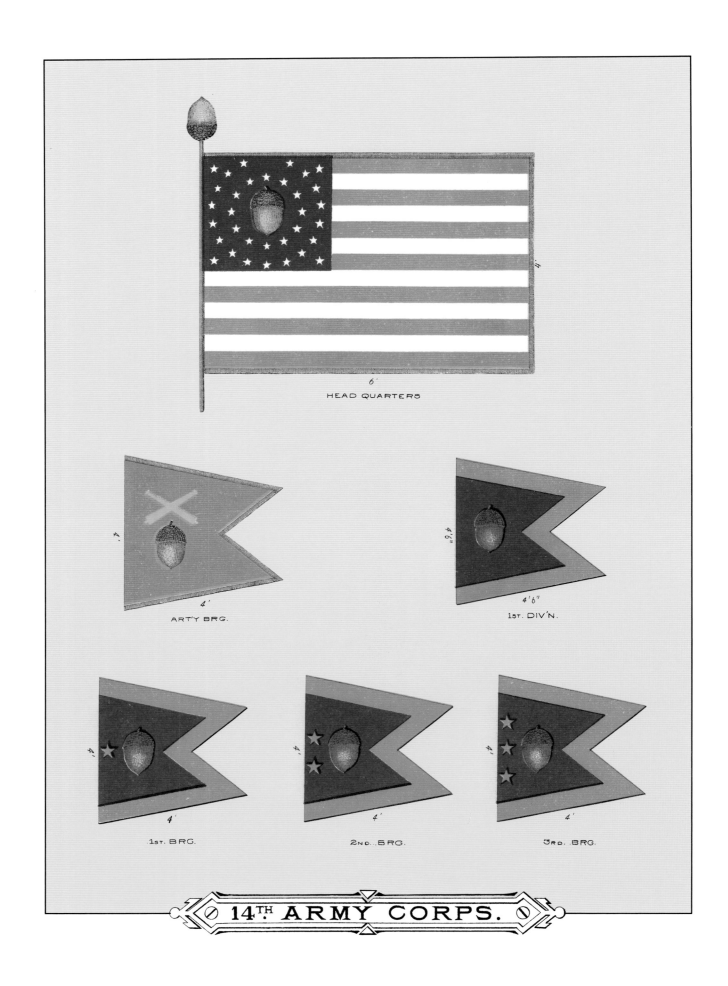

HEAD QUARTERS

ART'Y BRG.

1ST. DIV'N.

1ST. BRG.

2ND. BRG.

3RD. BRG.

14TH ARMY CORPS.

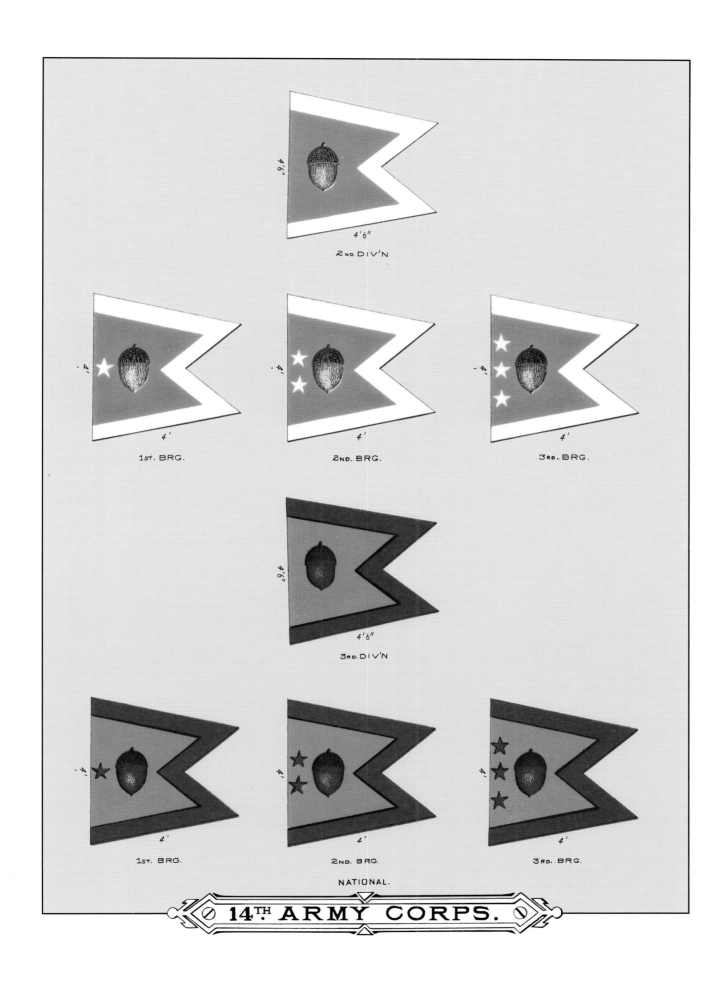

2ND DIV'N

1ST. BRG.　　2ND. BRG.　　3RD. BRG.

3RD. DIV'N

1ST. BRG.　　2ND. BRG.　　3RD. BRG.

NATIONAL.

14TH ARMY CORPS.

FIFTEENTH

Created G. O. No. 210. A. G. O. December 18, 18

COMMANDERS.

W. T. SHERMAN,	Major-G
F. P. BLAIR, Jr.,	"
J. A. LOGAN,	"
P. J. OSTERHAUS,	"
W. B. HAZEN,	"

1st Division—15th Army Corps.

COMMANDERS.		DATE.	
F. Steele,	Major-General.	January,	1863
E. S. Dennis,	Brigadier-General.	July	19, "
P. J. Osterhaus,	"	September	1, "
"	"	February,	1864
"	Major-General.	August,	"
M. Smith,	Col. 26th Iowa Vols.	January	4, "
C. R. Woods,	Brigadier-General.	"	13, "
"	"	July	15, "
"	"	September 23, "

2d Division—15th Army Corps.

COMMANDERS.		DATE.	
David Stuart,	Brigadier-General.	December,	1862
F. P. Blair, Jr.,	Major-General.	April	4, 1863
J. A. J. Lightburn,	Brigadier-General.	July	26, "
G. A. Smith,	"	September 10, "
M. L. Smith,	"	October	6, "
W. B. Hazen,	"	August	17, 1864
J. M. Oliver,	"	May,	18, 1865

1st Brigade—1st Division.

COMMANDERS.		DATE.	
F. P. Blair, Jr.,	Brigadier-General.	Dec.,	1862
F. H. Mauter,	Col. 32d Mo. Vols.	April 1, 1863
B. G. Farrar,	" 30th " "	June 13, "
F. Fletcher,	" 31st " "	July 28, "
C. R. Woods,	Brigadier-General.	Sept.,	"
"	"	Feb.,	1864
M. Smith,	Col. 26th Iowa Vols.	Dec. 14, 1863
"	" 26th " "	July 15, 1864
W. B. Woods,	Bvt. Brigadier-General.	Jan. 21, 1865
E. Briggs,	Lt. Col. 76th Ohio Vols.	June 16, "

2d Brigade—1st Division.

COMMANDERS.		DATE.	
E. E. Hovey,	Brigadier-General.	Dec.,	1862
C. R. Woods,	Col. 76th Ohio Vols.	May,	1863
"	Brigadier-General.	Aug. 24, "
H. Wangelin,	Col. 12th Mo. Vols.	July 30, "
J. A. Williamson,	" 4th Iowa "	Sept.,	"
"	" 4th " "	May,	1864
D. Carskadden,	" 9th " "	Dec.,	1863
"	" 9th " "	April 20, 1864
J. W. Jenkins,	Lt.- " 31st " "	Jan. 29, "
G. A. Stone,	" 25th " "	March 8, "
C. C. Walcutt,	Brigadier-General.	Sept 25, "
R. F. Catterson,	Col. 97th Ind. Vols.	Nov. 22, "

1st Brigade—2d Division.

COMMANDERS.		DATE.	
G. A. Smith,	Col. 8th Mo. Vols.	Dec.,	1862
"	Brigadier-General.	Oct. 19, 1863
"	"	Feb. 21, 1864
J. H. Blood,	Col. 6th Mo. Vols.	July,	1863
N. W. Tupper,	" 116th Ills. "	Sept. 10, "
"	" 116th " "	Nov. 24, "
D. C. Coleman,	Lt.-Col. 8th Mo. Vols.	Jan. 1, 1864
J. S. Martin,	" 111th Ills. "	July 20, "
T. Jones,	" 30th Ohio "	Aug.,	"
"	Bvt. Brigadier-General.	July,	1865
S. R. Mott,	Lt.-Col. 57th Ohio Vols.	June 20, "

2d Brigade—2d Division.

COMMANDERS.		
T. K. Smith,	Col. 54th Ohio Vols.	Dec
J. A. J. Lightburn,	Brigadier-General.	May
"	"	Oct.
"	"	Feb.
B. J. Spooner,	Col. 83d Ind. Vols.	July
"	" 83d " "	Sept
A. Malmborg,	" 55th Ills. "	Aug
T. Jones,	" 30th Ohio "	Jan.
W. S. Jones,	" 53d " "	Aug
"	" 53d " "	Jan.
J. S. Martin,	" 111th Ills. "	Dec

3d Brigade—1st Division.

Discontinued September, 1863. Reorganized December 1, 1863.

COMMANDERS.		DATE.	
J. M. Thayer,	Brigadier-General.	December	1862
J. A. Williamson,	Col. 4th Iowa Vols.	August	1, 1863
"	" 4th " "	November	1, 1864
G. A. Stone,	" 25th " "	December	1, 1863
"	" 25th " "	October	31, 1864
"	" 25th " "	January	5, 1865
H. Wangelin,	" 12th Mo. "	March	8, 1864
Wm. Smith,	" 1st Iowa "	September 25, "

3d Brigade—2d Division.

Discontinued October, 1863. Reorganized September, 1864.

COMMANDERS.		DATE.	
H. Ewing,	Brigadier-General.	December,	1862
E. Siber,	Col. 37th Ohio Vols.	July	21, 1863
A. Fowler,	" 99th Ind. "	September 28, 1864
J. M. Oliver,	" 15th Mich. "	November,	"
F. S. Hutchinson,	" 15th " "	May,	1865
A. V. Rice,	Brigadier-General.	June,	"

RMY CORPS.

ntinued G. O. No. 131.   A. G. O. August 1, 1865.

DATE.
December 18, 1862.
October,   1863.
November, 1863, and January, 1865.
September 23, 1864.
May,   1865.

3d Division—15th Army Corps.

Joined Corps April, 1863.   Transferred from Corps December, 1863.
Reorganized December 20, 1863 (formerly 2d Division, 17th Corps.)
Discontinued April, 1865.   Troops transferred to 1st and 2d Divisions, 15th Corps.

COMMANDERS.		DATE.	
J. M. Tuttle,	Brigadier-General.	April,	1863
"	"	September,	"
R. P. Buckland,	"	August	9, "
J. E. Smith,	"	December,	"

4th Division—15th Army Corps.

Joined 15th Corps July 28, 1863 (formerly 1st Division, 16th Corps.)
Discontinued September 14, 1864.   Reorganized September 23, 1864.

COMMANDERS.		DATE.	
H. Ewing,	Brigadier-General.	July,	1863
"	"	October 25,	"
J. M. Corse,	"	September,	"
"	"	"	1864
Wm. Harrow,	"	February 8,	"

1st Brigade—3d Division.

Discontinued April, 1865.

COMMANDERS.		DATE.
...land,	Brigadier-General.	April, 1863
"	"	Sept., "
"	"	Nov., "
...Millan,	Col. 95th Ohio Vols.	June 22, "
"	" 95th " "	Oct., "
...mas,	" 93d Ind. "	Aug., "
...nder,	" 59th " "	Dec., "
"	" 59th " "	April 2, 1864
"	" 18th Wis. "	Feb. 3, "
...own,	" 63d Ills. "	March 12, "
"	" 63d " "	Sept. 1, "
...k,	Brigadier-General.	Jan. 26, 1865

2d Brigade—3d Division.

Discontinued April, 1865.

COMMANDERS.		DATE.
J. A. Mower,	Brigadier-General.	April, 1863
"	"	Sept. 15, "
L. F. Hubbard,	Col. 5th Minn. Vols.	July 4, "
C. R. Wever,	" 17th Iowa "	Dec., "
"	" 17th " "	Jan. 29, 1865
G. B. Raum,	" 56th Ills. "	Feb., 1864

1st Brigade—4th Division.

Discontinued September 14, 1864.
Reorganized September 23, 1864.

COMMANDERS.		DATE.	
J. M. Loomis,	Col. 26th Ills. Vols.	July,	1863
"	" 26th " "	Sept.,	"
"	" 26th " "	March,	1864
R. Williams,	" 12th Ind. "	Aug.,	1863
"	" 12th " "	Jan.,	1864
"	" 12th " "	April,	"
J. M. Oliver,	" 15th Mich. "	Aug.,	"
R. Martin,	Lt.- " 66th Ind. "	Sept. 23,	"
E. W. Rice,	Brigadier-General.	Oct.,	"

2d Brigade—4th Division.

Discontinued September 14, 1864.
Reorganized September 23, 1864.

COMMANDERS.		DATE.	
S. G. Hicks,	Col. 40th Ills. Vols.	July,	1863
J. M. Oliver,	" 15th Mich. "	Aug.,	"
J. M. Corse,	Brigadier-General.	Oct., 25,	"
C. C. Walcutt,	Col. 46th Ohio Vols.	Nov. 25,	"
"	" 46th " "	April,	1864
W. A. Dickerman,	" 103d Ills. "	March,	"
W. S. Merriman,	Maj. 12th " "	Sept.,	"
R. N. Adams,	Col. 81st Ohio "	Oct.,	"
W. T. Clark,	Brigadier-General.	April,	1865

3d Brigade—3d Division.

Discontinued August, 1864.

COMMANDERS.		DATE.	
J. J. Woods,	Col. 12th Iowa Vols.	April,	1863
"	" 12th " "	June,	"
C. L. Matthies,	Brigadier-General.	May,	"
"	"	March,	1864
J. L. Geddes,	Col. 8th Iowa Vols.	September,	1863
J. Banbury,	" 5th " "	December,	"
"	" 5th " "	June,	1864
B. D. Dean,	" 26th Mo. "	May 15,	"
"	" 26th " "	July 25,	"

3d Brigade—4th Division.

Discontinued August, 1864.
Reorganized September, 1864.

COMMANDERS.		DATE	
J. R. Cockerill,	Col. 70th Ohio Vols	July,	1863
"	" 70th " "	Sept.,	"
"	" 70th " "	March,	1864
A. Fowler,	" 99th Ind. "	Aug. 14,	1863
"	" 99th " "	Jan. 27,	1864
W. S. Jones,	" 53d Ohio "	April 13,	"
J. M. Oliver,	" 15th Mich. "	May 16,	"
R. Rowett,	" 7th Ills. "	Sept.,	"
"	" 7th " "	April,	1865
F. J. Hurlbut,	Lt.- " 57th " "	Oct.,	1864

4th Brigade—4th Division.

Discontinued September, 1863.

COMMANDERS.		DATE.	
W. W. Sanford,	Col. 48th Ills. Vols.	July,	1863
J. M. Corse,	Brigadier-General.	Aug.,	"

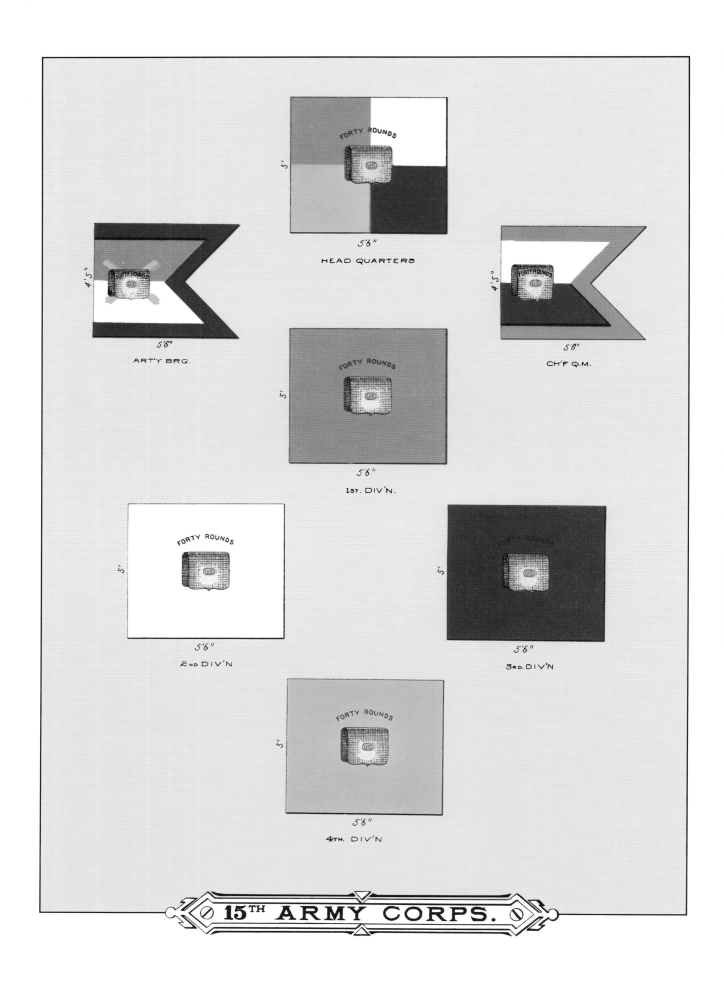

HEAD QUARTERS

ART'Y BRG.

CH'F Q.M.

1ST. DIV'N.

2ND DIV'N

3RD. DIV'N

4TH. DIV'N

15TH ARMY CORPS.

115

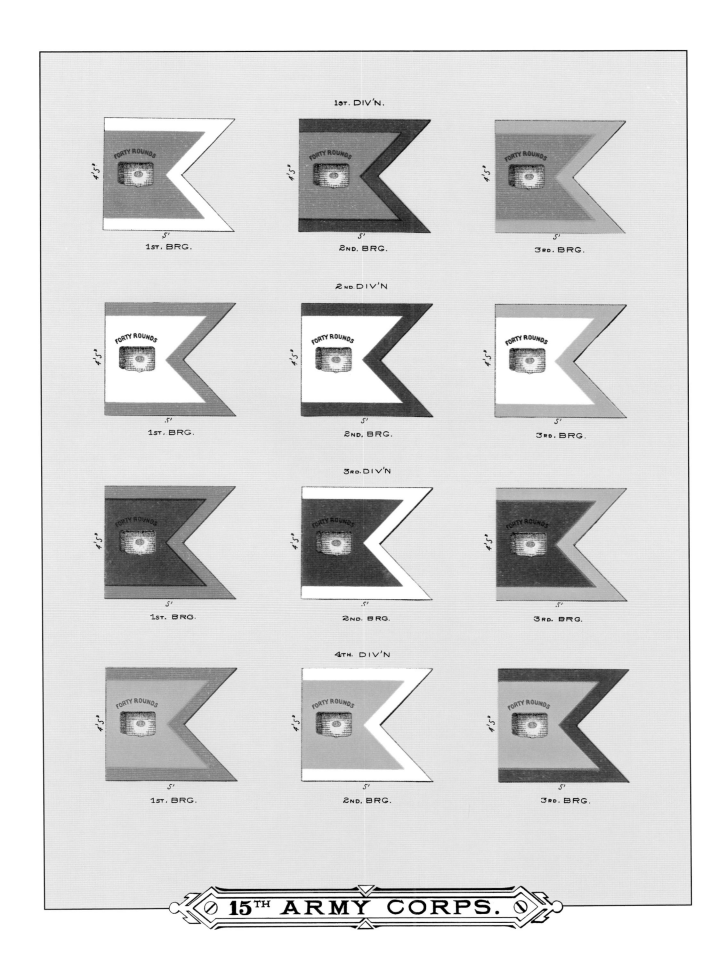

1ST. DIV'N.

1ST. BRG. 2ND. BRG. 3RD. BRG.

2ND. DIV'N

1ST. BRG. 2ND. BRG. 3RD. BRG.

3RD. DIV'N

1ST. BRG. 2ND. BRG. 3RD. BRG.

4TH. DIV'N

1ST. BRG. 2ND. BRG. 3RD. BRG.

15TH ARMY CORPS.

Created G. O. No. 210. A. G. O. December 18, 1862.   Discontinued G. O. No. 277. A. G. O. November 7, 1864.

COMMANDERS.

S. A. HURLBUT,   Major-G
This corps had no commande
N. J. T. DANA,   Major-G
A. J. SMITH,   "

LEFT WING.
Organized December, 1862.   Discontinued September, 1864.

COMMANDERS.		DATE.
C. S. Hamilton,	Major-General.	December, 1862.
R. J. Oglesby,	"	April, 1863.
G. M. Dodge,	Brigadier-General.	July 7, 1863, and October 15, 1863.
A. Mersey,	Col. 9th Ills. Vols.	August, 1863.
E. A. Carr,	Brigadier-General.	September 3, 1863.
T. E. G. Ransom,	"	August 19, 1864.

District of Corinth—Left Wing.
Denominated 2d Div., 16th Corps, March, 1863.
Again reported on return of 16th Corps, Dec., 1863.
Discontinued January 25, 1864.

COMMANDERS.		DATE.
G. M. Dodge,	Brig.-Genl.	Dec. 18, 1862.
J. D. Stevenson,	"	Dec., 1863.

District of Jackson – Left Wing.

Denominated 3d Div., 16th Corps, March, 1863.

COMMANDER.		DATE.
J. C. Sullivan,	Brig.-Genl.	January, 1863.

Fuller's Brigade—Left Wing.
Organized November, 1863; formerly 3d Brigade, 5th Division.
Designated 1st Brigade, 4th Division, March, 1864.

COMMANDERS.		DATE.
J.W. Fuller,	Col. 27th Ohio Vols.	Nov., 1863
"	" 27th "	Feb., 1864.
Wm. Feeney,	Capt. 27th "	Jan. 2, "

Cavalry Brigade—Left Wing.
Organized March, 1863.
Discontinued July, 1

COMMANDERS.		DAT
F. M. Cormyn,	Col.10th Mo. Cav.	Mar. 3,
Geo. A. Bacon,	" 15th Ills. "	July 13,

1st Brigade, Dist. of Corinth. Left Wing.

COMMANDER.		DATE.
T. W. Sweeney,	Brig.-Genl.	Dec., 1862.

2d Brigade, Dist. of Corinth. Left Wing.

COMMANDER.		DATE.
A. Mersey,	Col. 9th Ills. Vols.	Dec. 18, 1862.

3d Brigade, Dist. of Corinth. Left Wing.

COMMANDER.		DATE.
M. M. Bane,	Col. 50th Ills.Vols.	Dec. 18, 1862

1st Brig., Dist. of Jackson Left Wing.

Commander.		Date.
M. K. Lawler,	Brig.-Genl.	Jan., 1863.

3d Brig., Dist. of Jackson Left Wing.

Commander.		Date.
J. Richmond,	Col. 126th Ills. Vols.	Jan., 1863.

Cavalry Brigade, District of Jackson. Left Wing.

COMMANDER.		DATE.
J. K. Mizner,	Col. 3d Mich. Cav.	January, 1863.

2d Brig., Dist. of Jackson Left Wing.

Commander.		Date.
C. L. Dunham,	Col. 50th Ind. Vols.	Jan., 1863.

4th Brig., Dist. of Jackson Left Wing.

Commander.		Date.
O. Wood,	Col. 22d Ohio Vols.	Jan., 1863.

1st Division—16th Army Corps.
Transferred to 15th Corps, July, 1863.
Reorganized December, 1863.   Formerly 3d Div., 15th Corps.

COMMANDERS.		DATE.
J. W. Denver,	Brigadier-General.	December, 1862
"	"	February, 1863
John A. McDowell,	Col. 6th Iowa Vols.	January 19, 1863
W. S. Smith,	Brigadier-General.	March 22, "
J. M. Tuttle,	"	December, "
J. A. Mower,	"	March 7, 1864
J. J. Woods,	Col. 12th Iowa Vols.	October 19, "
John McArthur,	Brigadier-General.	November 3, "
"	"	February 18, 1865

2d Division—16th Army Corps.
Formerly District of Corinth.
Transferred to 15th Corps, September, 1864.

COMMANDERS.		DATE.
G. M. Dodge,	Brigadier-General.	March, 1863
A. Mersey,	Col. 9th Ills. Vols.	August, "
T. W. Sweeney,	Brigadier-General.	September 12, 1863
J. M. Corse,	"	July 26, 1864
K. Garrard,	"	February 18, 1865

1st Brigade—1st Division.
Organized March, 1863.

COMMANDERS.		DATE.
J. M. Loomis,	Col. 26th Ills. Vols.	March, 1863
R. P. Buckland,	Brigadier-General.	Dec , "
W. L. McMillan,	Col. 95th Ohio Vols.	Jan'y 26, 1864
"	" 95th "	Feb. 18, 1865

2d Brigade—1st Division.

COMMANDERS.		DATE
John A. McDowell,	Col 6th Iowa Vols.	Dec , 1862
C. C. Walcutt,	" 46th Ohio "	Jan., 1863
S. G Hicks,	" 40th Ills.	April, "
J. A. Mower,	Brigadier-General.	Dec., "
L. F. Hubbard,	Col. 5th Minn. Vols.	March 7, 1864
"	" 5th "	Aug 17, "
"	" 5th "	Feb. 18, 1865
Alex. Wilkin,	" 9th "	June 25, 1864
J. D. McClure,	" 47th Ills. Vols.	July 15, "

1st Brigade—2d Division.

COMMANDERS.		DATE.
T. W. Sweeney,	Brigadier-General.	March, 1863
E. W. Rice,	Col. 7th Iowa Vols.	July 20, "
"	" 7th "	Sept. 7, "
"	" 7th "	March 4, 1864
D. C. Anthony,	" 66th Ind.	Aug. 17, 1863
"	" 66th "	Jan. 1, 1864
J. B. Weaver,	" 2d Iowa	Dec. 15, 1863
J. I. Renaker,	" 122d Ills. "	Feb. 18, 1865
P. C. Smith,	Maj. 119th "	July 10, "

2d Brigade—2d Division.

COMMANDERS.		D
A. Mersey,	Col. 9th Ills. Vols.	March
"	" 9th " "	Sept.,
"	" 9th " "	May,
J. I. Renaker,	" 122d " "	Aug.,
P. E. Burke,	" 66th " "	April,
J. J. Phillips, Lt.-	" 9th " "	July
R. N. Adams,	" 81st Ohio " "	Aug.,
J. I. Gilbert,	" 27th Iowa " "	Feb.
J. Merriam, Lt.-	" 117th Ills. "	June

3d Brigade—1st Division.

COMMANDERS.		DATE.
J. R. Cockerell,	Col. 70th Ohio Vols.	Jan., 1863
J. L. Geddes,	" 8th Iowa "	Dec., "
S. G. Hill,	" 35th " "	Mar. 7, 1864
"	" 35th " "	Oct. 19, "
J. J. Woods,	" 12th " "	June 10, "
W. H. Heath, Lt.-	" 33d Mo. "	Feb. 18, 1865
Wm. A. Marshall,	" 7th Minn. "	Mar. 2, "

4th Brigade—1st Division.
Organized March, 1863.
Not reported in 1st Division subsequent to July, 1863.

COMMANDER.		DATE.
W. W. Sandford,	Col. 48th Ills. Vols.	March, 1863

3d Brigade—2d Division.

COMMANDERS.		DATE.
M. M. Bane,	Col. 50th Ills. Vols.	March, 1863
"	" 50th " "	Sept., "
"	" 50th " "	March, 1864
F. J. Hurlbut, Lt.-	" 57th " "	Aug. 25, 1863
M. Miller,	" 18th Mo. "	Jan. 18, 1864
Wm. Vandever,	Brigadier-General.	June, "
R. Rowett,	Col. 7th Ills. Vols.	Aug. 15, "
R. M. Moore,	" 117th " "	Feb. 18, 1865
C. L. Harris,	" 11th Mich. "	March 6, "

4th Brigade—2d Division.
Joined Div., March, 1863. Formerly 1st Brig.,
Transferred to 5th Div., 16th Corps, May, 1

COMMANDER.		D
J. W. Fuller,	Col. 27th Ohio Vols.	March

ARMY CORPS.

anized G. O. No. 20, Mil. Div. of West Miss., February 18, 1865.　　　Discontinued G. O. No. 124.　A. G. O. July 20, 1865.

DATE.
December 18, 1862.
17, 1864, to October 15, 1864.
October 15, 1864.
February 18, 1865.

RIGHT WING.
Organized June, 1864.　　　Designated Detachment of the Army of the Tennessee, December, 1864.

	COMMANDER.		DATE.
A. J. Smith,		Major-General.	June, 1864.

Brigade U. S. C. T.—Right Wing.

Organized June, 1864.　Formerly 1st Brigade U. S. C. T., District of Memphis.

Transferred to District of West Tennessee, August 27, 1864.

	COMMANDER.	DATE.
E. Bouton,	Col. 59th U. S. C. T.	June, 1864.

3d Division—16th Army Corps.
Formerly District of Jackson.　Transferred to Arkansas Expedition, August, 1863.
Reorganized January, 1864.　Formerly 6th Div., 16th Corps, or District of Columbus.

COMMANDERS.		DATE.	
N. Kimball,	Brigadier-General.	March,	1863
A. J. Smith,	"	January,	1864
D. Moore,	Col. 21st Mo. Vols.	May 30,	"
"	" 21st " "	October 29,	"
W. T. Shaw,	" 14th Iowa "	July 31,	"
J. B. Moore,	" 33d Wis. "	February 18, 1865
E. A. Carr,	Brigadier-General.	March 14,	"

4th Division—16th Army Corps.
Transferred to 13th Army Corps, July 28, 1863.　Reorganized January 24, 1864.
Transferred to 17th Army Corps, September, 1864.　Reorganized October, 1864.

COMMANDERS.		DATE.	
J. G. Lanman,	Brigadier-General.	December,	1862
J. C. Veatch,	"	January 24, 1864
J. W. Fuller,	"	July 16,	"
"	"	August 19,	"
T. E. G. Ransom,	"	August 2,	"
John P. Hawkins,	"	October,	"

1st Brigade—3d Division.

COMMANDERS.		DATE.	
an,	Brigadier-General.	March,	1863
man,	Col. 43d Ills. Vols.	May,	"
Graves,	" 12th Mich. "	July 12,	"
,	" 21st Mo. "	Jan. 24, 1864
,	" 21st " "	Sept. 14,	"
nch,	" 58th Ills. "	March 7,	"
rray,	" 89th Ind. "	May 31,	"
ney,	" 119th Ills. "	Oct. 29,	"
rd,	" 14th Wis. "	Feb. 18, 1865
re,	" 33d " "	March 17,	"

2d Brigade—3d Division.

COMMANDERS.		DATE.	
M. K. Lawler,	Col. 18th Ills. Vols.	March,	1863
J. Richmond,	" 126th " "	April,	"
W. T. Shaw,	" 14th Iowa "	Feb.,	1864
J. I. Gilbert,	" 27th " "	June 11,	"
"	" 27th " "	Oct.,	"
Jas. K. Mills,	" 24th Mo. "	Sept. 25,	"
L. Blanden,	" 95th Ills. "	Feb. 18, 1865
L. M. Ward,	" 14th Wis. "	March 15,	"

1st Brigade—4th Division.
Reorganized March, 1864.

COMMANDERS.		DATE.	
A. Brown,	Col. 3d Iowa Vols.	Jan.,	1863
I. C. Pugh,	" 41st Ills. "	Feb.,	"
J. W. Fuller,	" 27th Ohio "	March 10, 1864
H. T. McDowell,	" 39th " "	July 25,	"
V. E. Young,	" 49th U. S. C. T.	Oct.,	"

2d Brigade—4th Division.
Reorganized February, 1864.

COMMANDERS.		DATE.	
Cyrus Hall,	Col. 14th Ills. Vols.	Jan.	1863
"	" 14th " "	April,	"
Benj. Domblaser,	" 46th " "	March,	"
J. H. Howe,	" 32d Wis. "	Feb. 3, 1864
J. W. Sprague,	" 63d Ohio "	April,	"
Hiram Schofield,	" 47th U. S. C. T.	Oct.,	"

3d Brigade—3d Division.
anized S. O. No. 60, Mil. Div. West Miss.,
March 6, 1865.

COMMANDERS.		DATE.	
e,	Col. 62d Ills. Vols.	March	1863
lbert,	" 27th Iowa "	July 19,	"
olfe,	" 52d Ills. "	Jan.,	1864
,	" 52d " "	May 21,	"
oore,	" 117th " "	Feb. 28,	"
,	" 108th " "	March 6, 1865
,	" 108th " "	June,	"
les,	" 8th Iowa "	March 15,	"

Montgomery's Brigade—3d Division.
Transferred to Dist. of Eastern Arkansas, August, 1863.

COMMANDER.		DATE.
M. Montgomery,	Col. 25th Wis. Vols.	June 5, 1863

3d Brigade—4th Division.
Reorganized April, 1864.　Dropped from Div. Returns
May, 1864.　Taken up June, 1864.

COMMANDERS.		DATE.	
A. K. Johnson,	Col. 28th Ills. Vols.	Jan.,	1863
"	" 28th " "	May,	"
G. E. Bryant,	" 12th Wis. "	Feb.,	"
J. H. Howe,	" 32d " "	April 11, 1864
"	" 32d " "	June,	"
W. T. C. Grower,	" 17th N.Y. Vet.Vols	July 21,	"
John Tillson,	" 10th Ills. Vols.	Aug. 20,	"

"Detachment"—4th Division.
Transferred to Main Portion 4th Division, April, 1864.

COMMANDER.		DATE.
J. D. Stevenson,	Brigadier-General.	March, 1864

1st Brigade "Detachment"—4th Division.

COMMANDER.		DATE.
J. W. Fuller,	Col. 27th Ohio Vols.	March 10, 1864

2d Brigade "Detachment"—4th Division.

COMMANDER.		DATE.
J. W. Sprague,	Col. 63d Ohio Vols.	March 10, 1864

Cavalry Brigade—3d Division.
Formerly Cavalry Brigade, District of Jackson.　Transferred to 1st Cavalry Division, June, 1863.

COMMANDER.		DATE.
J. K. Mizner,	Col. 3d Mich. Cav.	March, 1863.

5th Division—16th Army Corps.

Discontinued January 25, 1864, and termed District of Memphis.

COMMANDER.		DATE.
J. C. Veatch,	Brigadier-General.	March 31, 1863

6th Division—16th Army Corps.

Changed to 3d Division, 16th Corps, January, 1864.

COMMANDERS.		DATE.
A. Asboth,	Brigadier-General.	March 31, 1863
A. J. Smith,	"	Aug. 5, "

8th D
Dis

COMMAND	
J. E. Smith, Brigadier-	

1st Brigade—5th Division.

COMMANDER.	DATE.
C. D. Murray, Col. 89th Ind. Vols.	March 31, 1863

2d Brigade—5th Division.

Transferred to Cavalry Division, Dec., 1863.

COMMANDERS.		DATE.
W. H. Morgan,	Col. 25th Ind. Vols.	March 31, 1863
"	" 25th " "	Aug., "
J. H. Howe,	" 32d Wis. "	July, "

1st Brigade—6th Division.

Organized July 14, 1863. Transferred to Cavalry Division, December, 1863.

COMMANDERS.		DATE.
Geo. E. Waring, Jr.,	Col. 4th Mo. Cav.	July, 1863
"	" 4th " "	Oct., "
C. H. Fox,	" 101st Ills. Vols.	Aug. 22, "
J. K. Mills,	" 24th Mo. "	Sept. 3, "

1st B
Transfer

COMMAND	
J. W. Fuller,	Col. 27th C

3d Brigade—5th Division.

Transferred to Left Wing, November, 1863.

COMMANDERS.		DATE.
Tho. Stephens,	Col. 2d Wis. Cav.	March 31, 1863
J. W. Fuller,	" 27th Ohio Vols.	May 1, "
"	" 27th " "	Aug., "
J. W. Sprague,	" 63d " "	July 25, "

4th Brigade Cavalry—5th Division.

COMMANDERS.		DATE.
L. F. McCrillis,	Col. 3d Ills. Cav.	March, 1863
J. F. Ritter,	" 1st Mo. "	March 31, "
David Moore,	" 21st " Vols.	May 16, "
"	" 21st " "	Sept. 6, "
T. J. Kinney,	" 119th Ills. "	Aug , "

2d B

COMMAND	
J. A. Mower,	Col. 11th

Gilbert's Brigade—5th Division.

Assigned to 5th Div., Nov. 22, 1863. Transferred to 3d Div., 16th Corps, and termed 2d Brig., 3d Div.

COMMANDER.		DATE.
J. I. Gilbert,	Col. 27th Iowa Vols.	January, 1864.

3d B
Di

COMMAND	
R. P. Buckland, Col. 72d	
J. W. Judy, " 114th	

District of Memphis.

Denominated 5th Divison, 16th Corps, March, 1863. Reorganized January 25, 1864.
Transferred to District of West Tennessee, June, 1864.

COMMANDERS.		DATE.
J. C. Veatch,	Brigadier-General.	Jan. 6, 1863
R. P. Buckland,	"	Jan. 25, "

District of Columbus.

Denominated 6th Division, 16th Corps, March, 1863.

COMMANDER.		DATE.
A. Asboth,	Brigadier-General.	January, 1863

District of
Joined from 13th Corps
Transferred to Department of

COMMANDERS.	
B. M. Prentiss,	Brigadier-G
M. Montgomery,	Col. 25th W
N. B. Buford,	Brigadier-G

1st Brigade, Colored—Dist. of Memphis.

Transferred to Right Wing, June, 1864.

COMMANDERS.		DATE.
J. M. Alexander, Col. 1st Ala. Col. Inf.		Jan. 30, 1864
E. Bouton,	" 59th U. S. C. T.	March 14, "

2d Brigade—District of Memphis.

Transferred to District of West Tennessee, June, 1864

COMMANDER.		DATE.
G. B. Hoge,	Col. 113th Ills. Vols.	Jan. 27, 1864

Arkansas Exp

Organized August, 1863. Tra

COMMANDER.	
F. Steel,	Major-

2d Division—Arkansas Expedition.

Organized August, 1863. Formerly 13th Division. Transferred to Department of Arkansas, January 6, 1864.

COMMANDERS.		DATE.
Wm. E. McLean,	Col. 43d Ind. Vols.	August, 1863.
Nathan Kimball,	Brigadier-General.	November, "
E. A. Carr,	"	" 30, "

1st Brigade—2d Division.
Arkansas Expedition.

Discontinued November, 1863.

COMMANDER.		DATE.
Wm. H. Graves,	Col. 12th Mich. Vols.	Sept., 1863

2d Brigade—2d Division.
Arkansas Expedition.

Transferred to Department of Arkansas, January 6, 1864.

COMMANDERS.		DATE.
Oliver Wood,	Col. 22d Ohio Vols.	Sept., 1863
A. Engelman,	" 43d Ills. "	Oct., "

3d Brigade—2d Division.
Arkansas Expedition

Organized November, 1863.
Transferred to Department of Arkansas, January

COMMANDER.	
Wm. H. Graves,	Col. 12th Mich. Vols. No

Cavalry Br

Organized August, 1863. Formerly Cavalry

COMMANDER.	
P. Clayton,	Col. 5th Ka

ORPS—Continued.

rmy Corps.	**13th Division—16th Army Corps.**		**1st Cavalry Division—16th Army Corps.**	
	Transferred to Arkansas Expedition, August, 1863.		Organized March, 1863. Transferred to District of West Tennessee, June, 1864.	

13th Division—16th Army Corps.

Transferred to Arkansas Expedition, August, 1863.

DATE.	COMMANDER.	DATE.
January, 1863	F. Salomon, Brigadier-General.	July 31, 1863

1st Cavalry Division—16th Army Corps.

Organized March, 1863. Transferred to District of West Tennessee, June, 1864.

COMMANDERS.		DATE.
C. C. Washburne,	Major-General.	March 31, 1863
J. K. Mizner,	Col. 3d Mich. Cav.	June, "
B. H. Grierson,	Brigadier-General.	July 24, "
"	"	Nov., "
"	"	May, 1864
E. Hatch,	Col. 2d Iowa Cav.	Sept. 24, 1863
Geo. W. Waring, Jr.,	" 4th Mo. "	April 27, 1864

1st Brigade—13th Division.

Transferred to Arkansas Expedition, August, 1863.

COMMANDERS.		DATE.
Wm. E. McLean,	Col. 43d Ind. Vols.	July 31, 1863
C. W. Kittridge,	" 36th Iowa "	Aug., "

1st Brigade—Cavalry Division.

COMMANDERS.		DATE.
B. H. Grierson,	Col. 6th Ills. Cav.	March 31, 1863
L. F. McCrillis,	" 3d " "	June, "
T. P. Herrick,	" 7th Kan. "	Aug. 29, "
T. S. Heath,	" 5th Ohio "	Sept., "
J. K. Mizner,	" 3d Mich. "	Oct., "
Geo. W. Waring, Jr.,	" 4th Mo. "	Jan. 7, 1864
"	" 4th " "	May, "
Joseph Karge,	" 2d N. J. "	April 27, 1864

2d Brigade—Cavalry Division.

Discontinued March, 1864. Reorganized April, 1864.

COMMANDERS.		DATE.
L. F. McCrillis,	Col. 3d Ills. Cav.	March 31, 1863
"	" 3d " "	Sept., "
E. Hatch,	" 2d Iowa "	June, "
"	" 2d " "	Nov. 17, "
F. Hurst,	" 6th Tenn. "	Aug., "
A. G. Brackett,	" 9th Ills. "	Jan., 1864
W. P. Hepburn, Lt.-	" 2d Iowa "	Feb. 7, "
E. F. Winslow,	" 4th " "	April, "

2d Brigade—13th Division.

Transferred to Arkansas Expedition, August, 1863.

DATE.	COMMANDER.	DATE.
January, 1863	S. A. Rice, Col. 33d Iowa Vols.	July 31, 1863

3d Brigade—1st Cavalry Division.

Discontinued November, 1863. Reorganized Dec., 1863 (formerly 2d Brig., 5th Div., 16th Corps.) Discontinued March, 1864. Reorganized May, 1864.

COMMANDERS.		DATE.
E. Hatch,	Col. 2d Iowa Cav.	Aug. 20, 1863
W. H. Morgan,	" 25th Ind. Vols.	Dec. 31, "
L. F. McCrillis,	" 3d Ills. Cav.	Jan. 4, 1864
Henry E. Burgh,	Lt.- " 9th " "	May, "

Cavalry Brigade—13th Division.

Designated Cavalry Brigade, Arkansas Expedition, August, 1863.

DATE.	COMMANDER.	DATE.
January, 1863	P. Clayton, Col. 5th Kans. Cav.	July 31, 1863
February, "		

Waring's Brigade—1st Cavalry Division.

Formerly 1st Brigade, 6th Division, 16th Corps. Discontinued January, 1864.

COMMANDER.		DATE.
Geo. E. Waring, Jr.,	Col. 4th Mo. Cav.	Dec. 31, 1863

as.	**District of Cairo.**		**Grierson's Cavalry Brigade.**	**Lee's Cavalry Brigade.**

District of Cairo.

Organized January, 1864. Transferred to District of West Tennessee, June, 1864.

DATE.	COMMANDERS.	DATE.
31, 1863	H. T. Reid, Brigadier-General.	Jan. 25, 1864
"	M. Brayman, "	March 19, "
19, "	H. Prince, "	April 24, "

Grierson's Cavalry Brigade.

Discontinued March, 1863, and termed 1st Brigade, 1st Cavalry Division.

COMMANDER.		DATE.
B. H. Grierson,	Col. 6th Ills. Cav.	February, 1863

Lee's Cavalry Brigade.

Discontinued March, 1863, and termed 2d Brigade, 1st Cavalry Division.

COMMANDER.		DATE.
A. C. Lee,	Col. 7th Kans. Cav.	January, 1863

Army Corps.

nt of Arkansas, January 6, 1864.

DATE.
August, 1863.

3d Division—Arkansas Expedition.

Organized August, 1863. Formerly 3d Division. Transferred to Department of Arkansas, January 6, 1864.

COMMANDERS.		DATE.
Nathan Kimball,	Brigadier-General.	August, 1863
Samuel A. Rice,	"	September, "
F. Salomon,	"	October 8, "

1st Brigade—3d Division.

Arkansas Expedition.

...rred to Department of Arkansas, January 6, 1864.

COMMANDERS.		DATE.
...ttridge,	Col. 36th Iowa Vols.	Sept., 1863
...cLean,	" 43d Ind. "	" 7, "

2d Brigade—3d Division.

Arkansas Expedition.

Transferred to Department of Arkansas, January 6, 1864.

COMMANDERS.		DATE.
T. H. Benton,	Col. 29th Iowa Vols.	Sept., 1863
S. A. Rice,	Brigadier-General.	Oct., "
Jas. M. Lewis,	Col. 28th Wis. Vols.	Nov., "

3d Brigade—3d Division.

Arkansas Expedition.

Organized August, 1863. Formerly 3d Brigade, 3d Division. Transferred to 2d Division, Arkansas Expedition.

COMMANDER.		DATE.
J. M. True,	Col. 62d Ills. Vols.	Aug., 1863

...sas Expedition.

...vision. Transferred to Department of Arkansas, January 6, 1864.

DATE.
August, 1863

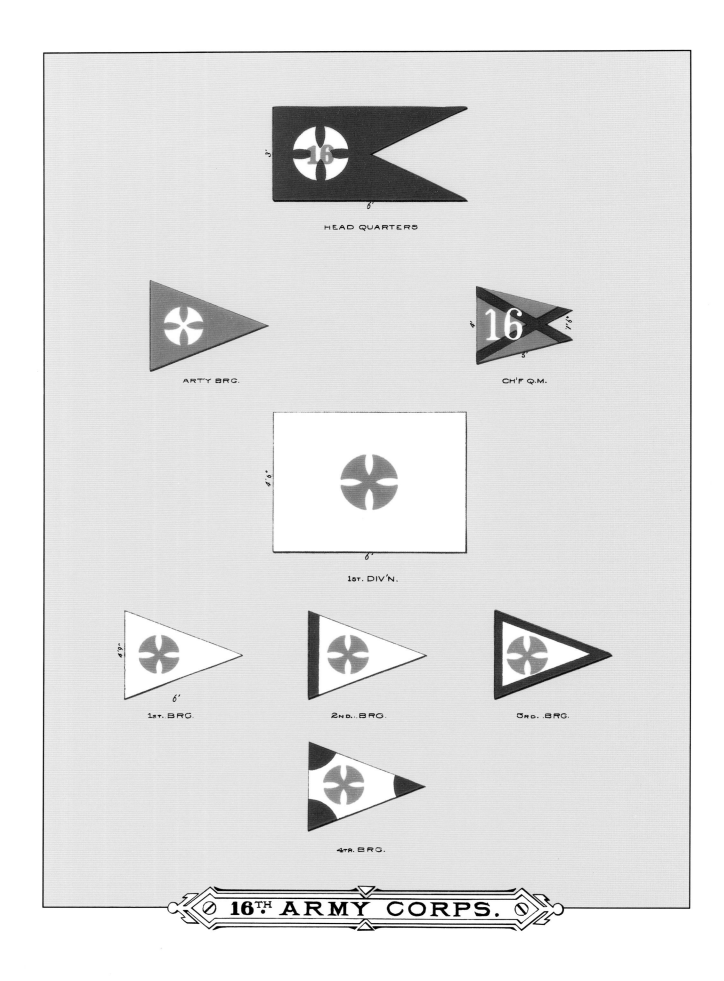

HEAD QUARTERS

ART'Y BRG.

CH'F Q.M.

1ST. DIV'N.

1ST. BRG.

2ND. BRG.

3RD. BRG.

4TH. BRG.

16TH ARMY CORPS.

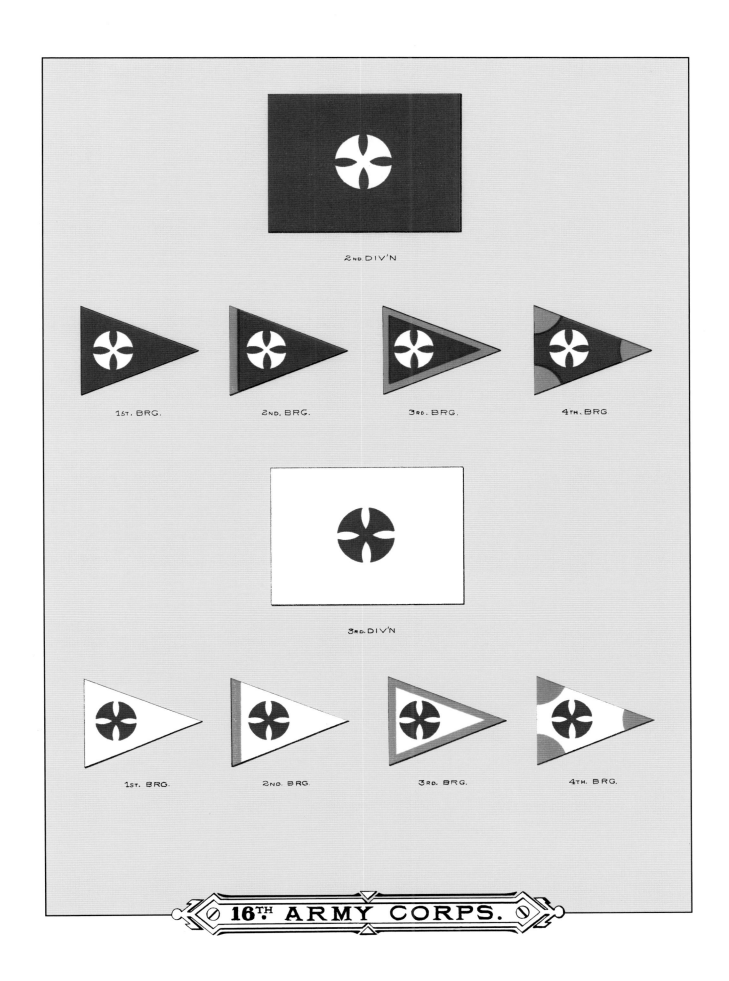

2ND DIV'N

1ST. BRG.   2ND. BRG.   3RD. BRG.   4TH. BRG

3RD. DIV'N

1ST. BRG.   2ND. BRG.   3RD. BRG.   4TH. BRG.

16TH ARMY CORPS.

Created G. O. No. 210.   A. G. O. December 18,

COMMANDERS.

J. B. McPHERSON,	Major-Gen
F. P. BLAIR, JR.,	"
T. E. G. RANSOM,	Brigadier-C
W. W. BELKNAP,	"

1st Division—17th Army Corps.

Organized September 14, 1863. (Formerly 6th Division, 17th Corps.) Discontinued September, 1864.
Reorganized September, 1864. (Formerly 4th Division, 16th Corps.)

COMMANDERS.   DATE.

A. Chambers,	Brigadier-General.	September, 1863
John McArthur,	"	" 28, "
E. S. Dennis,	"	October 23, "
T. E. G. Ransom,	"	September, 1864
J. W. Fuller,	"	" 22, "
J. W. Sprague,	"	October 23, "
J. A. Mower,	Major-General.	" 31, "
M. F. Force,	Brigadier-General.	April 3, 1865

2d D

Organized Septemb
Transfer

COMMANDER.

| J. F. Smith, | Brigadier |

1st Brigade—1st Division.

Organized October 28, 1863.

COMMANDERS.   DATE.

F. A. Starring,	Col. 72d Ills. Vols.	Oct. 29, 1863
"	" 72d " "	July, 1864
E. P. Jackson,	Lt.- " 58th Ohio "	June 20, "
H. T. McDowell,	" " 39th " "	Sept., "
C. S. Sheldon,	" " 18th Mo. "	Oct., "
"	" 18th " "	Dec. 24, "
"	" 18th " "	June 24, 1865
J. W. Fuller,	Brigadier-General.	Nov. 7, 1864
"	"	Jan. 17, 1865

2d Brigade—1st Division.

Organized September 14, 1863. (Formerly 2d Brigade, 6th Division.)
Discontinued June, 1865.

COMMANDERS.   DATE.

T. K. Smith,	Brigadier-General.	Sept. 27, 1863
T. W. Humphrey,	Col. 95th Ills. Vols.	Oct. 29, "
A. G. Malloy,	" 17th Wis. "	Nov. 15, "
J. H. Coates,	" 11th Ills.	March 10, 1864
B. Dornblaser,	" 46th " "	July, "
W. Swayne,	" 43d Ohio "	Sept., "
J. W. Sprague,	Brigadier-General.	Nov. 1, "
"	"	March, 1865
M. Montgomery,	Col. 25th Wis. Vols.	Jan. 30, "
"	" 25th " "	May, "

1st Brigade—2d Division.

Organized September 14, 1863. (Formerly 1st Brigade, 7th I

COMMANDER.

| J. I. Alexander, | Col. 59th Ills. Vols. | Sep |

3d Brigade—1st Division.

Organized September 14, 1863. (Formerly 3d Brigade, 6th Division.) Discontinued April, 1864.
Reorganized September, 1864. (Formerly 3d Brigade, 4th Division, 16th Corps.)

COMMANDERS.   DATE.

W. Hall,	Col. 11th Iowa Vols.	September, 1863
A. Chambers,	Brigadier-General.	October 10, "
J. Tillson,	Col. 10th Ills. Vols.	September, 1864
"	" 10th " "	April, 1865
H. D. Groat,	" 32d Wis. "	March 1, "

3d

Organized Septembe

COMMANDERS.

| C. L. Matthies, | Brigadie |
| J. Banbury, | Col. 5th |

4th Division—17th Army Corps.

Joined 17th Corps, August 7, 1863. (Formerly 4th Division, 13th Corps.)

COMMANDERS.   DATE.

M. M. Crocker,	Brigadier-General.	August, 1863
W. Q. Gresham,	"	May 27, 1864
G. A. Smith,	"	July 21, 1864, and October 31, 1864
W. W. Belknap,	"	Sept. 20, 1864, and May 29, and July 9, 1865
B. F. Potts,	"	June 26, 1865

6th D

Organized January 15, 1863.

COMMANDERS.

John McArthur,	Brigadier-G
A. Chambers,	Col. 16th Io
"	Brigadier-G
W. Hall,	Col. 11th Io

1st Brigade—4th Division.

Formerly 1st Brigade, 4th Division, 13th Corps.
Discontinued February, 1864. (Transferred to Red River Ex.)
Reorganized May, 1864.

COMMANDERS.   DATE.

I. C. Pugh,	Col. 14th Ills. Vols.	Aug., 1863
T. K. Smith,	Brigadier-General.	Oct. 24, "
W. L. Sanderson,	Col. 23d Ind. Vols.	May 26, 1864
B. F. Potts,	" 32d Ohio "	July 18, "
"	Brigadier-General.	" 9, 1865
J. J. Hibbetts,	Col. 32d Ohio Vols.	June 26, "

2d Brigade—4th Division.

Formerly 2d Brig., 4th Div., 13th Corps. Transferred to 1st Div., June 20, 1863.
Reorganized June, 1864. Discontinued November 6, 1864.
Reorganized April, 1865. Transferred from Corps, June 15, 1865.

COMMANDERS.   DATE.

C. Hall,	Col. 14th Ills. Vols.	Aug., 1863
B. Dornblaser,	" 46th " "	March 16, 1864
G. C. Rogers,	" 15th " "	June, "
I. C. Pugh,	" 44th " "	July 5, "
J. Logan,	" 32d " "	" 19, "
R. H. McFadden,	Maj. 41st " "	Oct. 1, "
C. J. Stolbrand,	Brigadier-General.	April 28, 1865

1st Brigade—6th Division.

Organized January 15, 1863.
Discontinued August, 1863.

COMMANDERS.

| G. W. Deitzler, | Brigadier-General. | Jan. |
| H. T. Reid, | " | April |

3d Brigade—4th Division.

Formerly 3d Brigade, 4th Division, 13th Corps.

COMMANDERS.   DATE.

W. Q. Gresham,	Brigadier-General.	August 26, 1863
Wm. Hall,	Col. 11th Iowa Vols.	May 23, 1864
W. W. Belknap,	Brigadier-General.	August 1, "
"	"	October 31, "
J. C. Abercrombie,	Lt.-Col. 11th Iowa Vols.	September 21, "
G. Pomutz,	Maj. 15th " "	October 23, "
B. Beach,	Lt.-Col. 11th " "	May 30, 1865
A. Hickenlooper,	Bvt. Brigadier-General.	June 16, "

3d B

Organized January 15, 1863.

COMMANDERS.

M. M. Crocker,	Brigadier-G
W. Hall,	Col. 11th Io
"	" 11th
A. Chambers,	" 16th
"	" 16th

ARMY CORPS.

inued G. O. No. 131.   A. G. O. August 1, 1865.

DATE.
January 11, 1863.
May 5, 1864, and October, 1864.
September 22, 1864.
July, 1865.

---

ny Corps.

th Division, 17th Corps.)
mber 20, 1863.

DATE.
September 14, 1863

3d Division—17th Army Corps.

COMMANDERS.		DATE.
John A. Logan,	Major-General.	December, 1862, and September, 1863
J. D. Stevenson,	Brigadier-General.	July, 1863
M. D. Leggett,	"	Nov., 1863; April and Sept., 1864, and April 3, 1865
Jasper A. Maltby,	"	March, 1864
C. R. Woods,	"	August 22, 1864
M. F. Force.	"	January 15, 1865

2d Brigade—2d Division.

nized September 14, 1863. (Formerly 2d Brigade, 7th Division.)

COMMANDERS.		DATE.
ver,	Col. 17th Iowa Vols.	Sept. 14, 1863
	" 17th " "	Nov. 25, "
m,	" 56th Ills. "	Oct., "

1st Brigade—3d Division.

COMMANDERS.		DATE.
I. N. Haynie,	Brigadier-General.	Jan. 25, 1863
C. C. Marsh,	Col. 20th Ills. Vols.	March 20, "
J. E. Smith,	Brigadier-General.	April 24, "
M. D. Leggett,	"	June 3, "
M. F. Force,	"	Nov., "
"	"	May, 1864
"	"	Oct., "
A. Mann,	Maj. 124th Ills. Vols.	March, "
G. E. Bryant,	Col. 12th Wis. "	July 22, "
C. Fairchild,	" 16th " "	Jan. 15, 1865
C. Ewing,	Brigadier-General.	April 4, "

2d Brigade—3d Division.

COMMANDERS.		DATE.
M. D. Leggett,	Brigadier-General.	Dec., 1862
"	"	May, 1863
E. S. Dennis,	"	April 11, "
M. F. Force,	Col. 20th Ohio Vols.	June 3, "
B. F. Potts,	" 32d " "	Nov. 17, "
R. K. Scott,	" 68th " "	March 6, 1864
"	" 68th " "	Sept. 30, "
"	" 68th " "	March 28, 1865
G. F. Wiles,	Lt.- " 78th " "	July 22, 1864
"	" 78th " "	Dec. 27, "

3d Brigade—3d Division.

Discontinued November, 1864.

COMMANDERS.		DATE.
J. D. Stevenson,	Brigadier-General.	December, 1862
F. Campbell,	Col. 81st Ills. Vols.	July, 1863
J. A. Maltby,	Brigadier-General.	September 8, "
A. G. Malloy,	Col. 17th Wis. Vols.	May, 1864
A. Worden,	Maj. 14th " "	September 12, "
D. D. Scott,	Lt.-Col. 17th " "	October, "

---

my Corps.

ion, 17th Corps, September 14, 1863.

DATE.
January 15, 1863
July 30, "
September 3, "
August 23, "

7th Division—17th Army Corps.

Organized January 15, 1863. Changed to 2d Division, 17th Corps, September 14, 1863.

COMMANDERS.		DATE.
I. F. Quinby,	Brigadier-General.	January 15, 1863
"	"	May 16, "
J. B. Sanborn,	Col. 4th Minn. Vols.	April 12, "
J. E. Smith,	Brigadier-General.	June 3, "

2d Brigade—6th Division.

Organized January 15, 1863.
Changed to 2d Brigade, 1st Division, September 14, 1863.

COMMANDER.		DATE.
Ransom,	Brigadier-General.	Jan. 15, 1863

1st Brigade—7th Division.

Organized January 15, 1863.
Changed to 1st Brigade, 2d Division, September 14, 1863.

COMMANDERS.		DATE.
N. Eddy,	Col. 48th Ind. Vols.	Jan. 15, 1863
J. B. Sanborn,	" 4th Minn. "	Feb.
"	" 4th " "	May 2, "
J. I. Alexander,	" 59th Ind. "	April 12, "
J. Isaminger,	Lt - " 63d Ills. "	Aug. 21, "

2d Brigade—7th Division.

Organized January 15, 1863.
Changed to 2d Brigade, 2d Division, September 14, 1863.

COMMANDERS.		DATE.
E. R. Eckley,	Col. 8th Ohio Vols.	Jan. 15, 1863
S. A. Holmes,	" 10th Mo. "	Feb., "
G. B. Raum,	" 56th Ills. "	June, "
C. R. Wever,	" 17th Iowa "	Aug., "

3d Brigade—7th Division.

Organized January 15, 1863. Changed to 3d Brigade, 2d Division, September 14, 1863.

COMMANDERS.		DATE.
C. L. Matthies,	Brigadier-General.	January 15, 1863
"	"	June 2, "
"	"	August 28, "
G. B. Boomer,	Col. 26th Mo. Vols.	February, "
H. Putnam,	" 93d " "	May 22, "
B. D. Dean,	" 26th " "	July 27, "

---

vision.

de, 1st Division, September 14, 1863.

DATE.
January 15, 1863
May 1, "
July 30, "
June 6, "
August 21, "

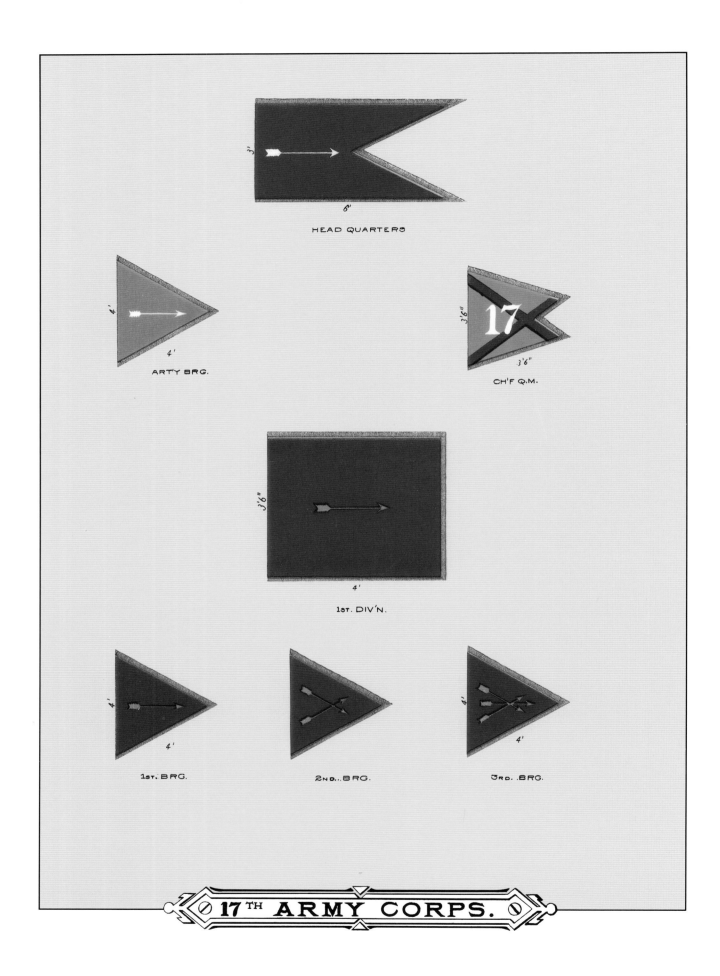

HEAD QUARTERS

ART'Y BRG.

CH'F Q.M.

1st. DIV'N.

1st. BRG.

2nd. BRG.

3rd. BRG.

17TH ARMY CORPS.

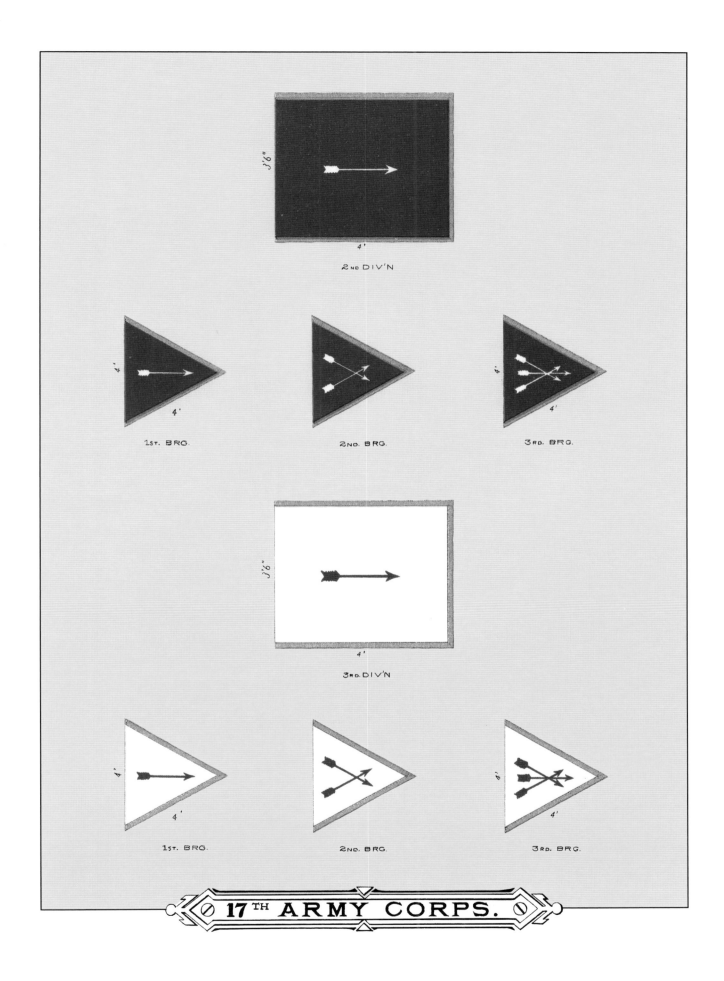

2ND DIV'N

1ST. BRG.

2ND. BRG.

3RD. BRG.

3RD. DIV'N

1ST. BRG.

2ND. BRG.

3RD. BRG.

17TH ARMY CORPS.

Created G. O. No. 214.   A. G. O. December 24, 1862.   Reor

COMMANDERS.

J. G. FOSTER,	Major-General
I. N. PALMER,	Brigadier-Gen
B. F. BUTLER,	Major-General
WM. F. SMITH,	"
J. H. MARTINDALE,	Brigadier-Gen
E. O. C. ORD,	Major-General
JOHN GIBBON,	"
G. WEITZEL,	Bvt. Major-Ge

1st Division—18th Army Corps.

Discontinued July, 1863.   Reorganized April, 1864.

COMMANDERS.		DATE.
I. N. Palmer,	Brigadier-General.	January 30, 1863
T. J. C. Amory,	Col. 17th Mass.Vols.	May 23, 1863
W. T. H. Brooks,	Brigadier-General.	April, 1864
Geo. J. Stannard,	"	June 20, and Sept. 15, 1864
H. Burnham,	"	July 31, 1864
J. B. Carr,	"	August 3, 1864
G. Marston,	"	September, 1864
C. Devens, Jr.,	"	October 29, 1864

2d Division—18th Army Corps.

Changed to District of Beaufort, May, 1863.   Reorganized April, 1864.

COMMANDERS.		DATE.
H. M. Naglee,	Brigadier-General.	January 2, and April
C. A. Heckman,	"	March 6, 1863
"	"	September 17, 1864
I. J. Wistar,	"	April 22, 1864
G. Weitzel,	"	May 7, 1864
J. H. Martindale,	"	" 20, 1864
A. Ames,	"	July 10, 1864

1st Brigade—1st Division.

COMMANDERS.		DATE.
T. J. C. Amory,	Col. 17th Mass.Vols.	Dec., 1862
C. L. Holbrook,	" 43d " "	May, 1863
L. Day,	Capt.17th " "	June, "
J. J. DeForrest,	Col. 81st N.Y. "	April, 1864
G. Marston,	Brigadier-General.	May 1, "
E. M. Cullen,	Col. 96th N. Y. Vols.	June, "
A. F. Stevens,	" 13th N. H. "	July, "
J. B. Raulston,	Lt.- " 81st N. Y. "	Sept. 29, "

2d Brigade—1st Division.

COMMANDERS.		DATE.
H. C. Lee,	Col. 27th Mass.Vols.	Dec., 1862
"	" 27th " "	June 7, 1863
G. N. Pierson,	" 5th " Mil.	May 12, "
H. Burnham,	Brigadier-General.	April, 1864
"	"	Sept. 27, "
E. M. Cullen,	Col. 96th N..Y. Vols.	July 31, "
"	" 96th " "	Sept. 29, "

1st Brigade—2d Division.

Formed part of District of Beaufort, May, 1863.

COMMANDERS.		DATE.
C. A. Heckman,	Brigadier-General.	Jan., 1863
"	"	April, "
"	"	" 26, 1864
J. J. DeForrest,	Col. 81st N. Y. Vols.	March 6, 1863
G. J. Stannard,	Brigadier-General.	May 17, 1864
Alex. Piper,	Col. 10th N. H. Hy. Art.	June 24, "
Jas. Stewart, Jr.,	Col. 9th N. J.Vols.	July 24, "
G. M. Guion,	" 148th N. Y. "	Sept. 30, "
W. H. McNary,	Lt.- " 158th " "	Oct. 17, "
J. Jourdan,	" 158th " "	Nov., "

2d Brigade—2d Division.

Transferred to Department of the South, Ap

COMMANDERS.		
W. W. H. Davis,	Col. 104th Pa. Vols.	Jan.
G. A. Stedman, Jr.,	" 11th Conn. "	Apr
"	" 11th " "	May
I. J. Wistar,	Brigadier-General.	May
G. M. Guion,	Col. 148th N.Y.Vols.	Aug
E. H. Ripley,	" 9th Vt. "	Sep

3d Brigade—1st Division.

Organized April, 1864.

COMMANDERS.		DATE.
H. T. Sanders,	Col. 19th Wis. Vols.	April, 1864
G. V. Henry,	" 40th Mass. "	May 31, "
"	" 40th " "	October 30, "
S. K. Brown,	Lt.- " 188th Pa. "	August 12, "
S. H. Roberts,	" 139th N. Y. "	" 20, "

3d Brigade—2d Division.

Organized June, 1864.

COMMANDERS.		DATE.
A. Ames,	Brigadier-General.	June 20, 1864
H. S. Fairchild,	Col. 89th N. Y. Vols.	July 11, "

5th

Termed Dis

COMMANDER.

Henry Prince,	Brigadie	

1st Brigade—5th Division

COMMANDER.

F. B. Spinola,	Brigadier-General.	Jan

Defences of New Berne, N. C.

Organized July, 1863.
Designated "Defences of New Berne," District of N. C., August, 1863.

COMMANDER.		DATE.
C. A. Heckman,	Brigadier-General.	July, 1863

District of Beaufort, N. C.

Organized May, 1863.   (Formerly 2d Division, 18th Corps.)
Designated Sub-District of Beaufort, District of N. C., August, 1863.

COMMANDERS.		DATE.
C. A. Heckman,	Brigadier-General.	May and June, 1863
F. B. Spinola,	"	May 31, 1863
T. J. C. Amory,	Col. 17th Mass. Vols.	July 21, 1863

COMM
H. M. Na

1st Brigade—
Defences of New Berne, N. C.

Organized July, 1863.
Discontinued August, 1863.

COMMANDER.		DATE
A. Zabriski,	Col. 9th N. J. Vols.	July, 1863

2d Brigade—
Defences of New Berne, N. C.

Organized July, 1863.
Discontinued August, 1863.

COMMANDER.		DATE.
James Jourdan,	Col. 158th N.Y.Vols.	July, 1863

1st Brigade—
District of Beaufort, N. C.

Organized May, 1863.   Discontinued July, 1863.

COMMANDERS.		DATE.
J. J. DeForrest,	Col. 81st N. Y. Vols.	May, 1863
C. A. Heckman,	Brigadier-General.	" "

Cavalry Brigade—Defences of New Berne, N. C.

Organized July, 1863.   Discontinued August, 1863.

COMMANDER.		DATE.
S. H. Mix,	Col. 3d N. Y. Cav.	July, 1863

ARMY CORPS.

864.   Discontinued G. O. No. 297. A. G. O. December 3, 1864.

DATE.
December 24, 1862, and August, 1863.
July, 1863.
October 28, 1863.
May 2, 1864.
July 19, 1864.
July 21, 1864, and September 22, 1864.
September 4, 1864.
October, 1864.

3d Division—18th Army Corps.

Transferred to Department of the South, May, 1863.
Reorganized June, 1864. (Formerly Hinks' Division, U. S. C. T.)

COMMANDERS.		DATE.
S. Ferry,	Brigadier-General.	January, 1863
W. Hinks,	"	June, 1864
H. Holman,	Col. 1st U. S. C. T.	July 1, and October 14, 1864
B. Carr,	Brigadier-General.	July 29, 1864
J. Paine,	"	August 3, and Nov. 3, 1864
G. Draper,	Col. 36th U. S. C. T.	October 28, 1864

4th Division—18th Army Corps.

Termed District of the Albemarle, May, 1863.

COMMANDERS.		DATE.
H. W. Wessells,	Brigadier-General.	January, 1863
"	"	April, "
T. F. Lehmann,	Col. 103d Pa. Vols.	March 14, "

1st Brigade—3d Division.

COMMANDERS.		DATE.
...ell,	Col. 85th Pa. Vols.	Jan. 12, 1863
...man,	" 1st U.S.C.T.	June 23, 1864
	" 1st " "	Aug. 5, "
...l,	" 1st " "Cav.	July 2, "
...nberlin,Lt.-	" 37th " "	Oct., "
	" 10th " "	Nov., "

2d Brigade—3d Division.

COMMANDERS.		DATE.
T. O. Osborne,	Col. 39th Ills. Vols.	Jan., 1863
S. A. Duncan,	" 4th U. S. C. T.	June, 1864
A. G. Draper,	" 36th " "	Aug. 22, "
	" 36th " "	Nov., "
J. W. Ames,	" 6th " "	Sept., "
D. E. Clapp,	Lt.- " 38th " "	Oct. 27, "

1st Brigade—4th Division.

Termed 1st Brigade, District of the Albemarle, May, 1863.

COMMANDERS.		DATE.
L. C. Hunt,	Brigadier-General.	January, 1863
"	"	April, . "
J. S. Belknap,	Col. 85th N. Y. Vols.	March, "

3d Brigade—3d Division.

Organized August, 1864.

COMMANDERS.		DATE.
S. A. Duncan,	Col. 4th U. S. C. T.	August, 1864
J. W. Ames,	" 6th " "	October 17, "

2d Brigade—4th Division.

Transferred to Department of the South, May, 1863.

COMMANDER.		DATE.
T. G. Stevenson,	Brigadier-General.	January, 1863

...rmy Corps.

April 22, 1863.

DATE.
January 11, 1863

2d Brigade—5th Division.

...d Jourdan's Brigade, 18th Corps, April, 1863.

COMMANDER.		DATE.
...rdan,	Col. 158th N.Y.Vols.	Jan. 11, 1863

...t of Virginia.

...63. (Formerly 7th Corps.)
...ed September 23, 1863.

		DATE.
...lier-General.		August, 1863

District of the Albemarle.

Organized May 3, 1863. (Formerly 4th Division, 18th Corps.)
Designated Sub-District of the Albemarle, District of N. C., August, 1863.

COMMANDER.		DATE.
H. W. Wessells,	Brigadier-General.	May 3, 1863

District of the Pamlico.

Organized April 22, 1863. Formerly 5th Division, 18th Corps.)
Designated Sub-District of the Pamlico, District of N. C., August, 1863.

COMMANDERS.		DATE.
Henry Prince,	Brigadier-General.	April 27, 1863
J. M. McChesney,	Lt.-Col. 1st N. C. Vols.	June, "
O. Moulton,	" " 25th Mass. "	July 26, "

1st Brigade—
District of the Albemarle.

Organized May 3, 1863. (Formerly 1st Brigade, 4th Division, 18th Corps.)
Designated 1st Brigade, Sub-Dist. of the Albemarle, Dist. of N. C., August, 1863.

COMMANDER.		DATE.
T. F. Lehmann,	Col. 103d Pa. Vols.	May, 1863

1st Brigade—
District of the Pamlico.

Organized April 22, 1863. (Formerly 1st Brigade, 5th Division, 18th Corps.)
Transferred to Department of Virginia, June, 1863.

COMMANDERS.		DATE.
F. B. Spinola,	Brigadier-General.	April, 1863
D. B. McKibben,	Col. 158th Pa. Vols.	May 27, "

DISTRICT OF

Organized August, 1863. Discontinued A

COMMANDERS.

JOHN J. PECK,   Major-Gener
I. N. PALMER,   Brigadier-Ge

Defences of New Berne—District of North Carolina.

Organized August, 1863. (Formerly Defences of New Berne, 18th Corps.)
Transferred to Department of Va. and N. C., April, 1864.

COMMANDERS.		DATE.
I. N. Palmer,	Brigadier-General.	August 14, 1863
"	"	November, "
T. J. C. Amory,	Col. 17th Mass. Vols.	October 7, "

Sub-District of the Albemarle—District of North Carolina.

Organized August, 1863. (Formerly District of the Albemarle, 18th Corps.)
Discontinued April, 1864. (Transferred to Department of Va. and N. C.)

COMMANDER.		DATE.
H. W. Wessells,	Brigadier General.	August, 186

1st Brigade—Sub-District of the Albemarle.

Discontinued September, 1863. Reorganized January, 1864.
Discontinued April, 1864. (Transferred to Department of Va. and N. C.)

COMMANDERS.		DATE.
T. F. Lehmann,	Col. 103d Pa. Vols.	August, 1863
F. Beach,	" 6th Conn. Vols.	January, 1864

Getty's Division.

Organized August, 1863. (Formerly Getty's Division, 7th Corps.)
Discontinued April, 1864.

COMMANDERS.		DATE.
G. W. Getty,	Brigadier-General.	August, 1863
C. A. Heckman,	"	January 14, 1864

Hinks' Division—U. S. C. T.

Organized April, 1864.
Termed 3d Division, 18th Corps, June, 1864.

COMMANDER.		DATE.
E. W. Hinks,	Brigadier-General.	April, 186

1st Brigade— Getty's Division.

Transferred to 10th Corps, August, 1863.
Reorganized March 1864. (Formerly Dept. of the Currituck.)
Discontinued April, 1864.

COMMANDERS.		DATE.
S. M. Alford,	Col. 3d N.Y.Vols.	Aug. 1863
S. H. Roberts,	" 139th " "	March, 1864

2d Brigade— Getty's Division.

Discontinued January, 1864.
Reorganized March, 1864.
Discontinued April, 1864.

COMMANDERS.		DATE.
Edw. Harland,	Brigadier-General.	Aug., 1863
Frank Beach,	Col. 16th Conn.Vols.	Dec., "
H. C. Lee,	" 27th Mass. "	March, 1864

1st Brigade—Hinks' Division— U. S. C. T.

COMMANDER.		DATE.
E. A. Wild,	Brigadier-General.	April, 1864

3d Brigade—Getty's Division.

Discontinued April, 1864.

COMMANDER.		DATE.
W. H. P. Steere,	Col. 4th R. I. Vols.	Aug., 1863

Cavalry Brigade—Getty's Division.

Organized February, 1864.
Discontinued April, 1864.

COMMANDER.		DATE.
N. B. Lord.	Col. 20th N.Y. Cav.	Feb., 1864

2d Brigade—Hinks' Division—U. S. C. T.

COMMANDER.		DATE.
S. A. Duncan,	Col. 4th U. S. C. T.	April, 1864

District of the Currituck.

Organized December, 1863. Designated 1st Brigade, Getty's Division, March, 1864.

COMMANDERS.		DATE.
Jas. H. Ledlie,	Brigadier-General.	December 11, 1863
S. H. Roberts,	Col. 139th N. Y. Vols.	February, 1864

Lee's Brigade—18th Army Corps.

Organized May, 1863. Discontinued June, 1863.

COMMANDER.		DATE.
F. C. Lee,	Col. 44th Mass. Vols.	May 31, 1863

Cavalry Brigade—18th Army Corps.

Organized May, 1863.
Transferred to " Defences of New Berne, N. C.," July, 1863.

COMMANDERS.		DATE.
S. H. Mix,	Col. 3d N. Y. Cav.	May 31, 1863
G. W. Lewis,	Lt.- " 3d " "	June, "

Jourdan's

Organized
Transferred to " I

COMMAND	
James Jourdan,	Col. 158th I

CAROLINA.

(...rred to Department of Va. and N. C.)

DATE.
August 14, 1863, and February 4, 1864.
January, 1864.

Sub-District of Beaufort—District of North Carolina.

Organized August, 1863. (Formerly District of Beaufort, 18th Corps.)
Discontinued April, 1864. (Transferred to Department of Va. and N. C.)

COMMANDERS.		DATE.
C. A. Heckman,	Brigadier-General.	August 14, 1863
...as. Jourdan,	Col. 158th N. Y. Vols.	October 11, "

Sub-District of the Pamlico—District of North Carolina.

Organized August, 1863. (Formerly District of the Pamlico, 18th Corps.)
Discontinued April, 1864. (Transferred to Department of Va. and N. C.)

COMMANDERS.		DATE.
O. Moulton,	Lt.-Col. 25th Mass. Vols.	August, 1863
J. Pickett,	" 25th " "	September 8, "
J. M. McChesney,	" 1st N. C. "	November 28, "
E. Harland,	Brigadier-General.	March 13, 1864

U. S. Forces—Yorktown and Vicinity.

Organized August, 1863. Discontinued April, 1864.

COMMANDERS.		DATE.
... J. Wistar,	Brigadier-General.	August, 1863
"	"	January 30, 1864
"	"	March 8, "
R. M. West,	Col. 1st Pa. Lt. Art.	December, 1863
"	" 1st " "	February 16, 1864

U. S. Forces—Norfolk and Portsmouth.

Organized September, 1863. Discontinued April, 1864.

COMMANDERS.		DATE.
E. E. Potter,	Brigadier-General.	September 23, 1863
James Barnes,	"	October 1, "
E. A. Wild,	"	January 18, 1864

...gade—U. S. Forces— Yorktown and Vicinity.

Organized January 22, 1864.
Discontinued February, 1864.

COMMANDER.		DATE.
...st,	Col. 1st Pa. Lt. Art.	Jan. 22, 1864

2d Brigade—U. S. Forces— Yorktown and Vicinity.

Organized January 20, 1864.
Discontinued April, 1864.

COMMANDER.		DATE.
S. A. Duncan,	Col. 4th U. S. C. T.	Jan. 20, 1864

Brigade U. S. C. T.—U. S. Forces— Norfolk and Portsmouth.

Organized November, 1863. Discontinued April, 1864.

COMMANDERS.		DATE.
E. A. Wild,	Brigadier-General.	November 2, 1863
J. H. Holman,	Col. 1st U. S. C. T.	January 19, 1864
A. G. Chamberlin,	Lt.- " 37th " "	February, "

Cavalry Brigade—U. S. Forces—Yorktown and Vicinity.

Organized January 25, 1864. Discontinued April, 1864.

COMMANDER.		DATE.
S. P. Spear,	Col. 11th Pa. Cav.	January 25, 1864

District of Saint Mary's, Md.

Organized December, 1863. Discontinued April, 1864.

COMMANDER.		DATE.
...G. Martin,	Brigadier-General.	December, 1863

...rmy Corps.

(... 2d Brigade, 5th Division.)
...ne, N. C., July, 1863.

	DATE.
	April, 1863

Heckman's Brigade—18th Army Corps.

Organized October, 1863. Discontinued February, 1864.

COMMANDERS.		DATE.
C. A. Heckman,	Brigadier-General.	October, 1863
A. H. Dutton,	Col. 21st Conn. Vols.	January, 1864

Provisional Brigade—18th Army Corps.

Organized October, 1864.

COMMANDER.		DATE.
E. Martindale,	Col. 81st U. S. C. T.	October, 1864

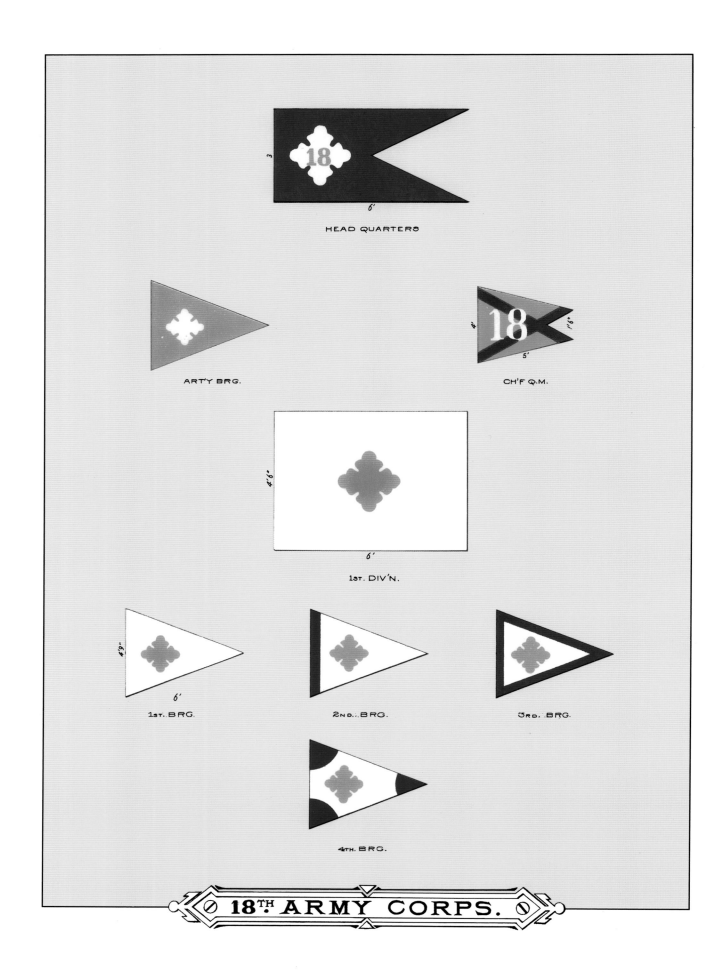

HEAD QUARTERS

ART'Y BRG.

CH'F Q.M.

1ST. DIV'N.

1ST. BRG.

2ND. BRG.

3RD. BRG.

4TH. BRG.

18TH ARMY CORPS.

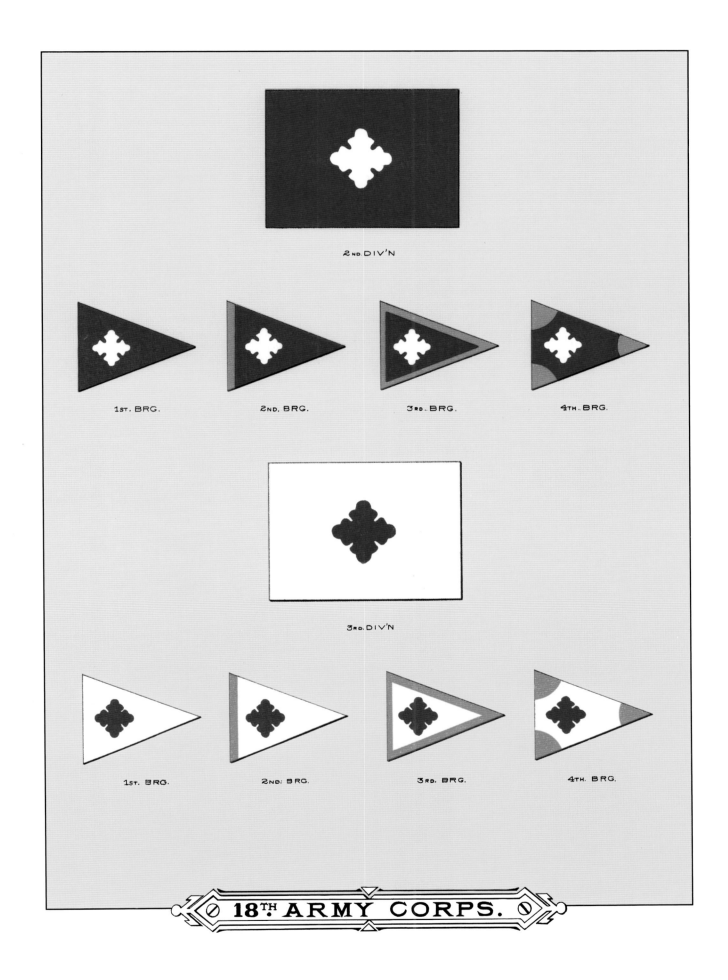

2ND. DIV'N

1ST. BRG.   2ND. BRG.   3RD. BRG.   4TH. BRG.

3RD. DIV'N

1ST. BRG.   2ND. BRG.   3RD. BRG.   4TH. BRG.

18TH ARMY CORPS.

Created G. O. No. 5.   A. G. O. January 5, 1863, to date from De⸢

COMMANDERS.

N. P. BANKS,	Major-Genera⸢
WM. B. FRANKLIN,	"
WM. H. EMORY,	Brigadier-Ger⸢
"	Bvt. Major-G⸢
J. J. REYNOLDS,	Major-Genera⸢
C. GROVER,	Brigadier-Gen⸢

U. S. Forces—Baton Rouge, La.

Organized December, 1862. Discontinued March, 1863.

COMMANDERS.		DATE.
C. Grover,	Brigadier-General.	December 17, 1862
"	"	February, 1863
C. C. Augur,	Major-General.	June 20, "

U. S. Forces—Carrollton, La.

Organized December, 1862.
Transferred to Defences of New Orleans, La., January, 1863.

COMMANDER.		DATE.
T. W. Sherman,	Brigadier-General.	December, 1862

Defences ⸢

Transferred to De⸢

COMMANDERS.	
T. W. Cahill,	Col. 9th Co⸢
T. W. Sherman,	Brigadier-G⸢
W. H. Emory,	"

1st Division—19th Army Corps.

COMMANDERS.		DATE.
C. C. Augur,	Major-General.	January, 1863
G. Weitzel,	Brigadier-General.	July, "
Wm. H. Emory,	"	December 13, "
Jas. W. McMillan,	"	May 2, 1864
"	"	January, 1865
B. S. Roberts,	"	June 25, 1864
Wm. Dwight,	"	July 1, "
"	"	March, 1865
Jas. D. Fessenden,	"	February, "

2d Division—19th Army Corps.

Discontinued (except 2d Brigade) July, 1863. Reorganized February 15, 1864.

COMMANDERS.		DATE.
T. W. Sherman,	Brigadier-General.	January, 1863
Wm. Dwight,	"	June, "
C. Grover,	"	February 15, 1864
"	"	November 10, "
"	"	December 28, "
H. W. Birge,	"	October 19, "
"	"	December, "
"	"	February 12, 1865

1st Brigade—1st Division.

Organized February, 1863.

COMMANDERS.		DATE.
Edwin P. Chapin,	Col. 116th N.Y.Vols.	Feb. 9, 1863
C. J. Paine,	" 2d La. "	June, "
Geo. M. Love,	" 116th N.Y. "	July 24, "
"	" 116th " "	Feb., 1864
"	" 116th " "	Oct. 30, "
Wm. Dwight,	Brigadier-General.	Feb. 20, "
"	"	March, "
Geo. L. Beale,	Col. 29th Me. Vols.	April 18, "
"	" 29th " "	Nov. 14, "
"	Brigadier-General.	Dec. 13, "
E. P. Davis,	Col. 153d N.Y.Vols.	Oct. 13, "
N. A. M. Dudley,	" 30th Mass. "	Nov. 2, "
"	" 30th " "	" 18, "

2d Brigade—1st Division.

Organized January, 1863.
Formerly Reserve Brigade, 18th Corps.

COMMANDERS.		DATE.
G. Weitzel,	Brigadier-General.	Jan., 1863
Stephen Thomas,	Col. 8th Vt. Vols.	July, "
"	" 8th " "	Nov., 1864
Jas. Smith,	" 128th N.Y.Vols.	Aug., 1863
Jacob Sharpe,	" 156th " "	Sept., "
"	" 156th " "	Nov., "
O. P. Gooding,	" 31st Mass. "	Oct., "
Geo. L. Beale,	" 29th Me. "	Feb., 1864
Jas. W. McMillan,	Brigadier-General.	March, "
"	"	June, "
"	"	Dec. 3, "
Henry Rust, Jr.,	Col. 13th Me. Vols.	May, "
Jas. D. Fessenden,	Brigadier-General.	Oct. 26, "
E. P. Davis,	Col. 153d N.Y.Vols.	Jan. 25, 1865

1st Brigade—2d Division.

Discontinued July, 1863.
Reorganized February 15, 1864.

COMMANDERS.		DATE.
T. S. Clark,	Col. 6th Mich. Vols.	Jan., 1863
"	" 6th " "	June, "
Neal Dow,	Brigadier-General.	Feb. 26, "
F. S. Nickerson,	"	" 15, 1864
A. B. Farr,	Col. 26th Mass.Vols.	June 29, "
H. W. Birge,	Brigadier-General.	July 5, "
"	"	Nov., "
T. W. Porter,	Col. 14th Me. Vols.	Oct. 19, "
H. D. Washburn,	" 18th Ind. "	Jan. 3, 1865

2d Brigade—2d Division.

Dropped from "Return" of 19th Corps, August⸢
Reorganized February 15, 1864.

COMMANDERS.		DA⸢
A. B. Farr,	Col. 26th Mass. Vo's.	Jan.⸢
Thos. W. Cahill,	" 9th Conn. "	May,⸢
H. W. Birge,	Brigadier-General.	Feb.,⸢
"	"	April,⸢
E. L. Molineux,	Col. 159th N.Y.Vols.	March⸢
"	" 159th " "	May,⸢
"	" 159th " "	July,⸢
"	" 159th " "	Dec.⸢
R. B. Merritt,	" 75th " "	June,⸢
N. W. Day,	" 131st " "	Nov.⸢
"	" 131st " "	Feb.⸢
Harvey Graham,	" 22d Iowa "	March⸢

3d Brigade—1st Division.

COMMANDERS.		DATE.
N. A. M. Dudley,	Col. 30th Mass. Vols.	January 12, 1863
"	" 30th " "	October 26, 1864
R. B. Merritt,	" 75th N.Y. "	July 11, 1863
C. C. Dwight,	" 160th " "	January 20, 1864
Francis Fessenden,	" 30th Me. "	February, "
Lewis Benedict,	" 162d N.Y. "	March, "
J. W. Blanchard,	Lt.- " 162d " "	April, "
Geo. M. Love,	" 116th " "	May, "
L. D. H. Currie,	" 133d " "	June 25, "
Jas. D. Fessenden,	Brigadier-General.	November 1, "

3d Brigade—2d Division.

Transferred to 3d Division, 19th Corps, July, 1863.

COMMANDERS.		DATE.
F. S. Nickerson,	Col. 14th Me. Vols.	Jan., 1863
Jacob Sharpe,	" 156th N.Y. "	Feb., 1864
D. Macauley,	" 11th Ind. "	Sept. 21, "
Alfred Neafie,	Lt.- " 156th N.Y. "	Oct. 19, "
Jas. P. Richardson,	Lt.- " 38th Mass. "	Dec., "
N. W. Day,	" 131st N.Y. "	March 4, 1865

4th Brigade—2d Division.

Organized August, 1864.
Discontinued January, 1865.

COMMANDERS.		DA⸢
David Shunk,	Col. 8th Ind. Vols.	Aug.,⸢
H. D. Washburn,	" 18th " "	Nov.,⸢

4th Division—19th Army Corps.

Transferred to the Defences of New Orleans, La., August, 1863. Discontinued February 15, 1864.

COMMANDERS.		DATE.
C. Grover,	Brigadier-General.	January, 1863
E. G. Beckwith,	Col. and A. A. D. C.	August 25, "
J. J. Reynolds,	Major-General.	January, 1864

District of Key Wes⸢

Organized April, 1863. Transferred to Dep⸢

COMMANDER.	
D. P. Woodbury,	Brigadier-G⸢

1st Brigade—4th Division

Discontinued February 15, 1864.

COMMANDERS.		DATE.
W. Wilson,	Col. 6th N.Y.Vols.	Jan., 1863
Wm. Dwight,	Brigadier-General.	Feb., "
Jos. S. Morgan,	Col. 90th N.Y.Vols.	June, "
J. Van Zandt,	" 91st " "	July 13, "
Henry W. Birge,	" 13th Conn. "	Aug., "
E. L. Molineux,	" 159th N.Y. "	Jan., 1864

2d Brigade—4th Division.

Discontinued February 15, 1864.

COMMANDERS.		DATE.
J. Van Zandt,	Col 91st N. Y. Vols.	Jan. 20, 1863
Wm. K. Kimball,	" 12th Me. "	March 23, "
Thos. W. Cahill,	" 9th Conn. "	Aug., "

3d Brigade—4th Division.

Discontinued August, 1863.

COMMANDERS.		DATE.
H. W. Birge,	Col. 13th Conn.Vols.	Jan., 1863
E. L. Molineux,	" 159th N.Y. "	July, "

2. Discontinued G. O. No. 4. A. G. O. March 20, 1865.

DATE.
December 16, 1862.
August 20, 1863.
November 7, 1864.
December 28, "
July 7, "
December, "

s, La.

r, 1862.
lf, August, 1863.

DATE.
December, 1862
January 9, 1863
May, "

Reserve Brigade.

Organized December, 1862.
Transferred to 1st Division, January, 1863.

COMMANDER.		DATE.
G. Weitzel,	Brigadier-General.	December, 1862

District of Pensacola, Fla.

Organized December, 1862.
Transferred to Department of the Gulf, August, 1863.

COMMANDERS.		DATE.
Neal Dow,	Brigadier-General.	December, 1862
J. Dyer,	Col. 15th Me. Vols.	January 24, 1863
"	" 15th " "	May, "
W. C. Holbrook,	" 7th Vt. "	April 21, "
"	" 7th " "	June 18, "

2d Division—19th Army Corps. (Serving in Department of the Gulf.)

Organized August, 1861.
Changed to 2d Division Reserve Corps, Military Division of West Mississippi, December, 1864.

COMMANDER.		DATE.
E. S. Dennis,	Brigadier-General.	August 18, 1864

3d Division—19th Army Corps.

Reorganized June, 1864.
Transferred to Military Division of West Mississippi, G. O. No. 277. A. G. O. November 7, 1864.

COMMANDERS.		DATE.
Wm. H. Emory,	Brigadier-General.	January 14, 1863
"	"	September 4, "
H. Fearing,	Col. 8th N. H. Vols.	June, "
Wm. Dwight,	Brigadier-General.	July, "
Jas. W. McMillan,	"	September, "
"	"	January 12, 1864
Cuvier Grover,	"	October 4, 1863
J. J. Reynolds,	Major-General.	February, 1864
M. K. Lawler,	Brigadier-General.	June, "
Geo. F. McGinnis,	"	August 25, "

Brigade—2d Division. (Serving in Dept. of the Gulf.)

COMMANDER.		DATE.
nblaser,	Col. 46th Ills. Vols.	Aug. 18, 1864

2d Brigade—2d Division. (Serving in Dept. of the Gulf.)

COMMANDER.		DATE.
J. R. Slack,	Col. 47th Ind. Vols.	Aug. 18, 1864

1st Brigade—3d Division.

Discontinued July, 1863. (Troops trans. to other commands)
Reorganized July, 1863 (by the joining of 3d Brig., 2d Div.)
Reorganized June, 1864.

COMMANDERS.		DATE.
T. Ingraham,	Col. 38th Mass. Vols.	Jan. 29, 1863
"	" 38th " "	March 4, "
Geo. L. Andrews,	Brigadier-General.	Feb. 13, "
S. P. Ferris,	Col. 28th Conn. Vols.	June, "
Frank S. Nickerson,	Brigadier-General.	July, "
T. W. Porter,	Col. 14th Me. Vols.	Aug. 31, "
Lewis Benedict,	" 162d N.Y. "	Sept., "
D. P. Woodbury,	Brigadier-General.	Feb., 1864
A. L. Lee,	"	June, "
L. A. Sheldon,	Col. 42d Ohio Vols.	Aug., "
Wm. McE. Dye,	" 20th Iowa "	Sept., "
S. L. Glasgow,	" 23d " "	Nov., "

2d Brigade—3d Division.

Reorganized June, 1864.

COMMANDERS.		DATE.
H. E. Paine,	Col. 4th Wis. Vols.	Jan. 3, 1863
J. H. Alcott,	Maj. 133d N.Y. "	June, "
H. Fearing,	Col. 8th N. H. "	July, "
A. B. Farr,	" 26th Mass. "	Aug. 29, "
"	" 26th " "	Nov., "
Jas. W. McMillan,	Brigadier-General.	Oct. 4, "
"	"	Dec., "
J. A. Sawtell,	Lt.-Col. 26th Mass. Vols.	Jan., 1864
A. Asboth,	Brigadier-General.	Feb., "
T. W. Bennett,	Col. 69th Ind. Vols.	June, "
W. T. Spicely,	" 24th " "	Aug., "

3d Brigade—2d Division. (Serving in Dept. of the Gulf.)

COMMANDERS.		DATE.
J. G. Guppy,	Col. 23d Wis. Vols.	August 18, 1864
Alexander Shaler,	Brigadier-General.	November 3, "

3d Brigade—3d Division.

Transferred to 1st Division, 19th Corps, August, 1863. Reorganized July, 1864.

COMMANDERS.		DATE.
Oliver P. Gooding,	Col. 31st Mass. Vols.	January 24, 1863
F. W. Moore,	" 83d Ohio "	July, 1864
A. H. Brown,	Lt.- " 96th " "	October 1, "
Geo. F. McGinnis,	Brigadier-General.	November, "

as.

lf, August, 1863.

DATE.
pril 20, 1863

Cavalry Brigade—19th Army Corps.

Organized July, 1864.
Transferred to Military Division of West Mississippi, G. O. No. 277. A. G. O. Nov. 7, 1864.

COMMANDERS.		DATE.
E. J. Davis,	Col. 1st Texas Cav.	July, 1864
"	" 1st " "	September, "
J. M. Krebs,	Lt.- " 87th Ills. Mt. Inf.	August, "

Detachment—19th Army Corps.

Organized July, 1864, consisting of 1st and 2d Divisions, 19th Corps.
Designated 19th Army Corps, G. O. No. 277. A. G. O. November 7, 1864.

COMMANDER.		DATE.
W. H. Emory,	Brigadier-General.	July, 1864

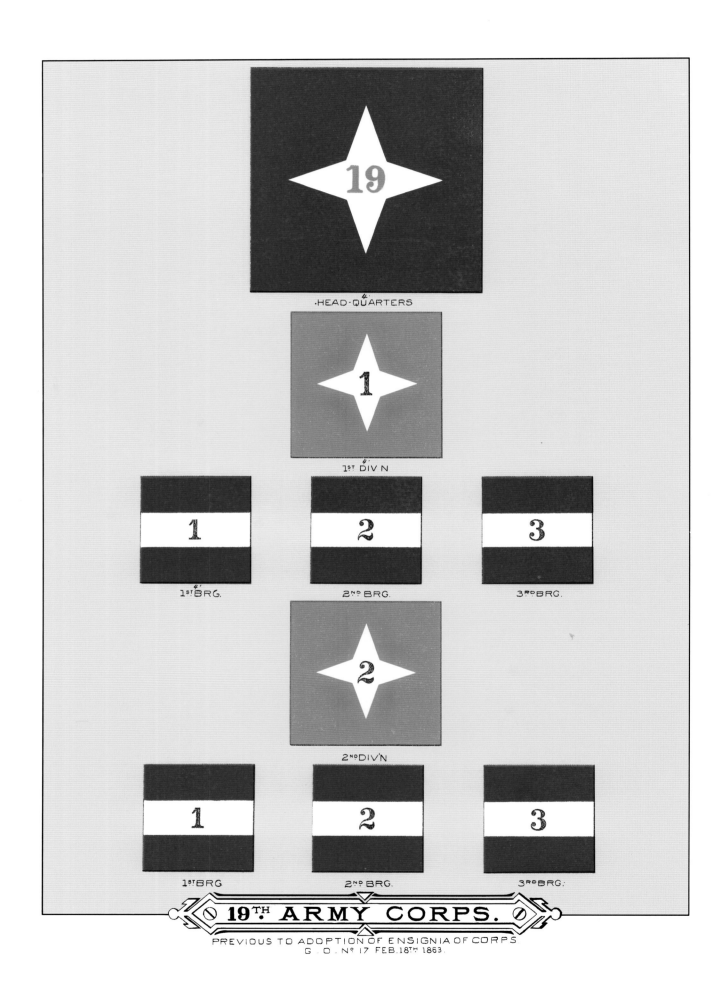

HEAD·QUARTERS

1ST DIV N

1ST BRG.   2ND BRG.   3RD BRG.

2ND DIV'N

1ST BRG   2ND BRG.   3RD BRG.

19TH ARMY CORPS.

PREVIOUS TO ADOPTION OF ENSIGNIA OF CORPS
G . O . Nº 17 FEB.18TH 1863.

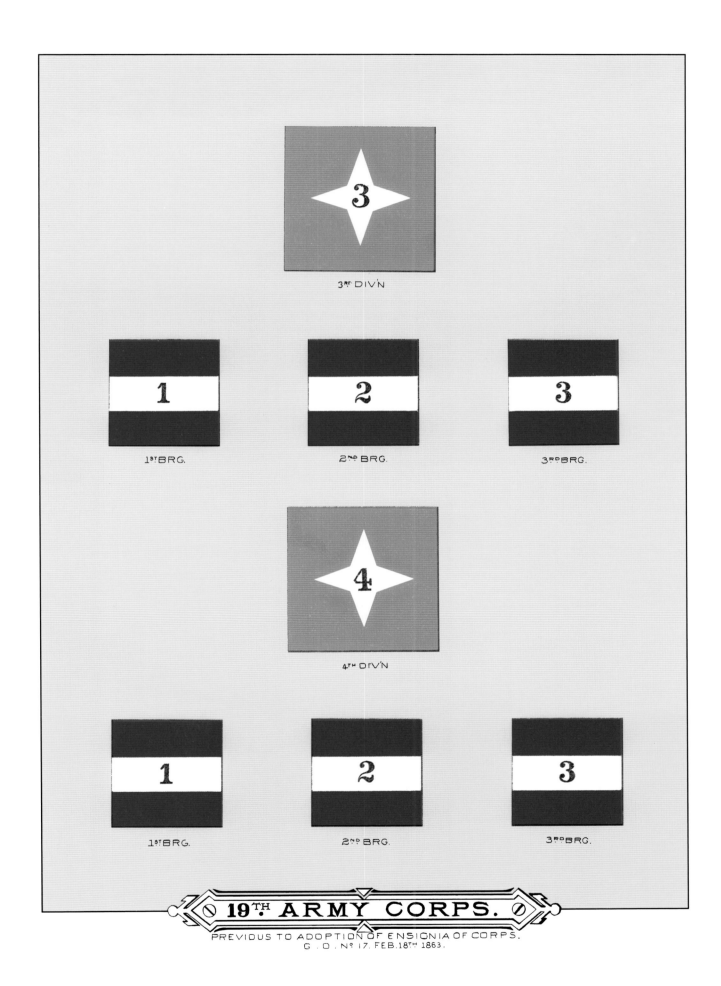

3ᴿᴰ DIV'N

1ˢᵀ BRG.　　　2ᴺᴰ BRG.　　　3ᴿᴰ BRG.

4ᵀᴴ DIV'N

1ˢᵀ BRG.　　　2ᴺᴰ BRG.　　　3ᴿᴰ BRG.

19ᵀᴴ ARMY CORPS.

PREVIOUS TO ADOPTION OF ENSIGNIA OF CORPS.
G . O . Nᵒ 17. FEB.18ᵀᴴ 1863.

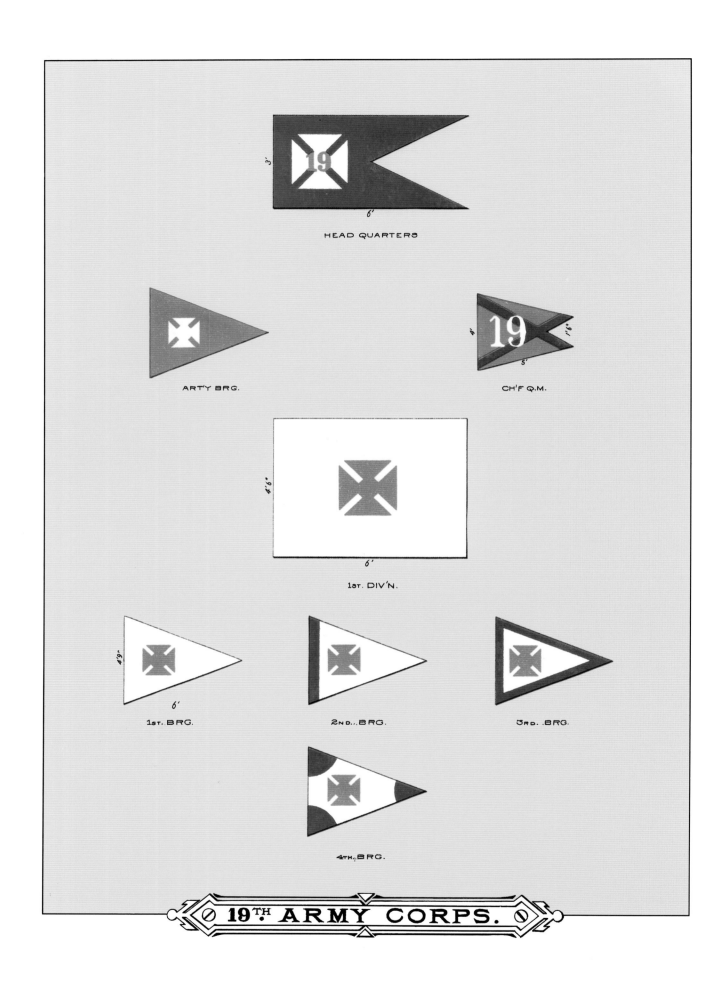

HEAD QUARTERS

ART'Y BRG.

CH'F Q.M.

1st. DIV'N.

1st. BRG.

2nd. BRG.

3rd. BRG.

4th. BRG.

19TH ARMY CORPS.

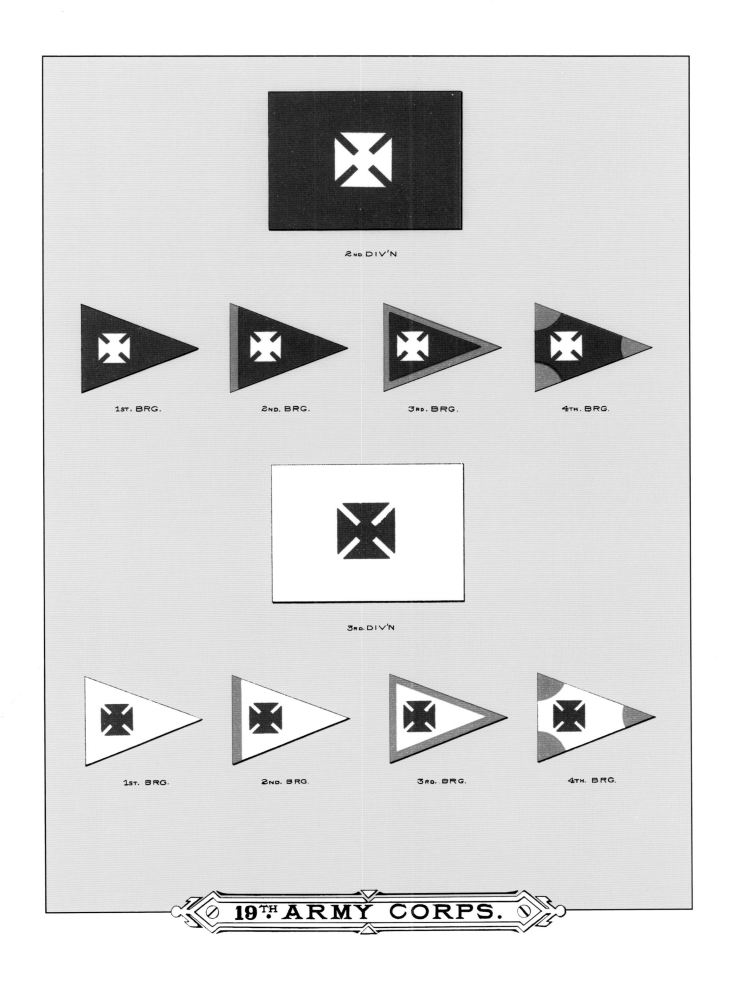

2ND. DIV'N

1ST. BRG.   2ND. BRG.   3RD. BRG.   4TH. BRG.

3RD. DIV'N

1ST. BRG.   2ND. BRG.   3RD. BRG.   4TH. BRG.

19TH ARMY CORPS.

TWENTIETH

Created G. O. No. 9.   A. G. O. January 9, 1863.   Discontinued October, 1863, in compliance with G. O. No. 322. A
Finally discontinued and

COMMANDERS.

A. McD. McCOOK,	Major-Gener
JOSEPH HOOKER,	"
A. S. WILLIAMS,	Brigadier-Ge
H. W. SLOCUM,	Major-Gener
J. A. MOWER,	"

1st Division—20th Army Corps.

COMMANDERS.		DATE.
J. C. Davis,	Brigadier-General.	January, 1863
A. S. Williams,	"	April, 1864
"	"	August 27, "
"	"	April 6, 1865
J. F. Knife,	"	July 28, 1864
N. J. Jackson,	"	November 11, "

1st Brigade—1st Division.

COMMANDERS.		DATE.
P. S. Post,	Col. 59th Ills. Vols.	Jan. 9, 1863
J. F. Knife,	Brigadier-General.	April, 1864
"	"	Aug. 27, "
W. W. Packer,	Col. 5th Conn. Vols.	July 28, "
"	" 5th " "	Sept. 21, "
J. L. Selfridge,	" 46th Pa. "	Oct. 20, "

2d Brigade—1st Division.

COMMANDERS.		DATE.
W. P. Carlin,	Col. 38th Ills. Vols.	Jan. 9, 1863
"	Brigadier-General.	March, "
H. C. Heg,	Col. 15th Wis. Vols.	Feb., "
T. H. Ruger,	Brigadier-General.	April, 1864
"	"	Oct., "
E. A. Carman,	Col. 13th N. J. Vols.	Sept. 17, "
"	" 13th " "	Nov., "
W. Hawley,	" 3d Wis. "	Jan. 16, 1865

3d Brigade—1st Division.

COMMANDERS.		DA
W. W. Caldwell,	Col. 81st Ind. Vols.	Jan.
"	" 81st " "	April,
T. T. Crittenden,	Brigadier-General.	March
H. C. Heg,	Col. 15th Wis. Vols.	May,
J. A. Martin,	" 8th Kans. "	Sept.
H. Tyndale,	Brigadier-General.	April
J. S. Robinson,	Col. 82d Ohio Vols.	May
"	" 82d " "	Sept.
H. Boughton,	" 143d N. Y. "	July

3d Division

COMMANDERS.

P. H. Sheridan,	Major-General
D. Butterfield,	"
W. T. Ward,	Brigadier-Gen
"	"
D. Dustin,	Col. 105th Ills

1st Brigade—3d Division.

COMMANDERS.		DATE.
N. Grensel,	Col. 36th Ills. Vols.	Jan. 9, 1863
F. T. Sherman,	" 88th " "	Feb. 13, "
"	" 88th " "	Sept. 20, "
W. H. Lytle,	Brigadier-General.	April, "
W. T. Ward,	"	" 14, 1864
B. Harrison,	Col. 70th Ind. Vols.	June 29, "
"	" 70th " "	April 21, 1865
F. C. Smith,	" 102d Ills. "	Sept. 23, 1864
H. Case,	" 129th " "	Dec. 31, "

2d Br

COMMAND	
B. Laibold,	C
"	
W. W. Barrett,	
S. Ross,	
J. Coburn,	
E. Bloodgood,	Lt.-
A. B. Crane,	" "
D. Dustin,	"

ARMY CORPS.

ber 28, 1863, consolidated with 21st Corps and formed 4th Corps.   Corps reorganized G. O. No. 144, April 4, 1864.
erred to other commands, June, 1865.

DATE.
January 9, 1863.
April 4, 1864.
July 27, and November 11, 1864.
August 27, 1864.
April 1, 1865.

2d Division—20th Army Corps.

COMMANDERS.		DATE.
W. H. Gibson,	Col. 49th Ohio Vols.	January 19, 1863
R. W. Johnson,	Brigadier-General.	February, "
A. Willich,	"	September 19, "
J. W. Geary,	"	April, 1864

1st Brigade—2d Division.

COMMANDERS.		DATE.
es,	Col. 39th Ind. Vols.	Jan. 19, 1863
ace,	" 15th Ohio "	Feb., "
ibson,	" 49th " "	March, "
h,	Brigadier-General.	May 28, "
neyer,	Lt.-Col. 32d Ind. Vols.	Sept. 20, "
r,	" 66th Ohio "	April, 1864
e, Jr.,	" 147th Pa. "	Aug. 4, "
	" 147th " "	Oct. 28, "
	" 147th " "	May 10, 1865
	" 28th " "	Sept. 27, 1864
indil,	" 33d N. J. "	April 11, 1865

2d Brigade—2d Division.

COMMANDERS.		DATE.
J. B. Dodge,	Col. 30th Ind. Vols.	Jan. 9, 1863
	" 30th " "	June, "
T. E. Rose,	" 77th Pa. "	May 18, "
A. Buschbeck,	" 27th " "	April, 1864
J. S. Lockman,	" 119th N.Y. "	May 23, "
P. H. Jones,	" 154th " "	June 7, "
	" 154th " "	Sept. 17, "
	" 154th " "	March 30, 1865
G. W. Mindil,	" 33d N. J. "	Aug. 8, 1864
"	" 33d " "	Jan. 19, 1865

3d Brigade—2d Division.

COMMANDERS.		DATE.
E. A. Parrott,	Col. 1st Ohio Vols.	Jan. 27, 1863
P. P. Baldwin,	" 6th Ind. "	April 17, "
W. W. Berry,	" 5th Ky. "	Sept. 20, "
D. Ireland,	" 137th N. Y. "	April 4, 1864
H. A. Barnum,	" 149th " "	Sept. 9, "

Corps.

DATE.
January 9, 1863
April 14, 1864
June 29, "
October, "
September 23, "

vision.

DATE.
Jan. 9, 1863
March, "
Feb., "
April 4, 1864
May 9, "
Sept. 22, "
Oct. 30, "
Nov. 9, "

3d Brigade—3d Division.

COMMANDERS.		DATE.
L. P. Bradley	Col. 51st Ills. Vols.	Jan. 9, 1863
N. H. Walworth,	" 42d " "	Sept. 28, "
J. Wood, Jr.,	" 136th N.Y. "	April 4, 1864
"	" 136th " "	Aug. 5, "
L. B. Faulkner,	Lt.- " 136th " "	July 28, "
P. B. Buckingham,	" " 20th Conn. "	Sept. 23, "
S. Ross,	" 20th " "	Nov. 10, "
Wm. Coggswell,	" 2d Mass. "	Jan. 16, 1865

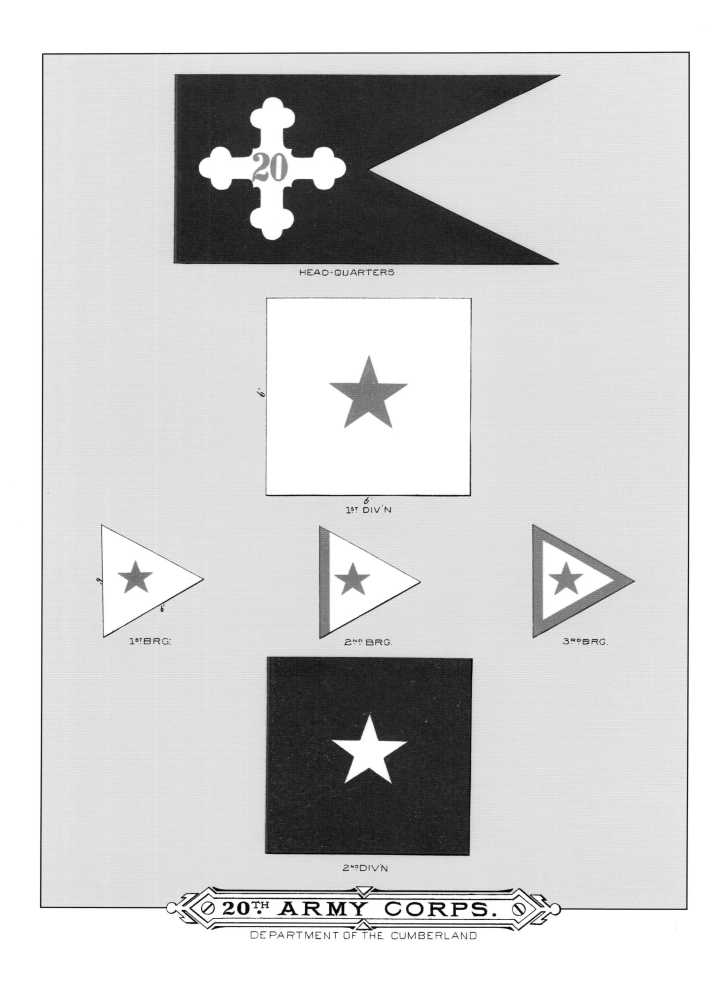

HEAD-QUARTERS

1ST DIV'N

1ST BRG.

2ND BRG.

3RD BRG.

2ND DIV'N

20TH ARMY CORPS.

DEPARTMENT OF THE CUMBERLAND

141

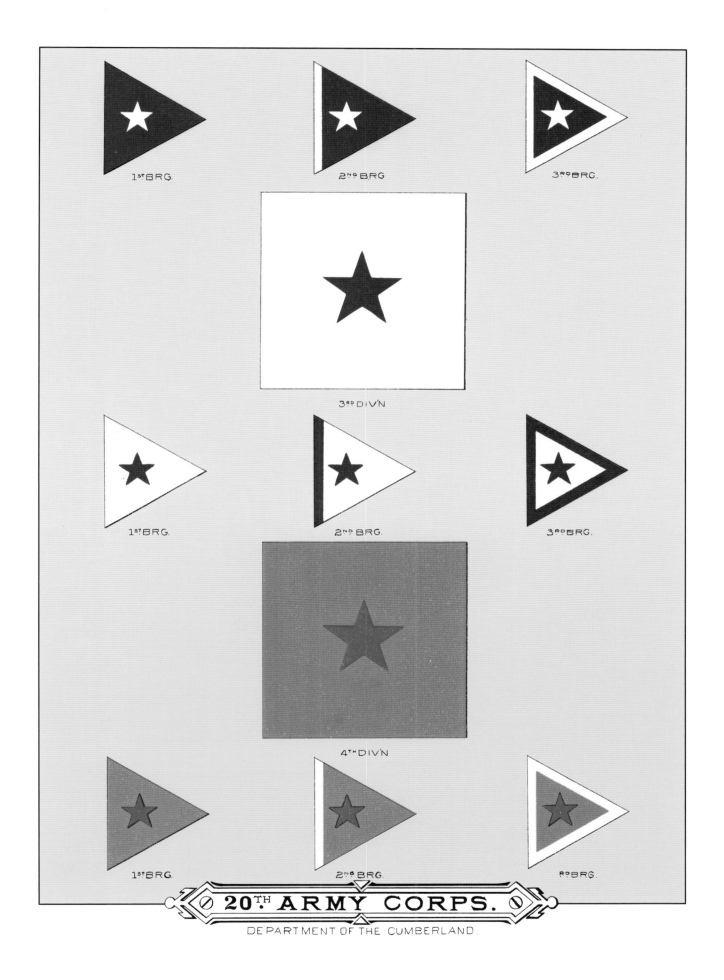

1ˢᵀ BRG.   2ᴺᴰ BRG   3ᴿᴰ BRG.

3ᴿᴰ DIV'N

1ˢᵀ BRG.   2ᴺᴰ BRG.   3ᴿᴰ BRG.

4ᵀᴴ DIV'N

1ˢᵀ BRG.   2ᴺᴰ BRG.   ᴿᴰ BRG.

20ᵀᴴ ARMY CORPS.

DEPARTMENT OF THE CUMBERLAND.

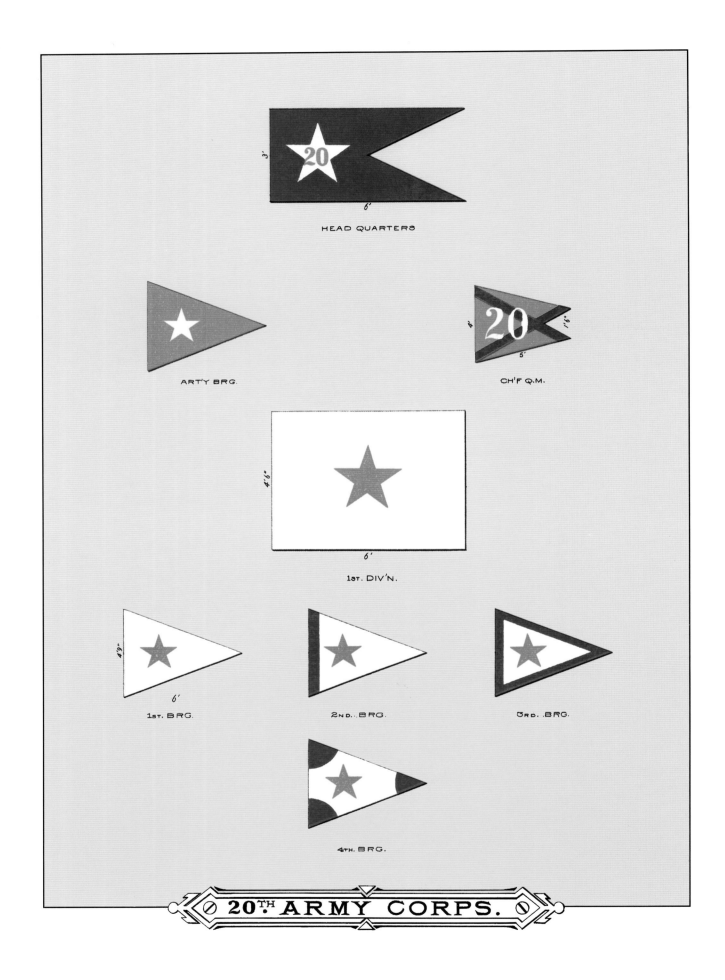

HEAD QUARTERS

ART'Y BRG.

CH'F Q.M.

1ST. DIV'N.

1ST. BRG.

2ND. BRG.

3RD. BRG.

4TH. BRG.

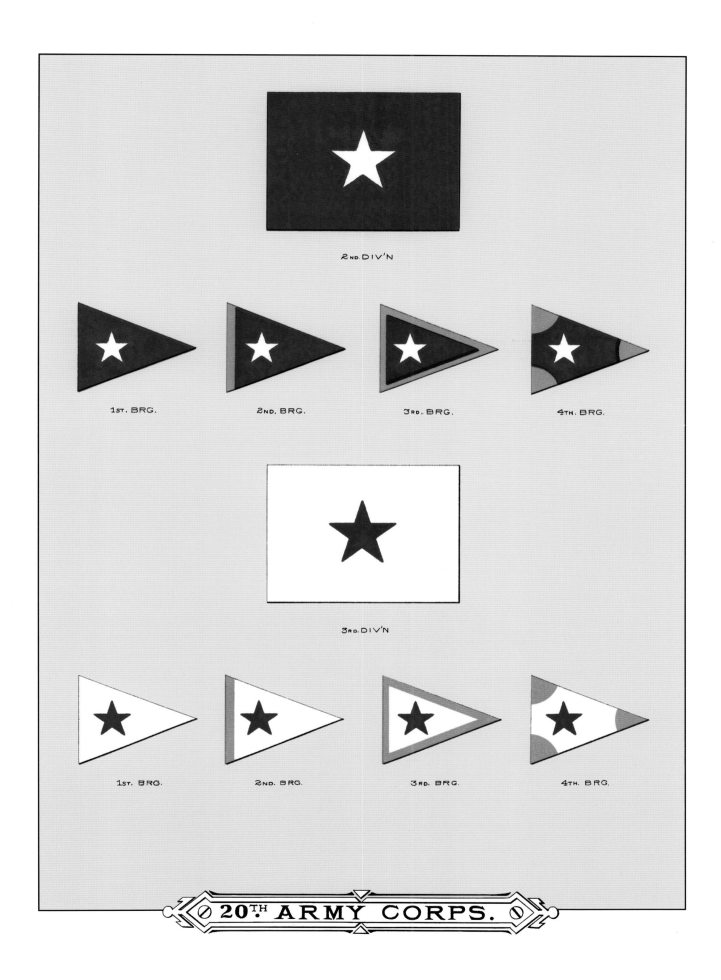

2ND. DIV'N

1ST. BRG.   2ND. BRG.   3RD. BRG.   4TH. BRG.

3RD. DIV'N

1ST. BRG.   2ND. BRG.   3RD. BRG.   4TH. BRG.

20TH ARMY CORPS.

TWENTY=FIRS[T]

Created G. O. No. 9. A. G. O. January 9, 1863.

Discontinued October, 18[

COMMANDERS.

T. L. CRITTENDEN,	Major-Gen[
"	"
"	"
T. J. WOOD,	Brigadier-
J. M. PALMER,	Major-Gen

1st Division—21st Army Corps.

COMMANDERS.		DATE.
M. S. Hascall,	Brigadier-General.	January, 1863
G. D. Wagner,	Col. 15th Ind. Vols.	February, "
J. M. Brannan,	Brigadier-General.	April 13, "
T. J. Wood,	"	May, "

2d

COMMANDERS.	
J. M. Palmer,	Major-G[
"	"
C. Cruft.	Brigadie[

1st Brigade—1st Division.

COMMANDERS.		DATE.
E. P. Fyffe,	Col. 26th Ohio Vols.	Jan., 1863
G. P. Buell,	" 58th Ind. "	June 10, "
"	" 58th " "	Aug. 3, "
F. A. Bartleson,	" 100th Ills. "	July 25, "

2d Brigade—1st Division.

COMMANDERS.		DATE.
G. D. Wagner,	Col. 15th. Ind Vols.	Jan., 1863
"	Brigadier-General.	April 13, "
M. Barnes,	Lt.-Col. 97th Ohio Vols.	Jan., "
G. A. Wood,	" " 15th Ind. "	Feb. 18, "

1st Brigade—2d Division.

COMMANDERS.		
C. Cruft,	Brigadier-General.	Jar
"	"	Ap
"	"	Au
D. A. Enyart,	Col. 1st Ky. Vols.	Ma
T. D. Sedgwick,	" 2d " "	Jul

3d Brigade—1st Division.

COMMANDERS.		DATE.
C. G. Harker,	Col. 65th Ohio Vols.	January, 1863
"	" 65th " "	March, "
M. Shoemaker,	" 13th Mich. "	February, "

3d

COMMANDERS.	
Wm. Grose,	Col. 36[
"	" 36[
L. H. Waters,	" 84[

ARMY CORPS.

A. G. O. September 28, 1863. Was consolidated with the 20th Corps and formed the 4th Corps.

DATE.	
January 9, 1863.	
March, "	
August, "	
February, "	
July, "	

my Corps.

DATE.
January 9, 1863
August, "
July, "

3d Division—21st Army Corps.

COMMANDERS.		DATE.
S. Beatty,	Col. 19th Ohio Vols.	January 9, 1863
H. P. Van Cleve,	Brigadier-General.	March 13, "

2d Brigade—2d Division.

COMMANDER.		DATE.
zen,	Brigadier-General.	Jan. 9, 1863

1st Brigade—3d Division.

COMMANDERS.		DATE.
B. C. Grider,	Col. 9th Ky. Vols.	Jan. 9, 1863
F. Knefler,	" 79th Ind. "	Feb., "
S. Beatty,	Brigadier-General.	April 11, "

2d Brigade—3d Division.

COMMANDERS.		DATE.
J. P. Fyffe,	Col. 59th Ohio Vols.	Jan. 9, 1863
G. F. Dick,	" 86th Ind. "	March, "

sion.

DATE.
January 9, 1863
April, "
March, "

3d Brigade—3d Division.

COMMANDERS.		DATE.
S. Matthews,	Col. 51st Ohio Vols.	January 9, 1863
S. M. Barnes,	" 8th Ky. "	April 14, "

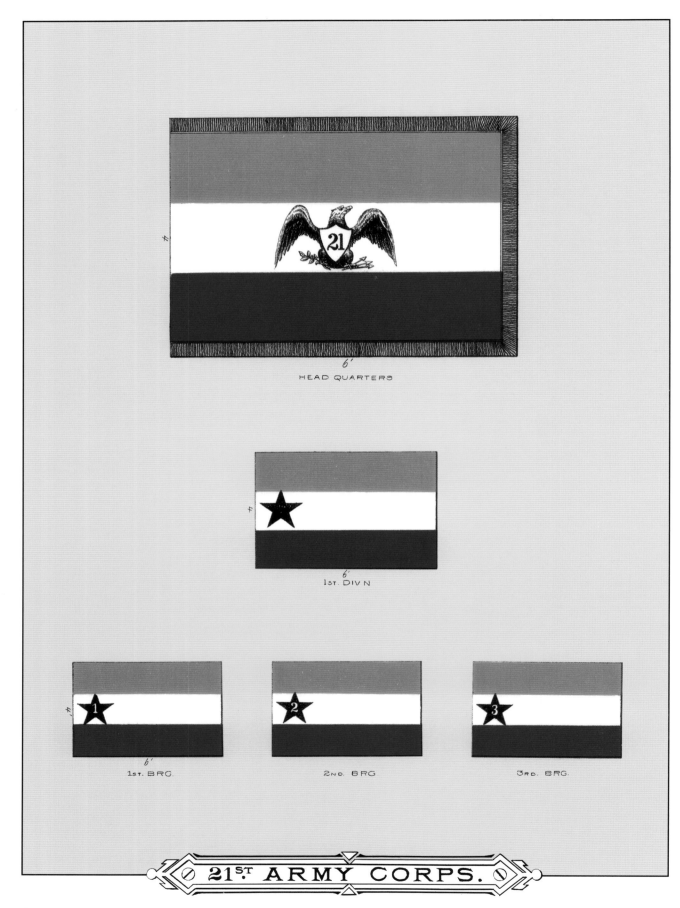

HEAD QUARTERS

1ST. DIVN

1ST. BRG.   2ND. BRG.   3RD. BRG.

21ST. ARMY CORPS.

DEPARTMENT OF THE CUMBERLAND.

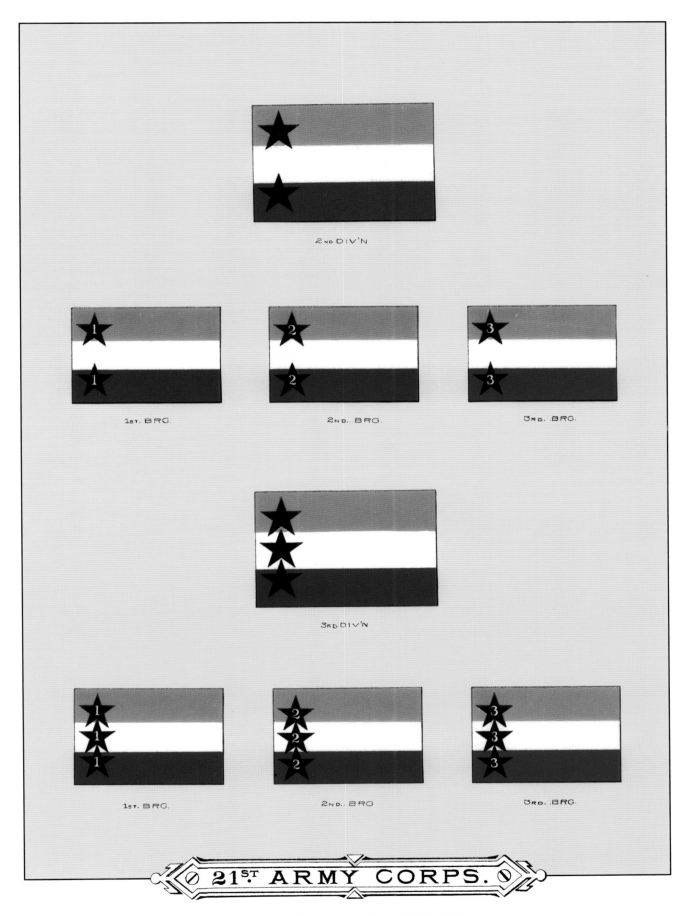

2ND DIV'N

1ST. BRG.

2ND. BRG.

3RD. BRG.

3RD DIV'N

1ST. BRG.

2ND. BRG.

3RD. BRG.

21ST ARMY CORPS.

DEPARTMENT OF THE CUMBERLAND.

148

Created G. O. No. 26. A. G. O. February

COMMANDERS.	
S. P. HEINTZELMAN,	Major-G[eneral]
C. C. AUGUR,	"
"	"
J. G. PARKE,	"

Abercrombie's Division—22d Army Corps.

Transferred to Army of the Potomac, June, 1863.

COMMANDER.		DATE.
J. J. Abercrombie,	Brigadier-General.	February 2, 1863

Casey's

D[ivision]

COMMANDER.	
Silas Casey,	Majo[r]

1st Brigade—Abercrombie's Division.

Organized April, 1863.
(Formerly 1st Brigade, Casey's Division.)

COMMANDER.		DATE.
Francis Fessenden,	Col. 25th Me. Vols.	April, 1863

2d Brigade—Abercrombie's Division.

Transferred to Department of Va., April, 1863.
Reorganized April, 1863. (Formerly 2d Brigade, Casey's Division.)

COMMANDERS.		DATE.
R. Cowdin,	Brigadier-General.	Feb. 2, 1863
B. Porter,	Col. 40th Mass. Vols.	March 31, "
G. J. Stannard,	Brigadier General.	April 21, "

1st Brigade—Casey's Division.

Transferred to Abercrombie's Division, April, 1863.

COMMANDER.		
Francis Fessenden,	Col. 25th Me. Vols.	Feb.

3d Brigade—Abercrombie's Division.

Transferred to Department of Va., April, 1863. Reorganized April, 1863. (Formerly 3d Brigade, Casey's Division.)

COMMANDERS.		DATE.
Wm. Gurney,	Col. 127th N. Y. Vols.	February 2, 1863
Alex. Hays,	Brigadier-General.	April, "
"	"	May, "
G. L. Willard,	Col. 125th N. Y. Vols.	April 26, "

3d [Brigade]

Transferred to Ab[ercrombie's]

COMMANDER.	
Alex. Hays,	Brigad[ier]

District of Alexandria.

Discontinued July 20, 1865.

COMMANDERS.		DATE.
J. P. Slough,	Brigadier-General.	Feb. 2, 1863
"	"	Dec., 1864
"	"	June, 1865
H. H. Wells,	Col. 26th Mich. Vols.	Nov., 1864
J. G. Parke,	Major-General.	April 26, 1865

Artillery—Defences of Alexandria.

Designated 2d Brigade, Defences South of the Potomac, April 15, 1863.

COMMANDER.		DATE.
R. O. Tyler,	Brigadier-General.	Feb. 2, 1863

Defence[s]

Organized Ap[ril]

COMMANDERS.		
R. O. Tyler,	Brigadier-Gen[eral]	
T. R. Tannatt,	Col. 1st Mass.	
G. A. DeRussy,	Brigadier-Gen[eral]	

Artillery Brigade—South of Potomac.

Designated 1st Brigade, Defences South of the Potomac, April 15, 1863.

COMMANDERS.		DATE.
M. Cogswell,	Col. 2d N. Y. Hy. Art.	February 2, 1863
T. R. Tannatt,	" 1st Mass. "	April 9, 1863

1st Brigade—Defences South of the Poton[ac]

Organized April 15, 1863. (Formerly Artillery Brigade South o[f]

COMMANDERS.		
T. R. Tannatt,	Col. 1st Mass. Hy. Art.	April
"	" 1st " "	Sept
J. N. G. Whistler,	" 2d N. Y. "	Aug.
"	" 2d " "	July
A. A. Gibson,	" 2d Pa. "	Marc[h]
J. C. Lee,	" 164th Ohio N. G.	May

3d Brigade—Defences South of the Poton[ac]

Organized May, 1863. Discontinued May, 1864.
Reorganized July, 1864.

COMMANDERS.		
H. L. Abbott,	Col. 1st Conn. Hy. Art.	May
J. C. Tidball,	" 4th N. Y. "	Nov
"	" 4th " "	June
Alex. Piper,	" 10th " "	Marc[h]
W. S. Irwin,	" 136th Ohio N. G.	July
W. Heine,	" 103d N. Y. Vols.	Aug.
W. H. H. Beadle,	Maj. 1st V. R. C.	Sept.
T. McL. Barton,	Lt.-Col. 1st N. H. Hy. Art.	Oct.
Jas. Brady,	" 1st Pa. Lt. "	Nov.
W. S. King,	" 4th Mass. Hy. "	Dec.
"	" 4th " " "	May
S. C. Hart,	Lt.- " 4th " " "	April
H. T. Lee,	Maj. 4th N. Y. " "	June

ARMY CORPS.

Discontinued June 11, 1866.

DATE.
February 2, 1863.
October 13, "
July, 1865.
June 5, "

y Corps.

	DATE.
	February 2, 1863

2d Brigade—Casey's Division.

Transferred to Abercrombie's Division, April, 1863.

COMMANDERS.		DATE.
ughton,	Brigadier-General.	Feb. 2, 1863
t,	Col. 12th Vt. Vols.	March 9, "

Division.

ril, 1863.

	DATE.
	February 2, 1863

otomac.

ed August, 1865.

	DATE.
	April, 1863
	" 26, "
	May 25, "

d Brigade—Defences South of the Potomac.

nized April, 1863. (Formerly Artillery Defences of Alexandria.)

COMMANDERS		DATE.
ls,	Col. 34th Mass. Vols.	April 29, 1863
ssels,	" 19th Conn. "	May 3, "
er,	" 15th N. Y. Hy. Art.	Sept. 20, "
erger,	Maj. 15th " "	Oct., "
ott,	Col. 1st Conn. "	Nov., "
natt,	" 1st Mass. "	March, 1864
in,	" 136th Ohio N. G.	May, "
n,	" 2d Prov. Pa. Hy. Art.	July, "
dy,	Lt.- " 1st Pa. Lt. Art.	Sept. 29, "
nes,	" 6th " Hy. "	Nov. 14, "
d,	" 2d Conn. Hy. Art.	June 26, 1865

h Brigade—Defences South of the Potomac.

Organized July 2, 1863. Discontinued May, 1864.
Reorganized May, 1864.

COMMANDERS.		DATE.
ll,	Col. 4th N. Y. Hy. Art.	July 2, 1863
e,	Lt.- " 4th " "	Aug. 6, "
all,	" 4th " "	Sept. 2, "
er,	" 15th " "	Nov., "
	" 15th " "	Feb., 1864
erger,	Maj. 15th " "	Jan., "
ott,	Col. 1st Conn. "	March, "
	Bvt. Brigadier-General.	July 16, 1865
servey,	Maj. 1st Wis. Hy. Art.	July, 1864
	Col. 1st " "	Oct. 6, "
orth,	" 12th V. R. C.	Aug. 6, "
ann,	Maj. 15th N. Y. Hy. Art.	June 28, 1865

Division of Pennsylvania Reserve Corps—22d Army Corps.

Discontinued April, 1863.

COMMANDER.		DATE.
H. G. Sickel,	Col. 3d Pa. Res. Corps.	February 2, 1863

1st Brigade—Division of Pa. Reserve Corps.

Transferred to Army of the Potomac, June, 1863.

COMMANDERS.		DATE.
W. McCandless,	Col. 2d Pa. Res. Corps,	Feb. 2, 1863
"	" 2d " "	May 29, "
W. Sinclair,	" 6th " "	March, "

2d Brigade—Division of Pa. Reserve Corps.

Transferred to Army of the Potomac, April, 1864.

COMMANDERS.		DATE.
H. C. Bollinger,	Col. 7th Pa. Res. Corps.	Feb. 2, 1863
"	" 7th " "	Sept., "
H. G. Sickel,	" 3d " "	April, "
"	" 3d " "	Oct., "

3d Brigade—Division of Pa. Reserve Corps.

Transferred to Army of the Potomac, June, 1863.

COMMANDER.		DATE.
J. W. Fisher,	Col. 5th Pa. Res. Corps.	February 2, 1863

Defences North of the Potomac.

Discontinued August 2, 1865.

COMMANDERS.		DATE.
J. A. Haskin,	Lt.-Col. and A. A. D. C.	February 2, 1863
M. D. Hardin,	Brigadier-General.	July 8, 1864

1st Brigade—Defences North of the Potomac.

COMMANDERS.		DATE.
A. A. Gibson,	Col. 2d Pa. Hy. Art.	Feb. 2, 1863
J. M. Warner,	" 1st Vt. "	March, 1864
W. H. Hayward,	" 150th Ohio N. G.	May, "
J. M. C. Marble,	" 151st " "	July, "
J. H. Kitching,	" 6th N. Y. Hy. Art.	Aug. 16, "
T. Allcock,	Lt.- " 4th " "	Sept., "
G. S. Worcester,	Maj. 3d Mass. "	Oct., "
C. H. Long,	Col. 1st N. H. "	Nov., "
E. G. Marshall,	" 14th N. Y. "	June, 1865

2d Brigade—Defences North of the Potomac.

COMMANDERS.		DATE.
L. O. Morris,	Col. 7th N. Y. Hy. Art.	Feb. 2, 1863
H. Miller,	" 162d Ohio N. G.	May, 1864
J. M. C. Marble,	" 151st " "	June, "
W. H. Hayward,	" 150th " "	July, "
H. G. Thomas,	Lt.- " 7th V. R. C.	Aug., "
J. A. P. Allen,	Maj. 3d Mass. Hy. Art.	Nov., "
W. S. Abert,	Col. 3d " "	Dec., "

3d Brigade—Defences North of the Potomac.

COMMANDERS.		DATE.
W. R. Pease,	Col. 117th N. Y. Vols.	February 2, 1863
A. Piper,	" 10th " Hy. Art.	April 14, "
J. Welling,	" 9th " "	March 26, 1864
J. H. Oberteuffer,	Lt.- " 2d Pa. "	May 27, "
G. S. Worcester,	Maj. 3d Mass. "	January 3, 1865
R. B. Shepherd,	Col. 1st Me. "	June, "

Twenty=Second A...

Military ...

Discontinued Decem...
Dis...

COMMANDERS.	
J. H. Martindale,	Brigadier-...
"	"
Jno. P. Sherburne,	Maj. and ...
Moses N. Wisewell,	Col. 6th V...
O. B. Wilcox,	Bvt. Majo...

Garrison of Washington.

Organized May, 1865. Discontinued April 30, 1866.

COMMANDERS.		DATE.	
G. W. Gile,	Bvt. Brigadier-General.	May,	1865
F. T. Dent,	Brigadier-General.	August 14,	"

Defences of Washington.

Organized G. O. No. 109, Department of Washington, August 5, 1865.
Discontinued April 30, 1866.

COMMANDER.		DATE.	
J. A. Haskins,	Brigadier-General.	August	5, 186...

1st Provisional Brigade—Garrison of Washington.

Discontinued September 27, 1865.

COMMANDERS.		DATE.	
D. P. DeWitt,	Col. 10th V. R. C.	May,	1865
G. W. Gile,	Bvt. Brigadier-General.	August 13,	"

1st Brigade—Defences of Washington.

Discontinued September 25, 1865.

COMMANDER.	DATE.	
J. N. G. Whistler,	Bvt. Brigadier-Gen'l.	Aug., 1865

2d Brigade—Defences of Washin...

Discontinued September 25, 1865.

COMMANDER.		
J. C. Tidball,	Bvt. Brigadier-Gen'l.	Aug...

2d Provisional Brigade—Garrison of Washington.

Discontinued September 27, 1865.

COMMANDERS.		DATE.	
S. D. Oliphant,	Col. 14th V. R. C.	May 5,	1865
C. F. Johnson,	" 18th " "	August,	"

3d Brigade—Defences of Washington.

Discontinued September 25, 1865.

COMMANDER.	DATE.	
H. L. Abbott,	Bvt. Major-General.	Aug., 1865

4th Brigade—Defences of Washin...

Discontinued September 25, 1865.

COMMANDER.		
R. B. Shepherd,	Col. 1st Me. Hy. Art.	Aug...

5th Brigade—Defences of Washington.

Discontinued September 25, 1865.

COMMANDER.		DATE.	
W. S. Abert,	Col. 3d Mass. Hy. Art.	August,	186...

Light Artillery Depot and Camps of Instruction.

Discontinued July, 1865.

COMMANDERS.		DATE.	
Wm. F. Barry,	Brigadier-General.	Feb. 2,	1863
A. P. Howe,	"	March 3,	1864
"	"	Aug. 9,	"
"	"	Oct. 12,	"
"	"	Nov. 1,	"
"	"	May 7,	1865
J. A. Hall,	Maj. 1st Me. Lt. Art.	July,	1864
"	" 1st " "	Sept.,	"
"	Lt.-Col. 1st " "	Oct. 26,	"
"	" " 1st " "	April,	1865

Independent Brigade.

Transferred to "Army of the Potomac," June, 1863.

COMMANDER.		DATE.	
A. B. Jewett,	Col. 10th Vt. Vols.	Feb. 2,	1863

Provisional Troops.

Discontinued March 24, 1865.

COMMANDER.		D...
Silas Casey,	Major-General.	Feb...

St. Mary's District.

Created June, 1864. Discontinued April 26, 1865.

COMMANDERS.		DATE.	
A. G. Draper,	Col. 36th U. S. C. T.	June,	1864
Jas. Barnes,	Brigadier-General.	July 6,	"

1st S...

Organized Novemb...

COMMAN...	
Wm. Gamble,	Col. 8th ...
Wm. Wells,	Brigadier...

CORPS—Continued.

shington.

ized April, 1865.
1865.

DATE.
February   2, 1863
October   1, "
September,   "
May   21, 1864
April   26, 1865

Cavalry Division.

Organized March, 1863. Transferred to Army of the Potomac, June, 1863.
Reorganized January 9, 1864. Discontinued November, 1864.

COMMANDERS.		DATE.
J. Stahel,	Major-General.	March 21, 1863
J. B. McIntosh,	Col. 3d Pa. Cav.	January 9, 1864
Wm. Gamble,	" 8th Ills. "	May 2, "

King's Division.

Organized July, 1863. Transferred to Army of the Potomac, May 1864.

COMMANDERS.		DATE.
R. King,	Brigadier-General.	July 15, 1863
M. Corcoran,	"	October, "
C. M. Alexander,	Col. 2d D. C. Vols.	December, "
R. O. Tyler,	Brigadier-General.	January, 1864

1st Brigade—Cavalry Division.

COMMANDER.		DATE.
J. T. Copeland,	Brigadier-General.	March, 1863

1st Brigade—"Irish Legion"—King's Division.

Joined 22d Army Corps, July, 1863.

COMMANDERS.		DATE.
M. Corcoran,	Brigadier-General.	July, 1863
M. Murphy,	Col. 182d N. Y. Vols.	October, "
J. P. McIvor,	" 170th " "	December, "
A. H. Grimshaw,	" 4th Del. "	January, 1864
"	" 4th " "	April, "
C. M. Alexander,	" 2d D. C. "	March, "

2d Brigade—Cavalry Division.

Formerly Independent Cavalry Brigade.

COMMANDER.		DATE.
R. B. Price,	Col. 2d Pa. Cav.	March, 1863

2d Brigade—"Irish Legion"—King's Division.

Organized January, 1864. Formerly 1st Brigade.

COMMANDERS.		DATE.
M. Murphy,	Col. 182d N. Y. Vols.	January, 1864
"	" 182d " "	April, "
J. P. McIvor,	" 170th " "	March, "

3d Brigade—Cavalry Division.

COMMANDERS.		DATE.
R. Johnston,	Lt.-Col. 5th N. Y. Cav.	March, 1863
O. DeForrest,	" 5th " "	April 8, "

Independent Cavalry Brigade.

nsferred to Cavalry Division, March, 1863, and known as 2d Brigade,
Cavalry Division.
Reorganized August, 1863. Discontinued November, 1864.

COMMANDERS.		DATE.
Price,	Col. 2d Pa. Cav.	Feb. 2, 1863
owell, Jr.,	" 2d Mass. "	Aug. 1, "
"	" 2d " "	April, 1864
Lazelle,	" 16th N.Y. "	Feb., "
"	" 16th " "	July, "
ansevoort,	" 13th " "	Oct., "

1st Brigade Veteran Reserve Corps.

Organized March 23, 1864.
Transferred to "Garrison of Washington," May, 1865.

COMMANDERS.		DATE.
R. H. Rush,	Col. 1st V. R. C.	March 23, 1864
Moses N. Wisewell,	" 6th " "	May 21, "
G. W. Gile,	" 9th " "	July 6, "

2d Brigade Veteran Reserve Corps.

Organized May, 1864. Discontinued August, 1864.

COMMANDER.		DATE.
W. H. Browne,	Col. 24th V. R. C.	May 28, 1864

le.

nued July 6, 1865.

	DATE.
	Nov., 1864
	June 22, 1865

District of Annapolis.

Organized July, 1865. Discontinued September, 1865.

COMMANDERS.		DATE.
L. P. Graham,	Brigadier-General.	July 13, 1865
J. A. Gorgas,	Col. 43d Pa. Vols.	Aug., "

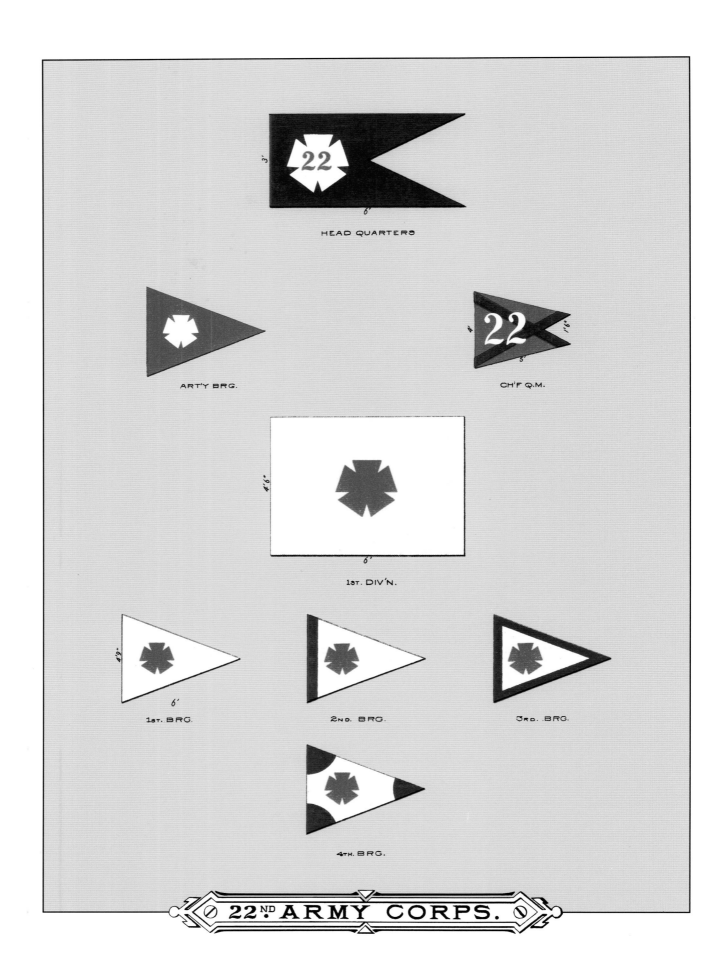

HEAD QUARTERS

ART'Y BRG.

CH'F Q.M.

1ST. DIV'N.

1ST. BRG.

2ND. BRG.

3RD. BRG.

4TH. BRG.

22ND ARMY CORPS.

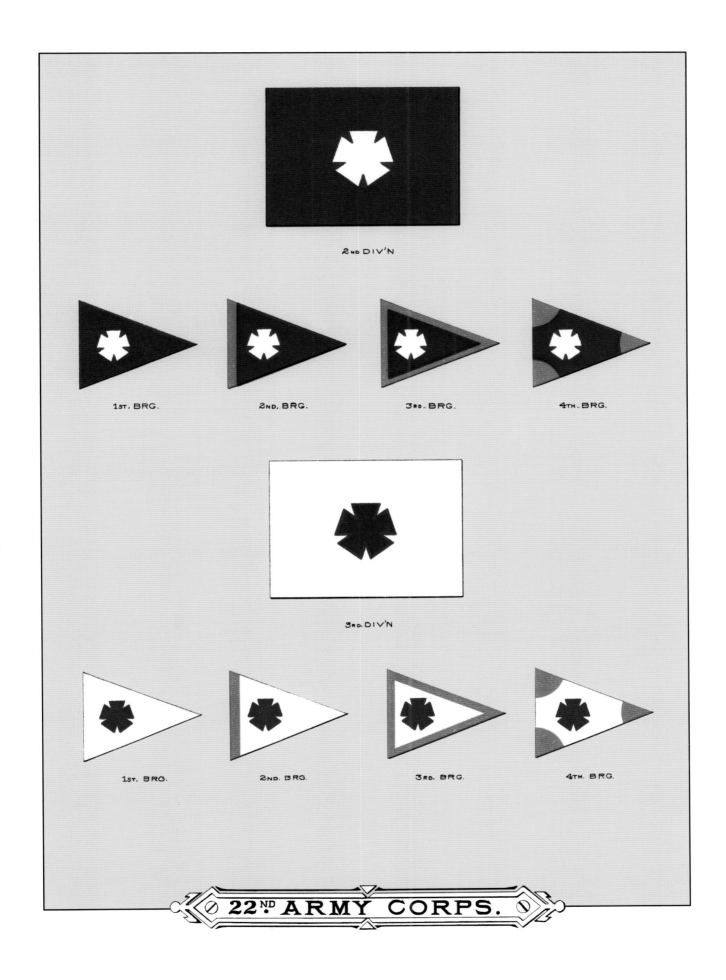

2ND DIV'N

1ST. BRG.   2ND. BRG.   3RD. BRG.   4TH. BRG.

3RD. DIV'N

1ST. BRG.   2ND. BRG.   3RD. BRG.   4TH. BRG.

22ND ARMY CORPS.

TWENTY=THIR[D]

Created G. O. No. 103. A. G. O. April 27, 1863. Reorganized April 10, 1864. S.

Independent Cavalry Brigade.

Organized August, 1863. Transferred to Cavalry Corps, Department of the Ohio, November, 1863.

COMMANDER.		DATE.
F. Woolford,	Col. 1st Ky. Cav.	August, 1863.

COMMANDERS.

G. L. HARTSUFF,	Major-Gener[al]
M. D. MANSON,	Brigadier-G[e]
J. D. COX,	"
"	Major-Gener[al]
GEO. STONEMAN,	"
J. M. SCHOFIELD,	"
S. P. CARTER,	Brigadier-G[e]

1st Division—23d Army Corps.

Discontinued January, 1864. Reorganized April, 1864. Discontinued June, 1864.
Reorganized December 29, 1864.

COMMANDERS.		DATE.
S. D. Sturgis,	Brigadier-General.	June, 1863
S. P. Carter,	"	July 10, "
R. K. Byrd,	Col. 1st Tenn. Vols.	" 15, "
J. T. Boyle,	Brigadier-General.	Aug. 6, "
A. P. Hovey,	"	April, 1864
Thos. H. Ruger,	"	Dec. 29, "
M. T. Thomas,	Bvt. Brigadier-General.	June, 1865
G. W. Schofield,	" "	July, "

2d Division—23d Army Corps.

Reorganized April, 1864. Discontinued July, 1865.

COMMANDERS.		DATE.
J. T. Boyle,	Brigadier-General.	June 24, 1863
M. D. Manson,	"	Aug., "
"	"	Dec. 24, "
Julius White,	"	Aug. 26, "
H. M. Judah,	"	Jan. 21 1864
"	"	April, "
M. S. Hascall,	"	May 28, "
J. A. Cooper,	"	Oct., "
"	"	May 8, 1865
Thos. H. Ruger,	"	Nov. 11, 1864
D. N. Couch,	Major-General.	Dec. 8, "
"	"	April, 1865
N. C. McLean,	Brigadier-General.	Feb. 28, "
G. W. Schofield,	Bvt. Brigadier-General,	May 30, "

3d Divisio[n]

Re[organized] Reorganized Ap[ril]

COMMANDER[S]

H. M. Judah,	Brigadier-Ge[neral]
M. S. Hascall,	"
J. W. Reilly,	Col. 104th O[hio]
"	" 104th
"	Brigadier-Ge[neral]
J. D. Cox,	"
S. P. Carter,	"
James Stewart,	Col. 9th N.

1st Brigade—1st Division.

Discontinued August, 1863. Reorganized April, 1864.
Served with 3d Div. from June to August 1864.
Discontinued Aug., 1864. Reorganized Dec., 1864.

COMMANDERS.		DATE.
S. P. Carter,	Brigadier-General.	June 24, 1863
R. K. Byrd,	Col. 1st Tenn. Vols.	July "
J. P. T. Carter,	" 2d " "	" 15, "
Rich. F. Barter,	"120th Ind. "	April, 1864
J. M. Orr,	"124th " "	Dec., " / May 18, 1865
J. N. Stiles,	Bvt. Brigadier-General.	March 14, "
A. W. Prather,	Col. 120th Ind. Vols.	June 27, "

2d Brigade—1st Division.

Discontinued August, 1863. Reorganized April, 1864.
Serving with 2d Div. from June to August, 1864.
Discontinued Aug., 1864. Reorganized Dec., 1864.

COMMANDERS.		DATE.
J. W. Reilly,	Col. 104th Ohio Vols.	June, 1863
S. A. Gilbert,	" 44th " "	July, "
S. R. Mott,	" 118th " "	" "
J. C. McQuiston,	" 123d Ind. "	April, 1864 / Dec. 31, "
P. T. Swaine,	" 99th Ohio "	June 23, "
C. S. Parrish,	" 130th Ind. "	July 25, "

1st Brigade—2d Division.

Reorganized April, 1864.

COMMANDERS.		DATE.
J. M. Shackelford,	Brigadier-General.	June, 1863
O. H. Moore,	Col. 25th Mich. Vols.	Aug., " / March, 1865 / May, "
S. R. Mott,	" 118th Ohio "	Oct. 20, 1863
W. E. Hobson,	" 13th Ky. "	Feb. 2, 1864
J. A. Cooper,	" 6th Tenn. "	April 25, " / June 14, "
"	Brigadier-General.	Nov. 11, " / April, 1865
N. C. McLean,	"	May, 1864
G. W. Gallup,	Col. 14th Ky. Vols.	Oct., "
J. B. Conyngham,	" 52d Pa. "	July, 1865

1st Briga[de]

Re[organized] Reorganized Ap[ril]

COMMANDER[S]

M. D. Manson,	Brigadier-Ge[neral]
S. A. Gilbert,	Col. 44th O[hio]
J. W. Reilly,	" 104th
"	Brigadier-Ge[neral]
F. A. Reeve,	Col. 8th E[ast]
S. P. Love,	" 11th K[y]
C. C. Doolittle,	" 18th M[ich]
O. W. Sterl,	" 104th O[hio]
W. S. Stewart,	" 65th Il[l]

3d Brigade—1st Division.

Discontinued Aug., 1863. Reorganized Dec. 30, 1864.
Discontinued July, 1865.

COMMANDERS.		DATE.
A. V. Kautz,	Col. 2d Ohio Cav.	June, 1863
M. T. Thomas,	" 8th Minn. Vols.	Dec., 1864
Jas. Tucker,	Lt.- " 25th Mass. "	June, 1865

U. S. Forces, S. W. Ky.—1st Division.

Organized October, 1863.
Discontinued Jan., 1864. Trans. to Dept. of the Ohio.

COMMANDER.		DATE.
C. Maxwell,	Col. 26th Ky. Vols.	Oct., 1863

2d Brigade—2d Division.

Reorganized April, 1864. Discontinued June, 1865.

COMMANDERS.		DATE.
M. W. Chapin,	Col. 23d Mich. Vols.	Aug. 6, 1863
J. R. Bond,	" 111th Ohio Vols.	Feb. 8, 1864
"	" 111th " "	May "
"	" 111th " "	Aug., "
M. S. Hascall,	Brigadier-General.	April 16, "
W. E. Hobson,	Col. 13th Ky. Vols.	June, "
J. C. McQuiston,	" 123d Ind "	Oct., "
O. H. Moore,	" 25th Mich. "	Nov., "
J. Mehringer,	" 91st Ind. "	Feb., 1865

2d Briga[de]

Re[organized] Reorganized Ap[ril]

COMMANDER[S]

E. H. Hobson,	Brigadier-Gen[eral]
Daniel Cameron,	Col. 65th Ills.
J. S. Casement,	" 103d Oh[io]
"	" 103d
"	" 103d
"	" 103d
M. D. Manson,	Brigadier-Gen[eral]
J. S. Hart,	Col. 24th Ky
A. T. Wilcox,	" 177th Oh[io]
G. W. Schofield,	Bvt. Brigadie[r]
L. H. Rousseau,	Lt.-Col. 12th

U. S. Forces, So. Cent. Ky.—1st Division.

Organized October, 1863.
Discontinued Jan., 1864. Trans. to Dept. of the Ohio.

COMMANDER.		DATE.
E. H. Hobson,	Brigadier-General.	Oct., 1863

U. S. Forces, Eastern Ky.—1st Division.

Organized October, 1863.
Discontinued Jan., 1864. Trans. to Dept. of the Ohio.

COMMANDER.		DATE.
G. W. Gallup,	Col. 14th Ky. Vols.	Oct., 1863

3d Brigade—2d Division.

Organized June, 1864.

COMMANDERS.		DATE.
S. A. Strickland,	Col. 50th Ohio Vols.	June 19, 1864
"	" 50th " "	Oct., "
"	" 50th " "	Jan., 1865
J. Mehringer,	" 91st Ind. "	Sept. 25, 1864
John O. Dowd,	" 181st Ohio "	Dec. 31, "
G. W. Hoge,	" 183d " "	June 27, 1865

3d Briga[de]

Discontinued Augu[st]
Disconti[nued]

COMMANDERS

J. A. Cooper,	Col. 6th T[enn]
W. B. Stokes,	" 5th
R. K. Byrd,	" 1st
J. N. Stiles,	" 63d In[d]
"	" 63d
T. J. Henderson,	" 112th Ill[l]

U. S. Forces, Somerset, Ky.—1st Division.

Organized October, 1863.
Discontinued Jan., 1864. Trans. to Dept. of the Ohio.

COMMANDER.		DATE.
T. T. Garrard,	Brigadier-General.	Oct. 22, 1863

U. S. Forces, No. Cent. Ky.—1st Division.

Organized October, 1863.
Discontinued Jan., 1864. Trans. to Dept. of the Ohio.

COMMANDER.		DATE.
S. S. Fry,	Brigadier-General.	Oct., 1863

1st East Tennessee Brigade—2d Division.

Temporarily assigned to 23d Corps, January, 1864.
Discontinued April, 1864.

COMMANDERS.		DATE.
J. G. Spears,	Brigadier-General.	Jan. 1864
Wm. Cross,	Col. 3d Tenn. Vols.	Feb. 6, "
J. A. Cooper,	" 6th " "	March 6, "

ARMY CORPS.

epartment of the Ohio.   Discontinued G. O. No. 131. A. G. O. August 1, 1865.

DATE.		District of Western Kentucky.
May 28, 1863.		Organized August, 1864. Discontinued January, 1865.
September 24, "		
December, "		COMMANDERS. DATE.
April 2, 1865.		E. A. Paine, Brigadier-General. August, 1864
January 28, 1864.		S. Meredith, " September 12, "
April 4, "		
June, 1865.		

Corps.

nued June 28, 1865.

DATE.
June 24, 1863
Aug., "
March, 1864
Sept. 16, "
Feb. 25, 1865
April, 1864
Oct. 22, "
April 7, 1865
June, "

4th Division—23d Army Corps.

Discontinued and formed into a " Cavalry Corps," Nov. 3, 1863.
Reorganized April 10, 1864.
Trans. to the Dept. of the Cumberland, G. O. No. 21, A. G. O., Feb. 10, 1865.

COMMANDERS.		DATE.
Julius White,	Brigadier-General.	June, 1863
S. P. Carter,	"	Aug., "
J. M. Shackelford,	"	Sept., "
Jacob Ammen,	"	April 10, 1864

5th Division, or District of Kentucky—23d Army Corps.

Organized April, 1864.
Transferred to Department of the Cumberland, January 17, 1865. G. O. No. 5, A. G. O.

COMMANDER.		DATE.
S. G. Burbridge,	Brigadier-General.	April, 1864.

1st Division—District of Kentucky.

Organized April 10, 1864.

COMMANDERS.		DATE.
E. H. Hobson,	Brigadier-General.	April 9, 1864
"	"	Dec., "
N. C. McLean,	"	July 6, "

2d Division—District of Kentucky.

Organized April, 1864.

COMMANDER.		DATE.
Hugh Ewing,	Brigadier-General.	April 7, 1864

---

n.

nued June 28, 1865.

DATE.
June, 1863
Aug., "
Dec. 14, "
Oct. 21, "
Jan. 6, 1864
April, "
Oct. 22, "
Jan., "
Sept., "
Dec. 14, "
Jan. 16, 1865
June 27, "

1st Brigade—4th Division.

COMMANDERS.		DATE.
Daniel Cameron,	Col. 65th Ills. Vols.	June, 1863
Robert K. Byrd,	" 1st Tenn. Mtd. Inf.	Aug., "
John Mehringer,	" 91st Ind. Vols.	April 17, 1864
W. Y. Dillard,	" 34th Ky. "	May 17, "
W. C. Bartlett,	Lt.- " 2d N. C. Mtd. Inf.	Nov. 29, "

1st Brigade—1st Division—Dist. of Kentucky.

Organized April, 1864.

COMMANDERS.		DATE.
G. W. Gallup,	Col. 14th Ky. Mtd. Inf.	April 13, 1864
S. B. Brown,	" 11th Mich. Cav.	May, "
E. H. Hobson,	Brigadier-General.	July 6, "
C. J. True,	Col. 40th Ky. Vols.	Oct., "

1st Brigade—2d Division—Dist. of Kentucky.

Organized April, 1864.

COMMANDERS.		DATE.
S. D. Bruce,	Col. 20th Ky. Vols.	April, 1864
T. B. Fairleigh,	Lt.- " 26th " "	May, "
"	" " 26th " "	Oct. 12, "
J. H. Hammond,	" " A. A. G.	Sept., "

---

n.

nued June 28, 1865.

DATE.
June, 1863
Aug. "
June 4, 1864
Feb., "
May 27, "
Aug., "
March, 1865
April 7, 1864
Bet. May 14 & 27, "
Feb. 25, 1865
May 1, "
June 18, "

2d Brigade—4th Division.

COMMANDERS.		DATE.
S. R. Mott,	Col. 118th Ohio Vols.	June, 1863
S. A. Gilbert,	" 44th " "	July, "
J. W. Foster,	" 65th Ind. "	Aug., "
Davis Tilson,	Brigadier-General.	April 10, 1864

2d Brigade—1st Division—Dist. of Kentucky.

Organized April, 1864.

COMMANDERS.		DATE.
C. J. True,	Col. 40th Ky. Mtd. Inf.	April, 1864
J. M. Brown,	" 45th " " "	July 6, "
F. N. Alexander,	" 30th Ky. Vols.	Sept., "

2d Brigade—2d Division—Dist. of Kentucky.

Organized April, 1864.

COMMANDERS.		DATE.
C. Maxwell,	Col. 26th Ky. Vols.	April 1864
"	" 26th " "	Sept., "
J. H. Grider,	" 52d " "	July, "
S. P. Love,	" 11th " "	Nov., "
D. J. Dill,	" 30th Wis. "	Dec., "

---

n.

ized June, 1864.

DATE.
June, 1863
" "
1864
Aug. 9, "
Dec. 15, "
Sept. 17, "
Jan. 29, 1865

3d Brigade—4th Division.

Discontinued October 17, 1864.

COMMANDERS.		DATE.
J. M. Shackelford,	Brigadier-General.	Aug., 1863
J. P. T. Carter,	Col. 2d Tenn. Vols.	Sept. 10, "
S. A. Strickland,	" 50th Ohio	April 10, 1864
B. P. Runckle,	" 45th " "	May, "
M. L. Pattersen,	Lt.- " 4th Tenn. "	June 10, "

3d Brigade—1st Division—Dist. of Kentucky.

Organized April, 1864.

COMMANDERS.		DATE.
C. S. Hanson,	Col. 37th Ky. Mtd. Inf.	April 13, 1864
B. J. Spaulding,	Lt.-Col. 37th Ky. Vols.	Oct., "

4th Brigade—1st Division—Dist. of Kentucky.

Organized April, 1864.

COMMANDERS.		DATE.
J. M. Brown,	Col. 45th Ky. Mtd. Inf.	April, 1864
R. W. Ratliff,	" 12th Ohio Cav.	July, "

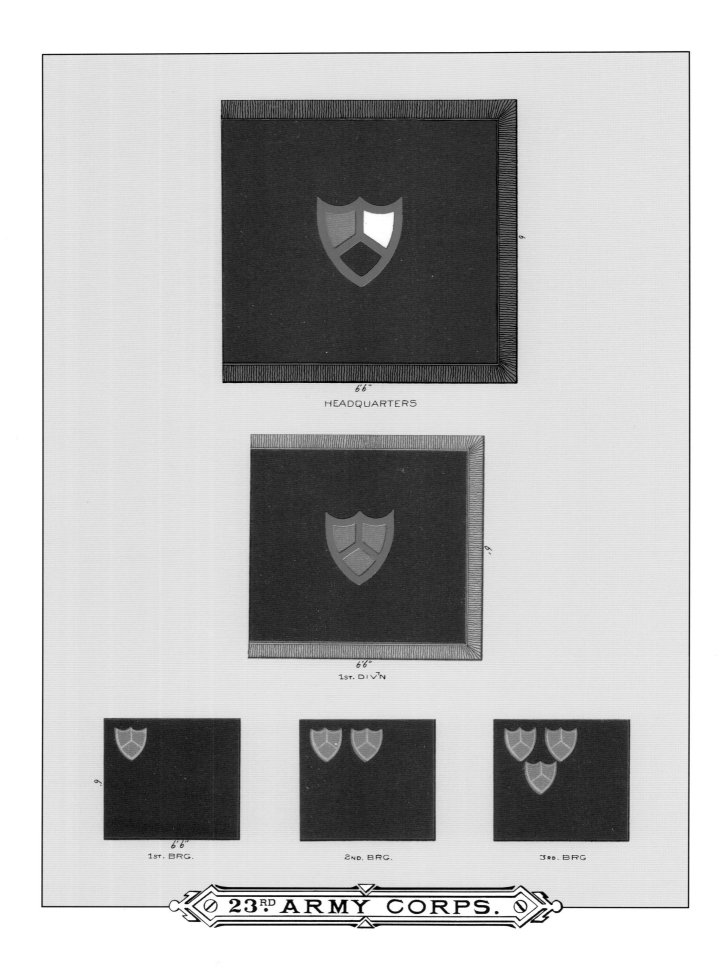

HEADQUARTERS

1st. DIV'N

1st. BRG.

2nd. BRG.

3rd. BRG

23RD ARMY CORPS.

157

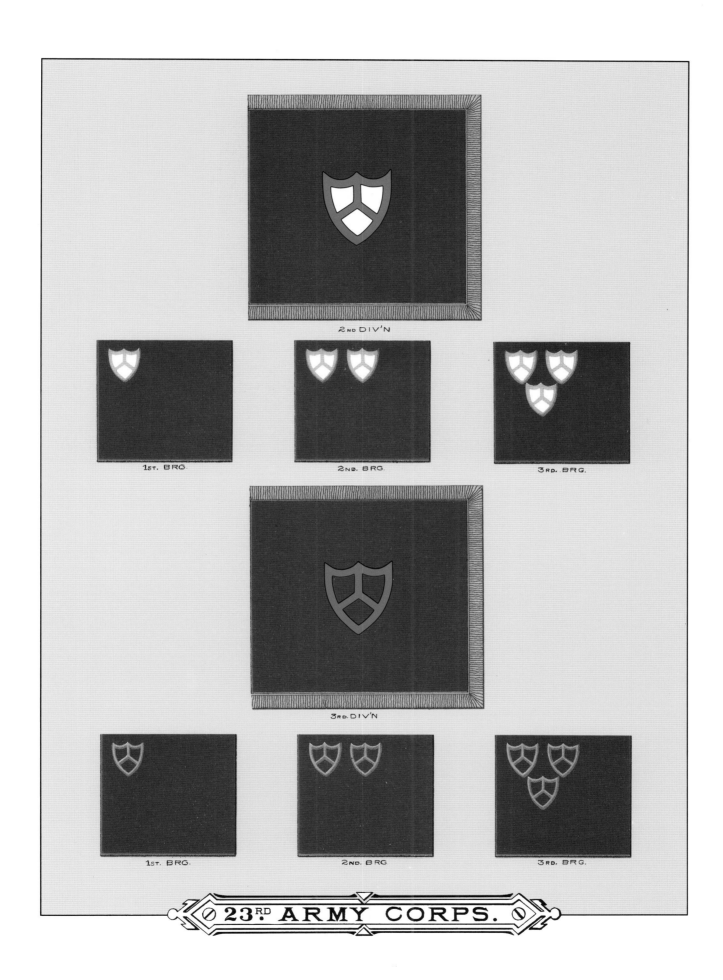

2ND DIV'N

1ST. BRG.

2ND. BRG.

3RD. BRG.

3RD. DIV'N

1ST. BRG.

2ND. BRG.

3RD. BRG.

23RD ARMY CORPS.

TWENTY=FOUR

COMPOSED OF WHITE TROOPS

Created G. O. No. 297.   A. G. O. December 3, 1

COMMANDERS.

E. O. C. ORD,	Major-Genera
A. H. TERRY,	Bvt. Major-Ge
C. DEVENS,	Major-Genera
JOHN GIBBON,	"
J. W. TURNER,	Bvt. Major-Ge

1st Division—24th Army Corps.

Organized December, 1864.

COMMANDERS.		DATE.	
A. H. Terry,	Bvt. Major-General.	December,	1864
R. S. Foster,	Brigadier-General.	"	"
"	"	February	2, 1865
"	Bvt. Major-General.	July,	"
J. R. Hawley,	Brigadier-General.	January,	"
T. O. Osborne,	"	May	2, "

2d Division—24th Army Corps.

Organized December, 1864.   Transferred to 10th Army Corps April, 1865.
Reorganized July 10, 1865.

COMMANDERS.		DATE.	
A. Ames,	Brigadier-General.	December,	1864
J. W. Turner,	Bvt. Major-General.	July,	186

1st Brigade—1st Division.

COMMANDERS.		DATE.	
A. C. Voris,	Col. 67th Ohio Vols.	Dec.,	1864
T. O. Osborne,	" 39th Ills. "	"	12, "
"	Brigadier-General.	July	8, 1865
J. C. Briscoe, Bvt.	"	May	10, "
H. R. West,	Lt.-Col. 62d Ohio Vols.	June	28, "
H. S. Fairchild, Bvt. Brigadier-General.		July	25, "

2d Brigade—1st Division.

Transferred to 10th Army Corps, April, 1865.
Reorganized May, 1865.   (Formerly 4th Brigade.)
Discontinued July, 1865.
Reorganized July, 1865.   (Formerly 3d Brigade.)

COMMANDERS.		DATE.	
J. R. Hawley,	Brigadier-General.	Dec.,	1864
J. C. Abbott,	Col. 7th N. H. Vols.	Jan.,	1865
H. S. Fairchild, Bvt. Brigadier-General.		May,	"
G. B. Dandy,	" "	July,	"

1st Brigade—2d Division.

COMMANDERS.		DATE.	
N. M. Curtis,	Bvt. Brigadier-General.	Dec.,	1864
R. Daggett,	Col. 117th N.Y.Vols.	Jan.	21, 1865
M. A. Darnall,	" 10th W. Va."	July,	"

2d Brigade—2d Division.

COMMANDERS.		D
G. Pennypacker,	Col. 97th Pa. Vols.	Dec.,
O. P. Harding,	Maj.203d " "	Jan.
J. A. Colvin,	Lt.-Col. 169th N.Y. Vols.	Feb.
Wm. B. Coan,	" 48th " "	Marc
J. H. Potter,	Brigadier-General.	July

3d Brigade—1st Division.

Designated 2d Brigade, 1st Division, July, 1865.

COMMANDERS.		DATE.	
H. M. Plaisted,	Col. 11th Me. Vols.	Dec.	3, 1864
G. B. Dandy,	" 100th N. Y."	Feb.	2, 1865
"	" 100th " "	June	12, "
E. S. Greeley,	" 10th Conn."	May,	"

4th Brigade—1st Division.

Designated 2d Brigade, 1st Division, May, 1865.

COMMANDERS.		DATE.	
Jas. Jourdan,	Bvt. Brigadier-General.	Dec.,	1864
H. S. Fairchild,	Col. 89th N. Y. Vols.	March	17, 1865

3d Brigade—2d Division.

COMMANDERS.		DATE.	
Louis Bell,	Col. 4th N. H. Vols.	December,	186
N. J. Johnson,	Lt.- " 115th N.Y. "	January	19, 186
G. F. Granger,	" 9th Me. "	February	14, "

1st Independent Brigade—24th Army Corps.

Organized July, 1865.

COMMANDER.		DATE.	
T. M. Harris,	Brigadier-General.	July	10, 1865

H ARMY CORPS.

ntinued G. O. No. 131. A. G. O. August 1, 1865.

DATE.
December 3, 1864.
" "
January, 1865.
" 15, "
July, "

3d Division—24th Army Corps.

Discontinued July 10, 1865.
Troops formed into 1st and 2d Independent Brigades.

COMMANDER.		DATE.
Chas. Devens,	Brigadier-General.	December, 1864

Independent Division—24th Army Corps.

Formerly 1st Division, Department of West Virginia. Joined 24th Army Corps, December, 1864.
Designation changed to 2d Division, 24th Corps, G. O. No. 86, Department of Virginia, July 10, 1865.

COMMANDERS.		DATE.
T. M. Harris,	Bvt. Brigadier-General.	December, 1864
John W. Turner,	" Major-General.	March, 1865

1st Brigade—3d Division.

Discontinued July, 1865.

COMMANDERS.			DATE.
lston,	Lt.-Col. 81st N. Y. Vols.	Dec.,	1864
llen,	" 96th " "	Jan. 16,	1865
pley,	" 9th Vt. "	March 22,	"
	Bvt. Brigadier-General.	May 5,	"
chols,	Col. 118th N.Y.Vols.	April 16,	"
ce,	" 11th Conn. "	June 13,	"

2d Brigade—3d Division.

Discontinued July, 1865.

COMMANDERS.			DATE
J. H. Potter,	Col. 12th N. H. Vols.	Dec.,	1864
V. G. Barney.	Lt.- " 9th Vt. "	Jan. 17,	1865
J. E. Ward,	" 8th Conn. "	Feb. 6,	"
M. T. Donohoo,	" 10th N. H. "	March,	"
J. N. Patterson,	" 2d " "	June,	"

1st Brigade—Independent Division.

Designated 1st Brigade, 2d Division, July, 1865.

COMMANDERS.			DATE.
T. F. Wilder,	Lt.-Col. 116th Ohio Vols.	Dec.,	1864
Andrew Potter,	" " 34th Mass. "	Feb. 3,	1865
W. S. Lincoln,	" 34th " "	April 27,	"
S. A. Simonson,	Lt.- " 23d Ills. "	June,	"

2d Brigade—Independent Division.

Discontinued June, 1865.

COMMANDER.			DATE.
Wm. B. Curtis,	Col. 12th W.Va.Vols.	Dec.,	1864

3d Brigade—3d Division.

Discontinued June, 1865.

COMMANDERS.		DATE.
Guy V. Henry,	Bvt. Brigadier-General.	December, 1864
S. H. Roberts,	Col. 139th N. Y. Vols.	February, 1865

3d Brigade—Independent Division.

Discontinued June, 1865.

COMMANDERS.		DATE.
M. S. Hall,	Lt.-Col. 10th W. Va. Vols.	December, 1864
T. M. Harris,	Bvt. Brigadier-General.	March 21, 1865
J. W. Holliday,	Lt.-Col. 15th W. Va. Vols.	April 27, "

2d Independent Brigade—24th Army Corps.

Organized July, 1865.

COMMANDER.		DATE.
J. C. Briscoe,	Bvt. Brigadier-General.	July 21, 1865

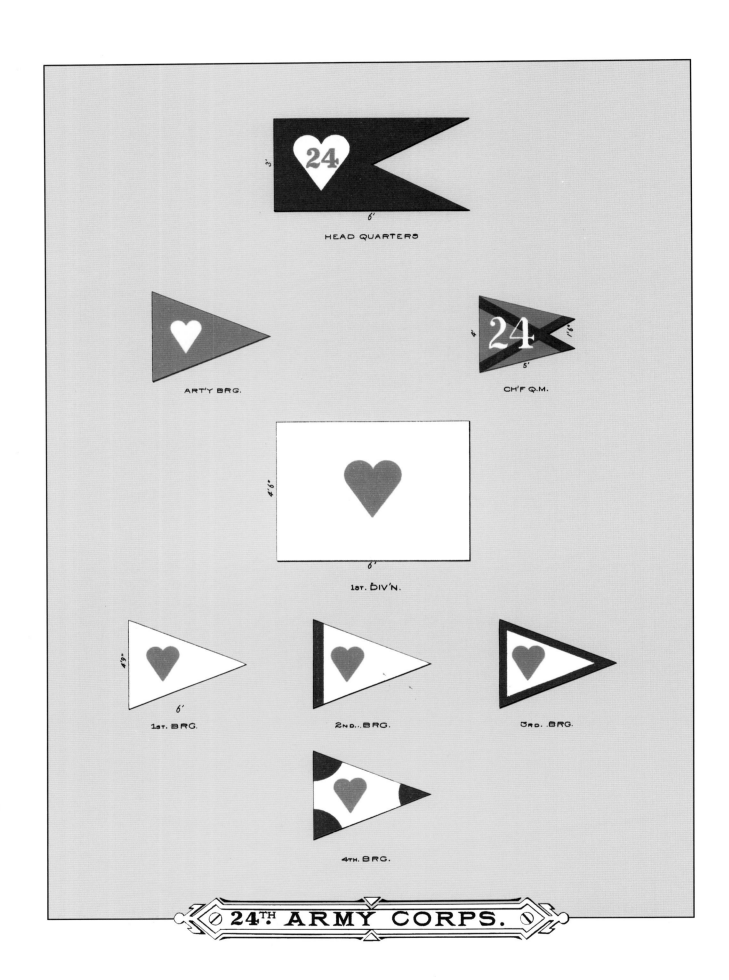

HEAD QUARTERS

ART'Y BRG.

CH'F Q.M.

1ST. DIV'N.

1ST. BRG.

2ND. BRG.

3RD. BRG.

4TH. BRG.

24TH ARMY CORPS.

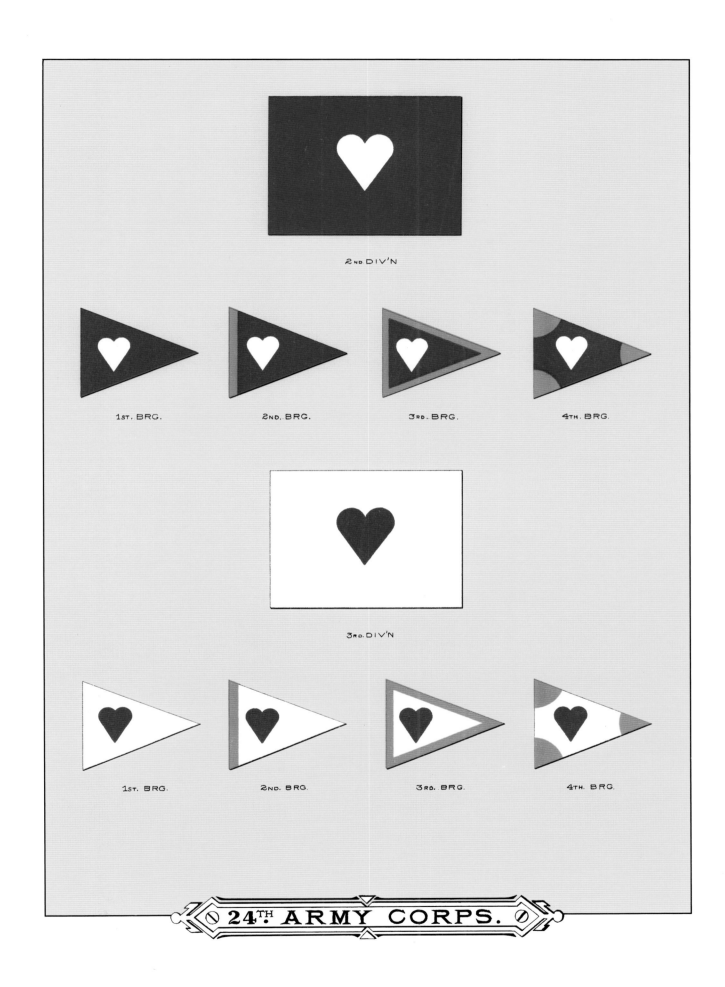

2ND DIV'N

1ST. BRG.　　2ND. BRG.　　3RD. BRG.　　4TH. BRG.

3RD. DIV'N

1ST. BRG.　　2ND. BRG.　　3RD. BRG.　　4TH. BRG.

24TH ARMY CORPS.

TWENTY=FIFTI[

COMPOSED OF COLORED TROOPS

Created G. O. No. 297. A. G. O. December 3,

COMMANDERS.

G. WEITZEL, Major-Gene[ral]
C. A. HECKMAN, Brigadier-G[eneral]

1st Division—25th Army Corps.

Designation changed to 3d Division, December 31, 1864.

COMMANDERS.		DATE.
C. J. Paine,	Brigadier-General.	December 3, 1864
E. A. Wild,	"	January, 1865
A. V. Kautz,	Bvt. Major-General.	March 27, "
A. G. Draper,	" Brigadier-General.	May 4, "
G. A. Smith,	" "	" 29, "
J. G. Perkins,	Col. 19th U. S. C. T.	January, 1866

2d D[ivision]

COMMANDERS.

W. Birney,	Brigadier-Gen[eral]
"	"
J. Shaw, Jr.,	Col. 7th U. S[. C. T.]
R. H. Jackson,	Bvt. Brigadier[-General]
T. H. Barrett,	Col. 62d U. S[. C. T.]

1st Brigade—1st Division.

Designation changed to 1st Brigade, 3d Division, December 31, 1864.
Formerly 1st Brigade, 3d Division, prior to December 31, 1864.

COMMANDERS.		DATE.
D. Bates,	Bvt. Brigadier-General.	Dec., 1864
A. G. Draper,	" "	Jan., 1865
"	" "	June 3, "
J. C. Moon,	Col. 118th U. S. C. T.	May 4, "
"	" 118th " "	July 7, "
R. M. Hall,	" 38th " "	Sept. 22, "
T. Bayley,	" 9th " "	Oct., "
J. G. Perkins,	" 19th " "	Dec. 28, "
G. M. Dennett,	Lt.- " 9th " "	Jan., 1866

2d Brigade—1st Division.

Designation changed to 2d Brigade, 3d Division, December 31, 1864.
Formerly 2d Brigade, 3d Division, prior to December 31, 1864.

COMMANDERS.		DATE.
S. A. Duncan,	Bvt. Brigadier-General.	Dec. 3, 1864
J. W. Ames,	Col. 6th U. S. C. T.	Dec., "
C. S. Russell,	Bvt. Brigadier-General.	Jan., 1865
T Bayley,	Col. 9th U. S. C. T.	Feb. 27, "
"	" 9th " "	Sept. 22, "
T. D. Sedgwick,	" 114th " "	March 3, "
"	" 114th " "	April 18, "
E. A. Wild,	Brigadier-General.	March 28, "
R. M. Hall,	Col. 38th U. S. C. T.	Oct., "
J. C. Moon,	" 118th " "	Dec. 8, "
D. Branson,	Lt.- " 62d " "	Jan., 1866

1st Brigade—2d Division.

COMMANDERS.

		D[ATE.]
J. Shaw, Jr.,	Col. 7th U. S. C. T.	Dec.
"	" 7th " "	Jan.
"	" 7th " "	March
"	" 7th " "	July
C. S. Russell,	" 28th " "	Dec.
O. A. Bartholomew,	" 109th " "	Feb.
H. W. Barry,	" 8,h " "	June

3d Brigade—1st Division.

Designation changed to 3d Brigade, 3d Division, December 31, 1864. Formerly 3d Brigade, 3d Division.
Discontinued October, 1865.

COMMANDERS.		DATE.
E. Wright,	Col. 10th U. S. C. T	December, 1864
H. G. Thomas,	Brigadier-General.	January, 1865
S. B. Yeoman,	Col. 43d U. S. C. T.	April, "
T. H. Barrett,	" 62d " "	July 27, "
J. G. Perkins,	" 19th " "	September 29, "

3d B[rigade—2d Division.]

Di[scontinued]

COMMANDERS.

C. S. Russell,	Col. 28th U[. S. C. T.]
H. C. Ward,	" 31st
"	" 31st
E. Martindale,	" 81st
W. W. Woodward,	" 116th

Cavalry Brigade—25th Army Corps.

Organized May, 1865. Designated 3d Brigade, 3d Division, July, 1865.

COMMANDER.		DATE.
G. W. Cole,	Bvt. Brigadier-General.	May, 1865

ARMY CORPS.

tinued G. O. No. 2. A. G. O. January 8, 1866.

DATE.
December 4, 1864, and February, 1865.
January, 1865.

rmy Corps.

	DATE.
December	3, 1864
March,	1865
February	21, "
April	24, "
November,	"

2d Brigade—2d Division.

COMMANDERS.		DATE.	
eday,	Bvt. Brigadier-General.	Dec.,	1864
	" "	June,	1865
kell,	" "	May,	"
	" "	July,	"
strong,	Col. 8th U. S. C. T.	Sept.,	"
rett,	" 62d " "	Oct.	12, "
wn,	" 117th " "	Nov.	4, "

ision.

1865.

	DATE.	
December,	1864	
"	8, "	
September,	1865	
January	10, "	
March	23, "	

3d Division—25th Army Corps.

Designation changed to 1st Division, December 31, 1864. Formerly 1st Division.
Transferred to 10th Army Corps, April, 1865. Reorganized July, 1865.

COMMANDERS.			DATE.	
C. A. Heckman,		Brigadier-General.	December	3, 1864
E. A. Wild,		"	"	30, "
C. J. Paine,		"	January,	1865
A. G. Draper,	Bvt.	"	July	6, "
W. T. Clark,		"	August and December, 1865.	
G. W. Cole,	Bvt.	"	October	25, 1865

1st Brigade—3d Division.

Designation changed to 1st Brigade, 1st Division, December 31, 1864.
Formerly 1st Brigade, 1st Division, prior to December 31, 1864.

COMMANDERS.		DATE.	
A. G. Draper,	Bvt. Brigadier-General.	Dec.	3, 1864
D. Bates,	" "	Jan.,	1865
C. S. Russell,	" "	July	6, "
T. J. White,	Lt.-Col 2d U. S. C. T.	Oct.	25, "

2d Brigade—3d Division.

Designation changed to 2d Brigade, 1st Division, December 31, 1864.
Formerly 2d Brigade, 1st Division, prior to December 31, 1864.

COMMANDERS.		DATE.	
E. Martindale,	Col. 81st U. S. C. T.	Dec.	4, 1864
J. W. Ames,	" 6th " "	Jan.,	1865
S. A. Duncan,	Bvt. Brigadier-General.	Feb.	28, "
J. Given,	Lt.-Col. 127th U. S. C. T.	July	20 "
J. H. Davidson,	" 122d " "	Oct.,	"
E. H. Powell,	Lt.- " 10th " "	Nov.,	"

3d Brigade—3d Division.

Designation changed to 3d Brigade, 1st Division, December 31, 1864. Formerly 3d Brigade, 1st Division, prior to December 31, 1864.
Reorganized July, 1865. Formerly Cavalry Brigade. Discontinued October, 1865.

COMMANDERS.		DATE.	
H. G. Thomas,	Brigadier-General.	December	15, 1864
E. Wright,	Col. 10th U. S. C. T.	January,	1865
G. W. Cole,	Bvt. Brigadier-General.	July,	"
J. H. Holman,	Col. 1st U. S. C. T.	February	20, "

Unassigned Brigade—25th Army Corps.

Organized March 27, 1865. Discontinued July, 1865.

COMMANDER.		DATE.
C. S. Russell,	Bvt. Brigadier-General.	March 27, 1865

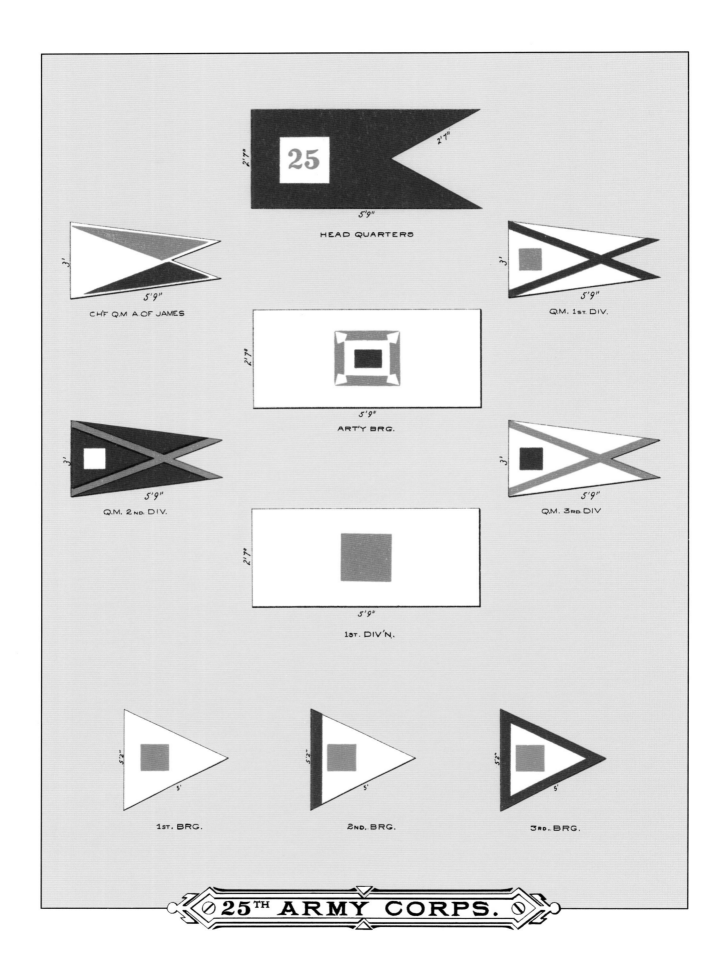

25

HEAD QUARTERS

CH'F Q.M A. OF JAMES

Q.M. 1st. DIV.

ART'Y BRG.

Q.M. 2nd. DIV.

Q.M. 3rd. DIV

1st. DIV'N.

1st. BRG.

2nd. BRG.

3rd. BRG.

25TH ARMY CORPS.

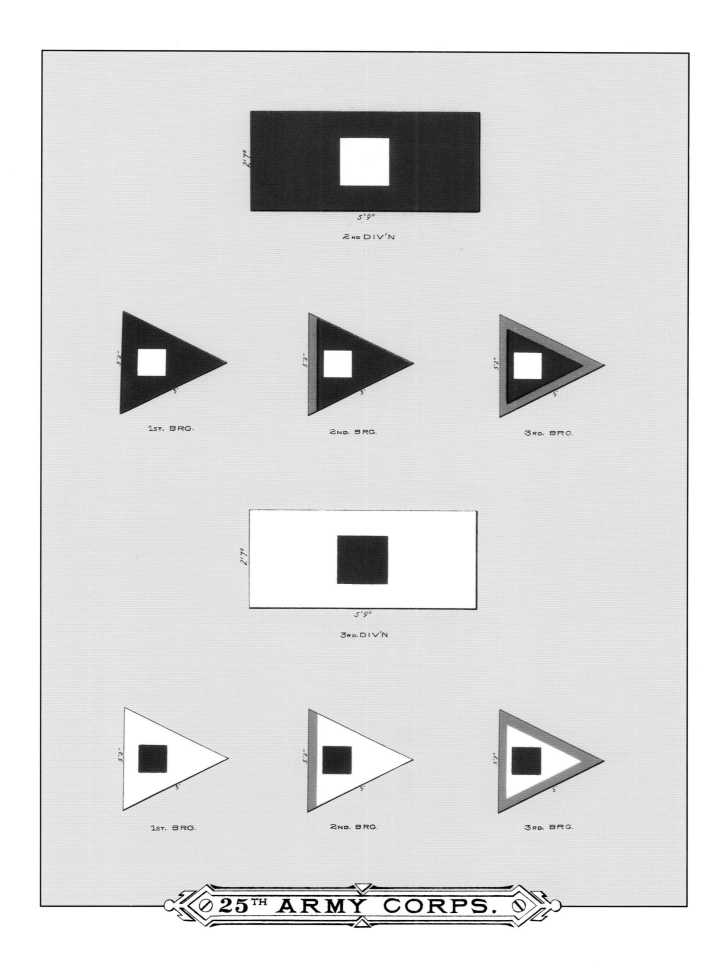

2'9"
5'9"
2ND DIV'N

5'2"
5'
1ST. BRG.

5'2"
5'
2ND. BRG.

5'2"
5'
3RD. BRG.

2'9"
5'9"
3RD. DIV'N

5'2"
5'
1ST. BRG.

5'2"
5'
2ND. BRG.

5'2"
5'
3RD. BRG.

25TH ARMY CORPS.

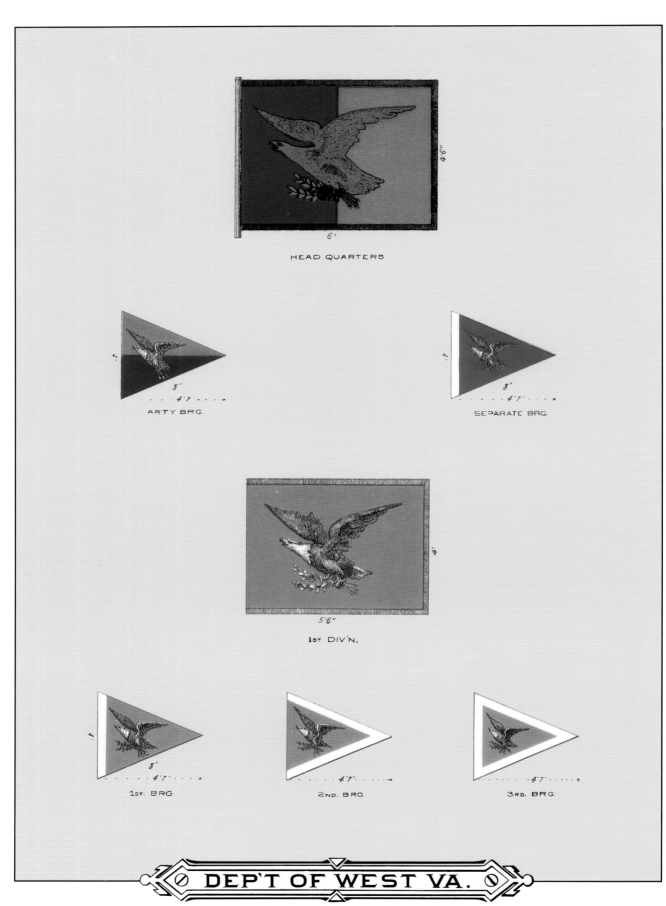

HEAD QUARTERS

ARTY BRG.

SEPARATE BRG

1ST DIV'N.

1ST. BRG.

2ND. BRG

3RD. BRG.

DEP'T OF WEST VA.

ADOPTED JAN 3RD 1865
GEN. ORDER Nº 2.
EXCEPT AS NOTED ON 3RD DIV

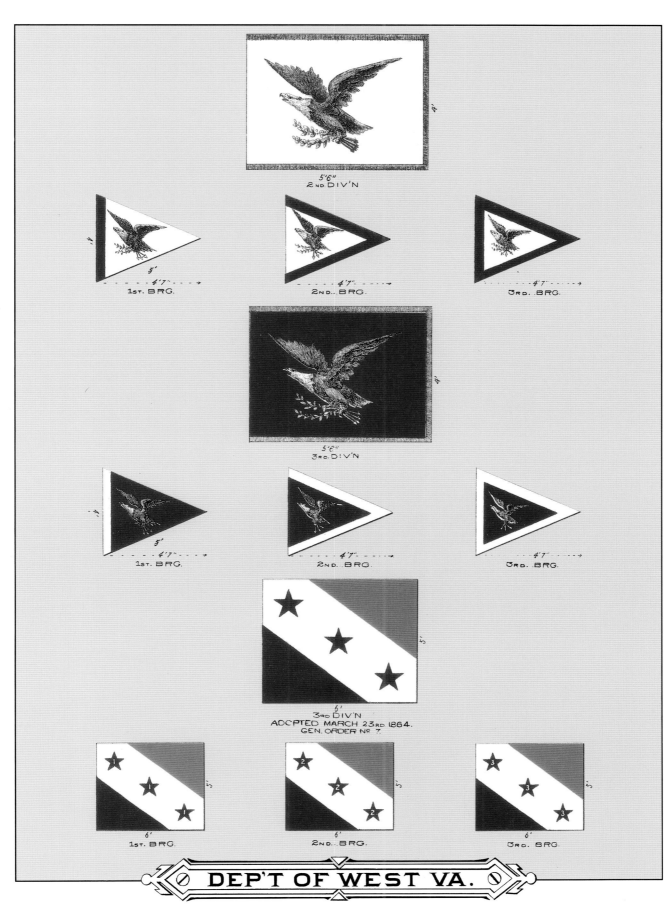

2ND DIV'N

1ST. BRG. 2ND. BRG. 3RD. BRG.

3RD DIV'N

1ST. BRG. 2ND. BRG. 3RD. BRG.

3RD DIV'N
ADOPTED MARCH 23RD 1864.
GEN. ORDER NO. 7.

1ST. BRG. 2ND. BRG. 3RD. BRG.

DEP'T OF WEST VA.

ADOPTED JAN 3RD 1865
GEN. ORDER NO. 2
EXCEPT AS NOTED ON 3RD DIV.

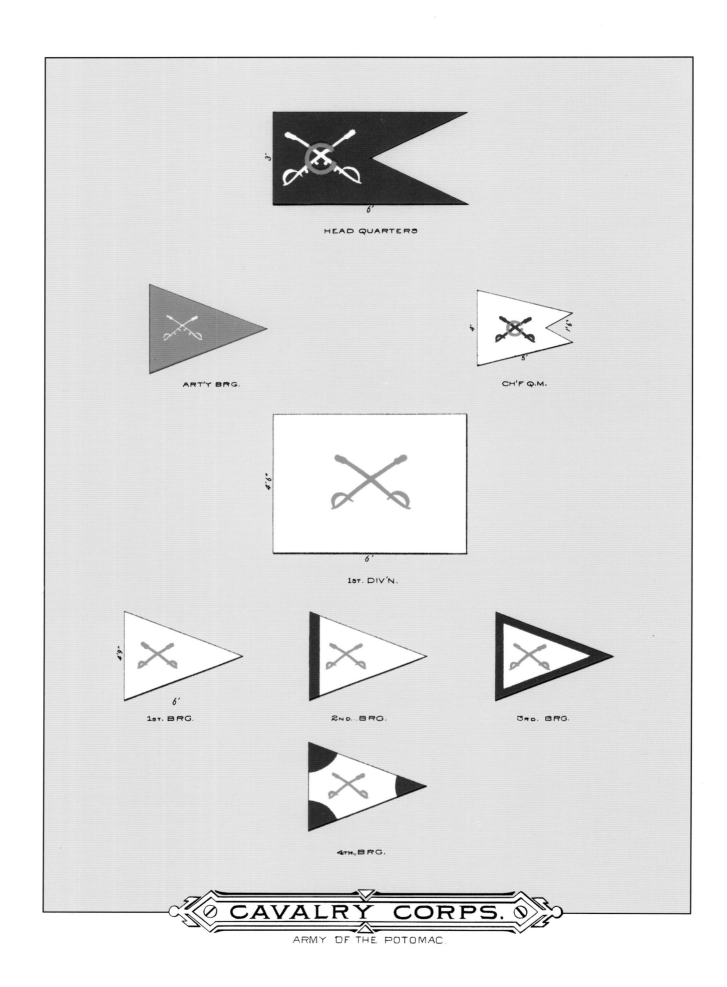

HEAD QUARTERS

ART'Y BRG.

CH'F Q.M.

1ST. DIV'N.

1ST. BRG.

2ND. BRG.

3RD. BRG.

4TH. BRG.

CAVALRY CORPS.

ARMY OF THE POTOMAC.

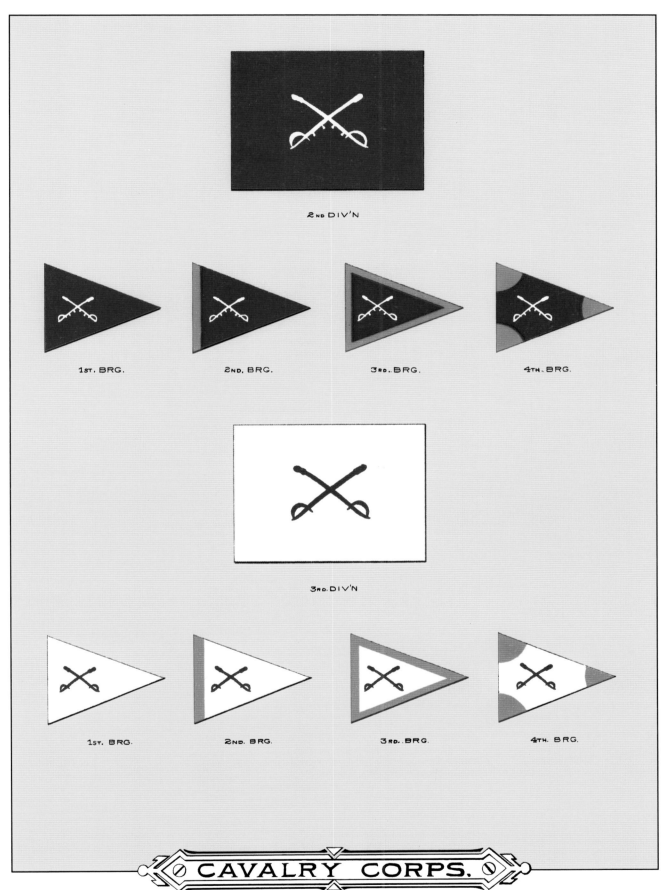

2ND DIV'N

1ST. BRG.   2ND. BRG.   3RD. BRG.   4TH. BRG.

3RD. DIV'N

1ST. BRG.   2ND. BRG.   3RD. BRG.   4TH. BRG.

CAVALRY CORPS.

ARMY OF THE POTOMAC

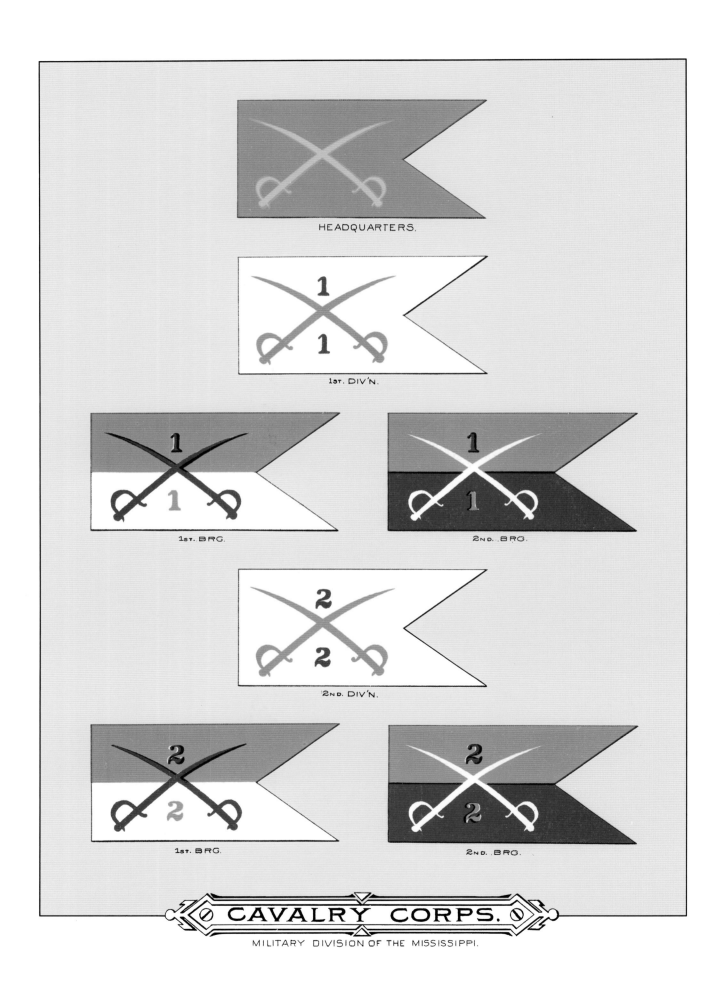

HEADQUARTERS.

1st. DIV'N.

1st. BRG.

2nd. BRG.

2nd. DIV'N.

1st. BRG.

2nd. BRG.

CAVALRY CORPS.

MILITARY DIVISION OF THE MISSISSIPPI.

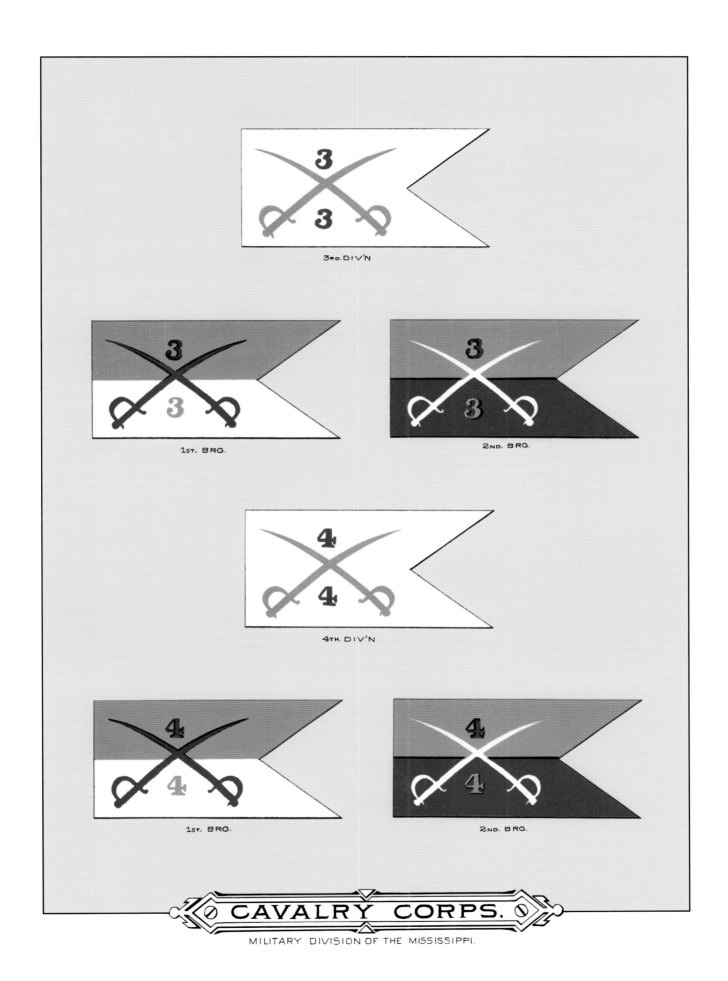

3RD. DIV'N

1ST. BRG.

2ND. BRG.

4TH. DIV'N

1ST. BRG.

2ND. BRG.

CAVALRY CORPS.

MILITARY DIVISION OF THE MISSISSIPPI.

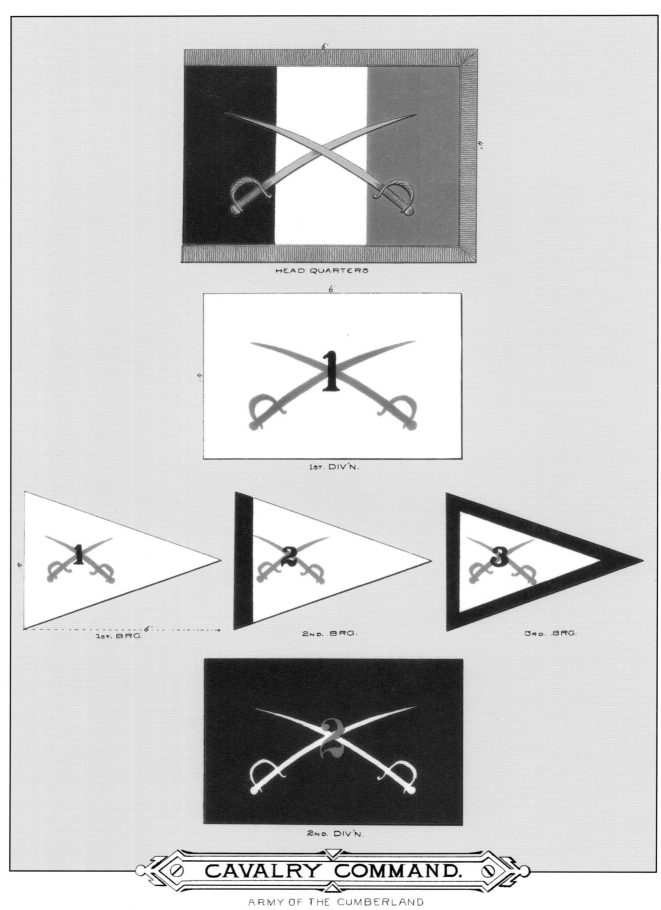

HEAD QUARTERS

1ST. DIV'N.

1ST. BRG.

2ND. BRG.

3RD. BRG.

2ND. DIV'N.

CAVALRY COMMAND.

ARMY OF THE CUMBERLAND

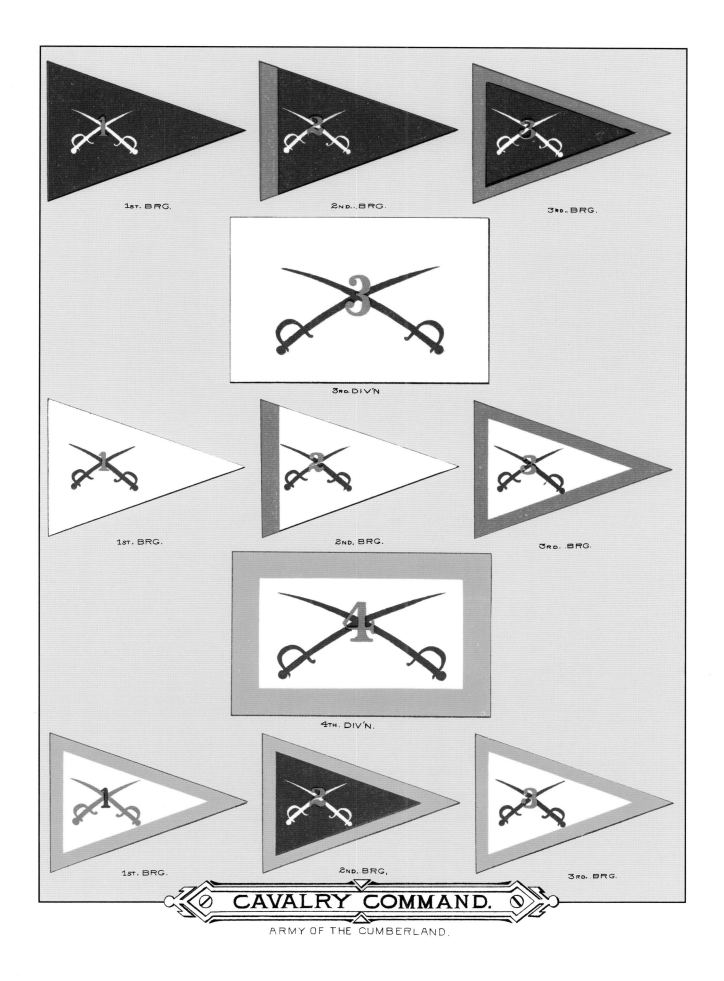

1ST. BRG.

2ND. BRG.

3RD. BRG.

3RD. DIV'N

1ST. BRG.

2ND. BRG.

3RD. BRG.

4TH. DIV'N.

1ST. BRG.

2ND. BRG.

3RD. BRG.

CAVALRY COMMAND.

ARMY OF THE CUMBERLAND.

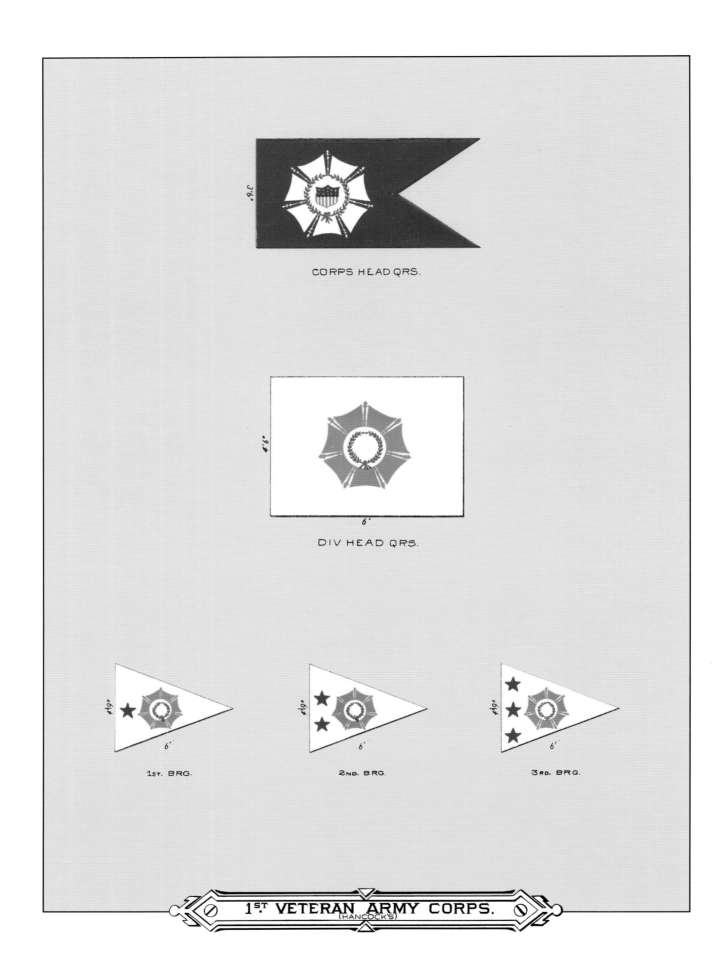

CORPS HEAD QRS.

DIV HEAD QRS.

1ST. BRG.

2ND. BRG.

3RD. BRG.

1ST. VETERAN ARMY CORPS.
(HANCOCK'S)

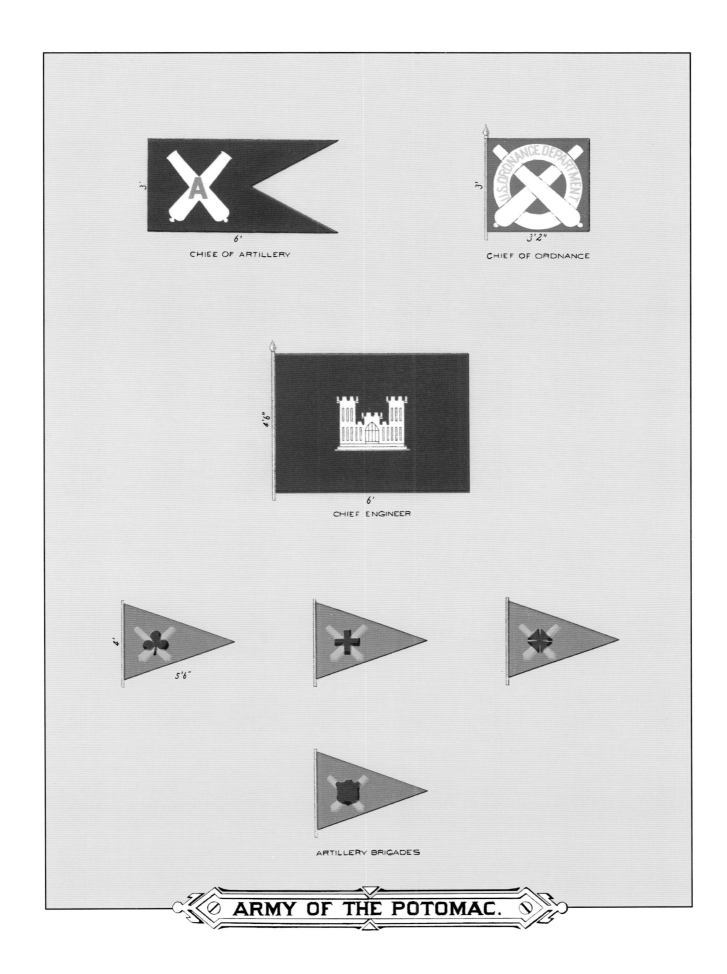

CHIEF OF ARTILLERY

CHIEF OF ORDNANCE

CHIEF ENGINEER

ARTILLERY BRIGADES

ARMY OF THE POTOMAC.

1. WILSON'S CAV'Y CORPS   2. SIGNAL CORPS   3. ENGINEER CORPS.

4. ENGINEER & PONTONIER CORPS.   5. SHERIDANS CAV'Y CORPS.

BADGES.

WORN BY MISCELLANEOUS COMMANDS.